Instagram

Digital Media and Society Series

Nancy Baym, *Personal Connections in the Digital Age*, 2nd
    edition
Mercedes Bunz and Graham Meikle, *The Internet of Things*
Jean Burgess and Joshua Green, *YouTube*, 2nd edition
Mark Deuze, *Media Work*
Andrew Dubber, *Radio in the Digital Age*
Quinn DuPont, *Cryptocurrencies and Blockchains*
Charles Ess, *Digital Media Ethics*, 2nd edition
Jordan Frith, *Smartphones as Locative Media*
Alexander Halavais, *Search Engine Society*, 2nd edition
Martin Hand, *Ubiquitous Photography*
Robert Hassan, *The Information Society*
Tim Jordan, *Hacking*
Graeme Kirkpatrick, *Computer Games and the Social
    Imaginary*
Tama Leaver, Tim Highfield and Crystal Abidin, *Instagram*
Leah A. Lievrouw, *Alternative and Activist New Media*
Rich Ling and Jonathan Donner, *Mobile Communication*
Donald Matheson and Stuart Allan, *Digital War Reporting*
Dhiraj Murthy, *Twitter*, 2nd edition
Zizi A. Papacharissi, *A Private Sphere: Democracy in a
    Digital Age*
Jill Walker Rettberg, *Blogging*, 2nd edition
Patrik Wikström, *The Music Industry*, 3rd edition

Instagram

Visual Social Media Cultures

TAMA LEAVER, TIM HIGHFIELD
AND CRYSTAL ABIDIN

polity

First published in 2020 by Polity Press

Polity Press
65 Bridge Street
Cambridge CB2 1UR, UK

Polity Press
101 Station Landing
Suite 300
Medford, MA 02155, USA

ISBN-13: 978-1-5095-3438-8
ISBN-13: 978-1-5095-3439-5(pb)

A catalogue record for this book is available from the British Library.

Library of Congress Cataloging-in-Publication Data
Names: Leaver, Tama, author. | Highfield, Tim, author. | Abidin, Crystal, author.
Title: Instagram : visual social media cultures / Tama Leaver, Tim Highfield, Crystal Abidin.
Description: Cambridge, UK; Medford, MA, USA : Polity, 2020. | Series: Digital media and society series | Includes bibliographical references and index. | Summary: "In the first book-length examination of Instagram, Leaver, Highfield and Abidin trace how this mobile photography app has developed as a platform and a culture. Rich with examples from across the world, from birth pictures to selfies at funerals, Instagram is essential reading for students and scholars of media and communication"-- Provided by publisher.
Identifiers: LCCN 2019024094 (print) | LCCN 2019024095 (ebook) | ISBN 9781509534388 (hardback) | ISBN 9781509534395 (paperback) | ISBN 9781509534401 (epub)
Subjects: LCSH: Instagram (Firm) | Online social networks. | Photography--Digital techniques--Social aspects. | Computer file sharing.
Classification: LCC TR267.5.I57 L43 2020 (print) | LCC TR267.5.I57 (ebook) | DDC 771--dc23
LC record available at https://lccn.loc.gov/2019024094
LC ebook record available at https://lccn.loc.gov/2019024095

Typeset in 10.25 on 13 pt Scala by
Servis Filmsetting Ltd, Stockport, Cheshire
Printed and bound in Great Britain by TJ International Limited

For further information on Polity, visit our website:
politybooks.com

For Emily.
For Kate.
For Sherman.

Our better halves.

Contents

Tables and Figures   viii
Acknowledgements   xi

Introduction   I

1   Platform   8

2   Aesthetics   39

3   Ecologies   75

4   Economies   100

5   Cultures   149

6   Lifespans   174

7   From the Instagram of Everything to the
    Everything of Instagram   191

    Appendix: Instagram Timeline   218
    References   225
    Index   259

Tables and Figures

Table 2.1.   List of Instagram filters (as at August 2018)   57
Table 2.2.   List of defunct Instagram filters (as at
              August 2018)   58

Figure i.1.   Instagram nametag for @polityinstabook   7
Figure 1.1.   Instagram 'Create New Account' popup
              message, 2017   17
Figure 1.2.   Screenshot of health warning returned
              with Instagram #bonespo search.   24
Figure 2.1.   Selfie sticks warning sign, Kyoto train
              station, June 2016   42
Figure 2.2.   Scene from western Austria, July 2012, as
              captured using Retro Camera for Android   54
Figure 2.3.   'Temporary placement object'; Perth train
              station, April 2014   55
Figure 2.4.   Type post templates (screenshots,
              1 August 2018)   61
Figure 2.5.   Screenshot of Instagram story (with
              music) as viewed in the Netherlands
              in July 2018 (where music remains
              unavailable as of early 2019). Screenshot
              by TH of story posted by TL for
              @polityinstabook   62
Figure 3.1.   'You're all caught up' message.
              Screenshot, 3 July 2018   90
Figure 3.2.   Example photograph taken with Huji
              Cam – Amsterdam, 17 September 2018
              (styled as 1998)   92

Figure 3.3.   Selfie by TH in Amsterdam (March
               2018), with various levels of Meitu filter
               applied   93
Figure 3.4.   Sample output from Prisma, using
               'Mondrian' style; based on original selfie
               by TH seen in figure 3.3   95
Figure 4.1.   Instagram ad by @ongxavier
               demonstrating how he uses Nivea
               products in his cleansing routine   117
Figure 4.2.   Artist impression of two Influencers who
               have tagged their accommodation and
               travel sponsor in their Instagram ad   118
Figure 4.3.   Artist impression of a young girl
               holding a burger from an internationally
               renowned fast food chain   120
Figure 4.4.   Instagram ad by @collettemiles
               demonstrating how she takes
               photographs with the Samsung product   122
Figure 4.5.   Instagram ad by @collettemiles featuring
               the Samsung product in her flatlay of
               essential items   123
Figure 4.6.   Instagram ad by @collettemiles featuring
               her slipping the Samsung product into
               her handbag   124
Figure 4.7.   Artist impression of a fashion flatlay
               @beatricesays   126
Figure 4.8.   Artist impression of an Instagram post
               promoting Strangers' Reunion in the
               captions tag by @beatricesays   128
Figure 4.9.   Artist impression of an Instagram post
               promoting Strangers' Reunion in the
               geolocation tag by @beatricesays   129
Figure 4.10.   Artist impression of @xiaxue's instablog
               post   130
Figure 4.11.   Artist impression of @naomineo_
               publicly demonstrating and captioning

the behind-the-scenes of capturing a good
hair flip in her Instagram post   135

Figure 4.12.   Artist impression of @naomineo_
publicly demonstrating and captioning
the behind-the-scenes of capturing a good
selfie lighting in her Instagram post   136

Figure 4.13.   Lists of hashtags that Instagram users
used to commiserate over the loss of
followers during 'The Instagram Purge'   138

Figure 4.14.   Lists of hashtags that Instagram users
used to commiserate over the loss of
followers during 'The Instagram Purge'   139

Figure 4.15.   Lists of hashtags that Instagram users
used to commiserate over the loss of
followers during 'The Instagram Purge'   140

Figure 5.1.   DIY galaxy glazed doughnut offered
by @boufesg that made for highly
Instagrammable foods   165

Figure 5.2.   Colour-changing drink offered by
@boufesg that made for highly
Instagrammable foods   166

Figure 5.3.   Selection of Insta-worthy menu
items, some of which involved a live
demonstration or act from the café staff   167

Figure 6.1.   Artist impression of an Instagram post
showing a foetal ultrasound with visible
metadata   176

Figure 7.1.   Artist impression of typical post by
@insta_repeat featuring a compilation
of Instagram posts framed in the same
visual template   206

Acknowledgements

We are grateful to many people for supporting us in the writing of this book, from colleagues, to family, and beyond. We initially decided a book on Instagram seemed like a good idea, and we were a good team to write it, at the Association of Internet Researchers (AoIR) annual conference in Berlin in 2016. AoIR has been the intellectual home for all three of us, and there are so many friends and colleagues in that, and subsequent conferences and exchanges, who have helped shape our thinking about Instagram and visual social media cultures.

Many of our scholarly friends and colleagues have contributed to our thinking about specific parts of this book, and supported us as we have written; we would like to thank in particular Greg Acciaioli, Kath Albury, Sophie Bishop, Jean Burgess, Paul Byron, Nicholas Carah, Christina Chau, Gemma Cobb, Alberto Cossu, Rob Cover, Sky Croeser, Amy Dobson, Brooke Erin Duffy, Stefanie Duguay, Sara Ekberg, Katie Ellis, Liz Ellison, Alex Gekker, Tarleton Gillespie, Ysabel Gerrard, John Hartley, Anne Helmond, Natalie Hendry, Jenny Kennedy, Mike Kent, Ben Light, Ariadna Matamoros Fernández, Anthony McCosker, Lee McGowan, Kate Miltner, Peta Mitchell, Sharif Mowlabocus, Sabine Niederer, Sarah Oates, Gwyneth Peaty, Thomas Poell, Jill Walker Rettberg, Bernhard Rieder, Brady Robards, Richard Rogers, Natalia Sánchez Querubín, Eleanor Sandry, Michael Stevenson, Katrin Tiidenberg, Emily van der Nagel, Fernando Van Der Vlist, Son Vivienne, Katie Warfield, Esther Weltevrede, and Patrik Wikström.

Tim would also like to acknowledge the support of the QUT Digital Media Research Centre, where aspects of this work were funded by his 2015–2018 Vice-Chancellor's Research Fellowship, and to thank his University of Amsterdam MA students, who provided inspiration and raised additional points of interest through their own Instagram research: Renate Brulleman, Anya Doshi, Annika Heinemeyer Nora Lauff, Abby Listerman, Anna Vallianatou and Donna Wielinga.

We would also like to thank all those who have offered feedback and suggestions at the numerous conferences, symposia, workshops, and other events at which elements of this book have been presented. In particular, Tama and Tim would like to acknowledge the participants of their Instagrammatics digital methods workshops, for their contributions and engagement and for bringing their own research interests to the questions and provocations we've asked, at: CCI Digital Methods Summer School (Melbourne, 2015; Brisbane, 2016); QUT Digital Media Research Centre digital methods series (Brisbane, 2015); Association of Internet Researchers (AoIR) digital methods preconference (Phoenix, 2015; Montréal, 2018); and Digital Methods Initiative Summer School (Amsterdam, 2017; 2018).

We would like to express our thanks to Mary Savigar and Ellen MacDonald-Kramer at Polity for their faith in this book, and their patience, professionalism and support in helping shape it into the best possible form it could be. We would also like to specially thank our sketch artist, mistercrow, for lending their artistic talents to this book, and acknowledge our appreciation to @boufesg, @collettemiles, and @ongxavier for allowing us to reproduce their Instagram images for our academic discussions.

Tama would specifically like to thank Emily for her patience, support and understanding while working on this book, and Henry, Tom, Rose and Lottie for reminding me that the very best of my life does not exist on social media. Emily's dad, Geoff, and Tama's parents, Margaret and Bob, have also been incredibly helpful and supportive during the time this was written. Tama would also like to thank Tim and Crystal: I wouldn't want to write a book with anyone else!

Tim would like to thank Kate, first and foremost. Writing has not been easy lately, and this one in particular was a struggle; it could not have happened without your irreplaceable generosity and advice, kindness, support and patience, in the face of my challenges. I cannot thank you enough here. Tim also thanks his family: Elaine, Tony, Hannah, Jamie, and Anais; and in particular, thanks go to Tony for his incredible work in developing the early Instagram tracker and data capture tool. Finally, Tim would like to thank Tama and Crystal, for their enthusiasm and dedication to this project, for pushing it in new and exciting directions, and for their amazing work in making this book happen.

Crystal would like to thank her Instagram husband, Sherman, for supporting her ethnographic research on this book by obliging to take every #OOTD shot in the best possible natural light, being patient at every eatery when instaworthy food flatlays demand documentation, and for spiritedly indulging me whenever I ask you to choose between Instagram filters (even though everything looks the same to you because you 'don't do Instagram'). Crystal would also like to thank Tim for his friendship, collegiality, and immense penchant for witty but embarrassing puns, and Tama for his supremely generous mentorship since we first met in 2013, for sharing snippets of his family Instas that always brighten my day, and for his leadership in steering this book to completion.

Introduction

This is not a book specifically about photography, which at first glance might seem quite odd when reading about Instagram. After all, Instagram is synonymous with the mass popularization of mobile, app-based photography. Filters and square frames, part of Instagram's initial affordances, made millions of people armed with nothing more than an iPhone feel like they were crafting photographs that suggested the professionalism of paid photographers (regardless of whether these feelings were justified). Each Instagram filter certainly alluded to a way of manipulating and crafting a photograph to imbue it with a specific meaning. And yet, the most used Instagram filters soon became clichés, often suggesting that the Instagram user was trying too hard to make their image speak in a way it simply could not.

Rather, in this book, we argue that Instagram should best be understood as a conduit for *communication* in the increasingly vast landscape of visual social media cultures. We argue that the visual image, video and other combinations of these elements in Stories are first and foremost about communicating with one another. Instagram is a social media platform, but, we argue, the *visual* focus is particularly important in the success and relevance of the platform. As Instagram has grown from an iPhone-only app into a vast platform owned by Facebook, it has also had to wrestle with being a space where communication and commerce have overlapped, from the appearance of advertising to the rise of Influencers and a new class of content creators who strive for authenticity on a platform best known for selfies and self-representation.

Moreover, as the platform amassed over a billion users, platform-provided filters have given way to socially-driven norms and what we argue is the templatability of visual social media on Instagram.

We argue that Instagram is more than an app, more than a platform, and more than a jewel in the Facebook 'family'. Rather, Instagram is an icon and avatar for understanding and mapping visual social media cultures, whether on Instagram itself, or through the many ways the material world has sought to become 'Insta-worthy' in redesigning practices, cultural institutions and material spaces. Facebook wants it to be an Instagram world out there and this book examines to what extent that desire has succeeded, how Instagram has changed over time, and what elements of Instagram matter the most.

Scroll Down: What's Below?

Chapter 1 focuses on the politics and operation of Instagram as a platform. Politics, here, does not mean national political systems, but rather the way that decisions are made about the way Instagram works, how it is built, how content is framed, how moderation works, what boundaries and rules govern the platform, and how all of these change over time. The chapter explores the early history before Kevin Systrom and Mike Krieger realized they were building an app focused on photos, through competition with Hipstamatic, Picplz, Snapchat and TikTok. We examine how Facebook's purchase of Instagram slowly reshaped the platform, and how major changes such as including Stories radically changed how Instagram is used. We also examine how rules and boundaries in terms of content and moderation have developed and changed over time, including moments when this process does not work as well as it should, and Instagram's insistence that it can refer to all of its users as a singular community, despite the many different and at times opposing perspectives this must contain.

The chapter ends by examining the departure of Instagram's founders in 2018, and the many challenges the platform faced in 2019, from evidence that it is utilized for political manipulation to broader community concerns about failures to protect young people from harmful content.

Our second chapter explores the role of aesthetics – the visual look, feel and design – of Instagram and the way this has changed. Early Instagram, from the icon to the filters, was built on bringing a retro-aesthetic to everyday visual photography and communication, yet from the beginning was reworking what photography meant on the app, pushing a new photographic vernacular of the everyday. Over many iterations, Instagram slowly grew its options, from new filters, to allowing more manual editing of each photo whether filtered or not. At the same time, Instagram's own aesthetic, visible in its icons and interface, grew and changed, with notable ruptures including the shift from the recognizable brown polaroid-derived icon to the rainbow one, and that fateful moment when Instagram's interface stopped using a camera icon to indicate new content being made, replacing it with a plus sign in a box, demonstrating a long journey from the original core function of photography. Similarly, the square frames synonymous with Instagram stopped being mandatory, while the introduction of Stories introduced new interest in vertical images and vertical video to the extent that this shift eventually underpinned the launch of IGTV. The aesthetic norms of selfies shaped, and were shaped by, the Instagram platform as well. The three key ideas featured in this chapter are thus: visual aesthetics, including genres and tropes of content and visual normalization; user practices and norms; and audiences and motivations for Instagram use.

Chapter 3 situates Instagram within the broader ecologies of mobile, social, visual and locative apps and platforms. Instagram has always had keen competitors in the visual social media space, including Web 2.0 elder Flickr to a range of visual apps today from Snapchat to TikTok. Third-party apps also rely on Instagram, such as editing and transformation apps, from beautifying selfies to artistic re-renders. Instagram also has its own emerging ecology of related apps: Bolt, a direct-messaging app similar to Snapchat that was only released for six months in a few countries before disappearing; Hyperlapse, which introduced a new sped-up video aesthetic; Layout, which allows basic image collages (similar to many other third-party apps); Boomerang, Instagram's 2-second looping video app and answer to animated GIFs; and IGTV, Instagram's attempt to take on YouTube by popularizing the vertical video format. This chapter also argues that within the Instagram ecology, space and time are being reconfigured and remediated relative to Instagram itself; time is no longer measured, for example, by dates and times, but in relation to Instagram's Now, so images were shared 10 seconds, or 5 days ago, with no specific date or time beyond that.

In chapter 4 we turn to the economies and economics of Instagram. While Instagram did not launch itself as a place for commerce, or even have advertising for the first few years, this has radically changed over the past few years. We consider how social media Influencers commercialized Instagram, making it into a marketplace for attention and commerce, and the social norms which emerged long before Instagram's official tools were released to, for example, mark a post as paid sponsorship. We examine Influencers' social and cultural strategies for driving up client demand on the app and engaging followers; some vernacular strategies for gaming savvy Instagram use in the midst of changes in the platform over the years; and challenges that have emerged as Instagram became an ecology of economies. We examine the centrality of the selfie as a marker for Influencer economics, and how this has broader implications for the way selfies are viewed, along with strategies Influencers utilize to remain relatable and seemingly authentic despite the rush to commercialize.

The diversity of cultures and groups on Instagram is the focus of chapter 5. Rather than there being a singular understanding and use of Instagram, many different approaches, understandings and vernaculars are visible in the way different groups use the platform. Instagram is best understood in terms of the multiplicity of cultures that are not delimited by specific demographic categories. Young people in different regions are particularly likely to develop their own, specific, often niche uses, which often include shorthands and norms not easily understood by others. Politicians across the globe are turning to Instagram to engage with their citizens, sharing their thoughts and lives, with notable examples such as Singapore's Member of Parliament Baey Yam Keng, New Zealand Prime Minister Jacinda Ardern, and US Representative Alexandria Ocasio-Cortez. Cultural diversity is also visible in the way that cultural, social and domestic spaces and institutions are responding to Instagram. Instagram-specific museums and galleries are emerging where every space is a perfect selfie opportunity, while traditional galleries and museums are carefully crafting opportunities for visual interaction even amongst traditional art. Restaurants, cafés and bars are ensuring they are Insta-worthy, from the design of food and drinks to art and ambience design. Even homes are now being built with the angles and aesthetics crafted to allow ideal Instagram impact every day.

Chapter 6 examines the impact of Instagram over the entire lifespan, from birth to death. While Instagram's Terms of Use prevent anyone under 13 years of age using the platform, Instagram is nevertheless filled with children. Even before birth, the sharing of ultrasound photos to announce a pregnancy is a normalized social ritual. The debates around sharenting illustrate that the question is not whether to share images of children, but when and how often. Parental and child influencers diversify the representations and discussions of parenting and childhood online, but when advertising and sponsorship are involved, they raise difficult questions about the line between representation and exploitation of children. At the other end of life, mourning and selfies at funerals shows that Instagram has opened up new spaces for grieving and celebrating life and, despite moral panics in the press to the contrary, these practices respect and cherish the dead. This chapter also examines the cold reality of what happens to someone's Instagram data after they die. Ultimately, this chapter argues that all Instagram users co-create each other, and in the case of children and the deceased, it is very clear how Instagram users are representing and telling the stories of other people in the posts, comments and Stories they share.

Our final chapter pulls all of the threads together, examining the cumulative impact of the platform: from the Everything of Instagram, to the Instagram of Everything. We look at the materialization of Instagram in everything from stickers and posters to Instagram-themed cameras and bespoke app integration in new phones. We examine the impact of Instagram on popular culture more broadly, and interrogate the phenomenon of virtual Influencers, digital amalgams of design, storytelling, communication and art who command large Instagram audiences but do not exist in the material world beyond the platform. We argue that Instagram use has shifted from a focus on filters, to an era of templatability, where new aesthetic and communication norms are established by celebrities and Influencers that ripple through the platform, establishing the fleeting vernacular norms of the day. We conclude, dabbling in alliteration, and suggest a framework of eight 'A's to understand the future of Instagram: affordances and algorithms; aesthetics and affect; attention and audiences; and agency and activism.

Over to You: Instagram the Instagram Book!

Now that you're reading this book, we have a request: we'd love to know where you're reading and what you think of the book. We would enjoy hearing your reactions, questions, thoughts, constructive criticism or even suggestions for future additions if there's enough interest to one day do a second edition of *Instagram: Visual Social Media Cultures*. The most obvious way to share with us, as you might imagine, is to take a photo on Instagram and use the hashtag #polityinstabook, or tag us at @polityinstabook, or if you'd like to send us a message directly, either use the Direct Message function, or tag us in Stories. If you'd like to follow the book's account on Instagram you are more than welcome; we aim to repost some of the places people are reading, and the thoughts they share with us amongst other Instagram-related material. To follow us on Instagram, you can also just scan our nametag in the image below (figure i.1). We're on Twitter as well (also @polityinstabook) if you would like to follow us there, where we'll be tweeting and retweeting news about Instagram.

Figure i.1. Instagram nametag for @polityinstabook

CHAPTER ONE

Platform

In this first chapter, we explore the emergence and history of Instagram as an app and, quite quickly, a platform. While the term platform is a loaded one (Gillespie 2010), the use of the term here is specifically to draw attention to the fact that Instagram is more than one thing: it is an app; it is a series of programs and algorithms; it is a gigantic database of images, videos, captions, comments, geolocative tags, location tags, likes, emoji and more and more items over time; it is a collection of personal data (connected with similar sets of personal data after the purchase by Facebook); it is an application program interface (API) which enacts rules to allow different apps, platforms and partners to access, add or remove data from the Instagram database; it is a series of decisions and developments over time that create different versions of each of these things; and it also encapsulates various popular understandings of what Instagram 'is' to the more than a billion people who use it. In short, describing Instagram as a platform offers a continual reminder that Instagram is many different things, some at the same time, and some that have quite radically changed over time.

Similarly, in discussing the politics of Instagram, we are not talking about the political influence of the platform (although that is important, and explored near the end of this chapter), but rather we are highlighting the importance of specific decisions and changes which have made Instagram what it is today. While we're outlining some of the major events and decisions that have shaped Instagram, this chapter is by no means exclusive; for a more robust change-by-change outline of Instagram, see the Appendix which offers a chronology of Instagram's various versions and alterations. In this chapter, we are focusing on a few of the bigger changes and moments that have shaped the platform, and use these to situate the platform, and the company, in a broader context. In exploring Instagram, we are always mindful of the broader visual social media landscape of which Instagram is a part, but hope that this exploration of Instagram illuminates more about this broader context as well.

From Burbn to Instagram

Instagram founders Kevin Systrom and Mike Krieger initially began working together on an app in 2010, but it was not focused on photography at all. Rather, inspired by the emergence of location-based check-in apps, the pair were developing a Foursquare competitor, a check-in app called Burbn, based on locating and sharing details of the best bourbon locations. After realizing their app was unlikely to compete with a glut of locative media apps, the two completely stripped their work back to photos, comments and likes with an optional check-in (Swisher 2013).

After experimenting with a number of designs and names, the two settled on Instagram. As Systrom (2011) recalls, they 'renamed because we felt it better captured what you were doing – an instant telegram of sorts. It also sounded camera-y.' While Instagram is well known as an app which changed photography, it's worth remembering that the *immediacy* of 'instant' was the most important thing at the beginning. The *communication* that photography allowed, rather than fidelity to the photographic form, is at the very root of the platform's success. When the app began testing in July 2010, the icon was originally a rendering of an existing instant Polaroid camera, but the complexity of this icon, and potential copyright issues, meant a memorable image was needed. The iconic Instagram app design – which was still broadly inspired by a polaroid camera – was thus designed by Cole Rise and was largely unchanged for the first four years of Instagram (Heath 2014). Cole Rise was also responsible for seven of the original Instagram filters including, unsurprisingly, Rise. Instagram officially launched in the Apple App Store on 6 October 2010, as an iPhone app which allowed instant photography within a square frame (images could *not* be loaded from the phone's gallery), with a series of filters to add different stylistic feels to images, and the ability for followers to like or comment on each image.

Notably, Instagram did not invent photo sharing, or photo filters, or even square frames. Instagram's success was based, in part, on their successful integration and balancing of these elements, but all of them existed at the time in other apps which pre-dated Instagram. The Hipstamatic app, for example, was launched in December 2009 and introduced filters and square frames to iPhone users, and was so successful it was named as one of Apple's Apps of the Year for 2010. In early 2011, *New York Times* photographer Damon Winter won a Picture of the Year International prize for images of US troops in Afghanistan that were taken and processed using Hipstamatic's filters (Winter 2011). The big differences, though, were that Hipstamatic was a paid app ($1.99) and the focus was on the experience of taking and editing a photo, with sharing as secondary (Carter & Maclean 2012). However, on Instagram the social experience – of gaining likes and comments – was central, even if the affordances were largely similar (Vaidhyanathan 2018). While Hipstamatic is still available today, it has a tiny fraction of Instagram's user numbers. In a bittersweet retrospective interview in 2017, the founders of Hipstamatic noted that their app had a 'major role to play in the very existence of Instagram' (Downs & Koebler 2017). Nor was Hipstamatic the only competing app that Instagram had to contend with when it launched.

While Instagram had initially courted iPhone users with their higher quality cameras, PicPlz had gone in the other direction, launching in May 2010 with an Android app, with filters, and which was integrated with Twitter and Foursquare from initial release. Showing a fairly public lack of faith in Instagram, Andreessen Horowitz, one of the two initial investors in Instagram when it was still Burbn, very publicly backed PicPlz with a more significant investment (Swisher 2013). While PicPlz thrived for a time, including releasing an Apple version of the app, it was ultimately Instagram that thrived and PicPlz completed shut down after losing most of its users by July 2012.

Another early investor in Instagram, Twitter co-founder Jack Dorsey, made no secret that he was interested in Instagram coming under the Twitter umbrella. Instagram allowed users to cross-post images directly to Twitter where the full image would appear in the Twitter timeline in a reduced size form. This initial integration added much needed visual content to Twitter, but also greatly increased Instagram's visibility in its early days. Dorsey offered a US$500 million deal to Systrom and Krieger, but was turned down after the company successfully received a further US$50 million from investors. While Systrom also let Facebook's Mark Zuckerberg know Instagram was not on the market, Zuckerberg instead doubled the Instagram offer, with a US$1 billion dollar deal which proved enough to see Instagram become entirely Facebook owned (Shontell 2013). At the time of its sale, Instagram was 18 months old, the company had 13 employees, 30 million users (all on iPhones) and an Android version of the app was only a week old.

Facebook Purchase

In April 2012, Facebook announced that they had signed a US$1 billion deal to buy Instagram (Facebook 2012). There was an immediate backlash from Instagram users who feared that the app would be dismantled or become another extension of the main Facebook site. Attempting to reassure those users, in their official press release Facebook stated:

we need to be mindful about keeping and building on Instagram's strengths and features rather than just trying to integrate everything into Facebook. That's why we're committed to building and growing Instagram independently. Millions of people around the world love the Instagram app and the brand associated with it, and our goal is to help spread this app and brand to even more people. (Facebook 2012).

On Instagram's blog, Kevin Systrom noted that he and Mike Krieger would continue, as Facebook employees, to helm Instagram, emphasizing that their app would remain unique: 'We'll be working with Facebook to evolve Instagram and build the network. We'll continue to add new features to the product and find new ways to create a better mobile photos experience. The Instagram app will still be the same one you know and love' (Systrom 2012). Thus, despite the intense user backlash when it was first announced, the purchase of Instagram by Facebook became less and less visible, less and less remembered, to the extent that by 2018 surveys suggested that less than half of Americans even knew that Facebook owned Instagram (DuckDuckGo 2018).

While US$1 billion may not seem an enormous sum in light of Instagram's subsequent growth, it is important to remember that at the time Facebook purchased the company, they had no business model and had not made a single cent of revenue. While it may be hard to remember an Instagram without ads, the platform did not start experimenting with advertising until late 2013, and only rolled out its advertising tools globally, and opened it to all businesses, in September 2015. Of course, as users with significant Instagram followings started to attract sponsorship and advertising outside of the platform's tools, the transparency of the commercial dealings of Influencers led to Instagram adding a 'Paid Partnership with' tag in mid-2017 so that all paid, promoted and endorsed content could be clearly marked, as is explored in chapter 5.

The purchase of Instagram by Facebook did not help relationships with other social media companies, though, especially Twitter. In June 2012, as part of wider changes to third-party access, Twitter blocked the ability for Instagram users to 'find friends' who they were connected to on Twitter (Robertson 2012). Six months later, Twitter also removed the ability for Instagram images to appear in the main Twitter timeline (D'Orazio 2012). Where Instagram images had previously been embedded in Twitter, the changes meant that posts could now only appear as a link which needed to be clicked and opened in another program – a browser or app – in order to see the image. These changes showed further antagonism between Twitter heads and Instagram's new owners, Facebook, and that relationship has never really mended.

Instagram's purchase by Facebook should not be understood just as eclipsing a rival platform before it grew too large. Nor should it be understood simply as Facebook trying to become a bigger player in the visual social media stakes. Importantly, perhaps most importantly, Facebook also acquired all of the underlying Instagram user data from the date of purchase onward. The data generated by taking a photograph, and the metadata (data about that photo) generated by the mobile device taking the photo, and added manually by the user in terms of tagging people, locations, adding hashtags, or simply in the image's captions, all add to the usefulness of the image as a datapoint that can be added to, compared with, and analysed as part of other data points (Vaidhyanathan 2018). As social media scholar and critic Siva Vaidhyanathan (2018, p. 55) warns, 'Facebook has grown into the most pervasive surveillance system in the world. It's also the most reckless and irresponsible surveillance system in the commercial world.' As a jewel in Facebook's suite of apps and offerings, Instagram is part of the Facebook empire, and the personal data of Instagram's users is subject to the same conditions, uses, analyses and potential misuses as any other Facebook user (whether or not an Instagram user actually has a separate Facebook account). Moreover, subsequent changes to Instagram, which saw users encouraged to return to the platform more and more, should also be understood as part of the larger Facebook strategy of 'keeping more people interacting with Facebook services in different ways to generate more data' (Vaidhyanathan 2018, p. 39).

Despite now being Facebook employees, Kevin Systrom and Mike Krieger worked hard as Instagram's Heads to ensure that the platform did not get thought of as Facebook. Even as data, practices, policies and employees fell under a single umbrella, the upbeat public face of Instagram was distinct, colourful and a long way from the Facebook mothership. Instagram continued to appeal to younger people, to teens especially, even as Facebook became home to an older and older demographic. As late as 2018, *Guardian* journalist Scott Greer (2018) argued that very strategically, 'Instagram has been able to maintain a charming image and dissociate itself from Facebook at every turn.'

Third-Party Instagram Apps and API Changes

In late 2015 Instagram announced changes to their Application Program Interface, or API, which is essentially the software and rules which allow other platforms and apps to access the Instagram platform. The rule changes, which were staggered and many were actually enforced from 1 June 2016, meant that third-party Instagram readers (such as Padgram) and web-based Instagram clients (such as Webstagram) essentially could no longer operate. Instagram's altered and tightened APIs, and related policies, were ostensibly to better ensure the quality of third-party apps, but also came at a time when Instagram itself was beginning to undergo significant change and internal consolidation (Constine 2015). While the API changes did not have the same impact as they did when Twitter made the first dramatic changes to their API (Bohn 2012), it nevertheless demonstrated a significant shift in the way Instagram interacted with other developers who utilized the Instagram platform in any capacity. Instagram's API changes essentially ended an early phase where third-party applications had almost free reign, to a more controlled ecology where Instagram were far more careful and selective about who could access Instagram data and what could be done with it.

It is no coincidence that Instagram's API changes came in the midst of the platform releasing several standalone apps of its own. In August 2014, Instagram quietly released the Hyperlapse app for Apple devices, which allowed users to speed up, smooth and stabilize video footage to create appealing, condensed videos of longer periods of activity. In March 2015, another Instagram app, Layout, was added, which allowed users to create image collages of various forms and post these directly to Instagram. Layout was particularly notable in that it replicated the functionality present in many of the third-party Instagram apps, showing that Facebook was all too happy to pick and choose some of the most popular elements of Instagram's ecology of third-party apps. The third Instagram-related app, Boomerang, was released in October the same year; it allowed the capture of two-second long looped videos, in aesthetically similar territory to animated GIFs (Miltner & Highfield 2017), but as video rather than image files. The emergence of Instagram's own suite of apps, and the changes forced onto all third-party apps accessing Instagram's data, is explored in more detail in chapter 3. Of course, the most turbulent relationship between Instagram and another platform is the ongoing turf war with Snapchat, which is explored below in relation to the emergence of Stories.

Finstagrams, Rinstagrams and Multiple Accounts

While Mark Zuckerberg has been widely and publicly insistent that Facebook users only have one 'real' identity, and should thus only have one 'real' Facebook account (Haimson & Hoffmann 2016), Instagram has historically been far more flexible in terms of names, identities and multiple accounts. However, while uniqueness might not have characterized all Instagram users, relatively quickly a certain aesthetic expectation did: Instagram feeds were highly polished and curated, not really spaces for untamed frivolity or silliness. In this context, Finstagrams, or Finstas, emerged; Finstagrams were almost always private accounts, with very low numbers of (trusted) followers, featuring content that was often disruptive, ironic or at odds with the main Instagram aesthetic (such as reposted content, memes and so forth). These led to the main Instagram accounts being redubbed Rinstagrams, or Rinstas, which, were usually public accounts, featuring polished content that were carefully edited to add to a specific look, style or brand. Yet Finstas, to some extent, were swiftly seen as more authentic: in a *New York Times* piece (Safronova 2015) reporting on the popularity of Finstas, these 'Fake Instagram' accounts were specifically characterized as presenting something portrayed as lacking in 'real' Instagram: 'truer version[s] of themselves than their main profiles'. Seemingly endorsing the holding of multiple accounts, addressing different audiences, in February 2016 Instagram added the ability to move between multiple Instagram accounts without having to log out. Switching between Instas and Finstas became a breeze. While Instagram's owner Facebook consistently argues that there is only one 'real' authentic 'you' online (van Dijck 2013), Instagram's promotion of the ease of movement between multiple accounts, and the emergence of prompts to 'Share a Different Side of Yourself. Create a private account to share photos and videos with a close group of followers' (see

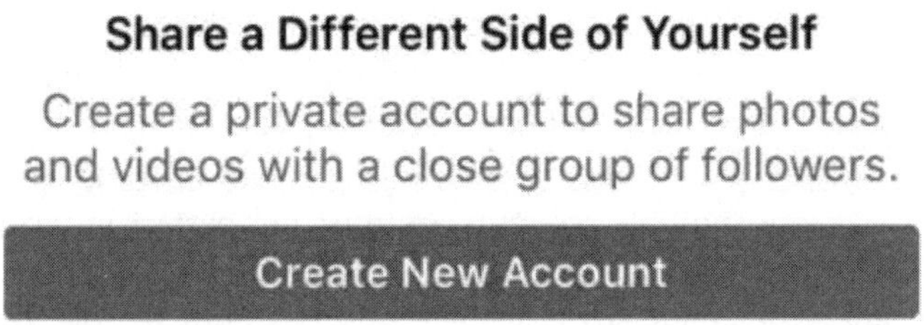

Share a Different Side of Yourself

Create a private account to share photos and videos with a close group of followers.

Create New Account

Figure 1.1. Instagram 'Create New Account' popup message, 2017

figure 1.1), reveals Instagram is far more supportive of the idea that multiple accounts are needed to address and engage with different groups and contexts (Abidin 2017d).

While one motivation for Instagram's flexibility is clearly financial – multiple accounts almost certainly means more time on Instagram, more time seeing advertisements and more loyalty to the platform – it is also important to note that the platform is simultaneously more flexible and accommodating to a multiplicity of voices, perspectives and performances by individuals and groups. It's also a big bonus for social media managers, of course, meaning that multiple people can contribute to and manage a particular brand's account without having to completely log out of their own personal accounts every time. While Facebook's real identity policy faced a considerable backlash from queer communities (Newton 2014) and other marginalized groups for whom digital pseudonymity is paramount for personal safety and self-actualization (Holpuch 2015), the company responded to criticism minimally, insisting identities were still singular, but relaxing their policy to allow users to use 'the name they go by in everyday life' to 'keep our community safe' (Facebook 2018b). On Instagram, multiple accounts are not just tolerated, but actively encouraged, which allows for far more meaningful privacy and audience segmentation. Of course, where privacy is a concern, Finstas are an important strategy for controlling who sees what content on Instagram (Duffy & Chan 2019), yet as early as 2015 popular reporting noted the problem of 'finsta snitches' (Safronova 2015) who betrayed the trust of Finsta users, capturing and reposting Finsta content in more mainstream settings, disrupting the users' attempts to control the contexts in which their content is seen. While Finstas and multiple accounts are thus not perfect in terms of allowing private and more carefully moderated spaces, Instagram's approach nevertheless is far more flexible and meaningful than is possible on Facebook's main platform (Highfield & Leaver 2015).

The Algorithmic Timeline

In June 2016, Instagram shifted from a chronological display of Instagram content in a user's feed to an algorithmically sorted timeline in a move which angered many users and was widely considered more like Mark Zuckerberg's famous instruction to 'move fast and break things' (Vaidhyanathan 2018). Like the Facebook newsfeed and related proprietary tools for making decisions about content and curation, the algorithmic timeline is opaque to most users, which led to wild speculation about exactly how decisions are made. In 2018 Instagram briefed technology reporters on the broad parameters of how the algorithmic timeline operates, in part to reassure businesses and brands that the algorithms would continue to ensure a level playing field and that users would see their content, even as the number of users continues to grow. According to their briefing, each user's unique Instagram feed is based on three core categories:

- Interest – how much Instagram perceives a user will want to see a post based on past viewing of similar content;
- Recency – how new the post is; and
- Relationship – how close a user is to the user posting the content. This is determined by a range of things, including frequency of past liking, comments and being tagged in photos together.

In addition, other minor signals that influence the timeline include how often a user opens Instagram, how many people they follow, and how much time they tend to spend on Instagram each time it is opened (Constine 2018b).

Of course, there are many other algorithms at work on Instagram, from those which determine suggested accounts to follow, through to those that flag content for moderation or removal, through to those that curate the Explore area, matching content and accounts with the recorded activity of each user. Indeed, even the previous chronological timeline was delivered by an algorithm, although the difference here is that the operation of that algorithm was transparent to users. While the scope of algorithmic activities are often invisible to users, and difficult to map or even track, it's important to recall that all large platforms using algorithms necessarily include cultural assumptions and social norms of some kind in those algorithms, often perpetuating inequalities of various kinds (Gillespie 2018; Noble 2018).

As social media scholar Taina Bucher has argued, the introduction of an algorithmic timeline, or anything labelled as algorithmic, invites users to imagine and respond to the perceived cultural logic of the algorithm. Many Instagram users took to Twitter and other platforms to decry the upcoming timeline changes as something that would destroy their existing experiences of the platform as it would codify elements of popularity and ranking that were perceived to be antithetical to their everyday uses. Thus, in mapping responses to the introduction of Instagram's algorithmic timeline, the response from users revealed that for them 'algorithms are seen as powerbrokers that you either play with or play against' (Bucher 2018, p. 112). The algorithmic timeline was met with the hashtag #RIPInstagram being used on Twitter to lament the changes, and discuss them in a largely negative way (Skrubbeltrang, Grunnet & Tarp 2017). That said, just like Facebook's newsfeed changes, Instagram did not appear to lose many, if any, users as the algorithmic timeline was rolled

out for everyone. Indeed, interpreting and gaming the algorithm has become something of a social media dark art, as
discussed in chapter 4.

Communities, Boundaries and Content Moderation

The notion of the Instagram Community as a singular group,
or even vaguely meaningful collection of people beyond the
basic fact that these are all people who have chosen to download and create an account on Instagram, stretches the idea of
community further than is meaningful. The use of the term
community is, however, not accidental, and instead is part
of a broader strategy to name and, to some extent, control or
constrain the behaviour of Instagram users (Gillespie 2018).
Perhaps the most notable place where the Instagram community is officially named into being is in the Community
Guidelines which outline what was is, and what is not, permitted on the platform. In the short, summary version, of these
guidelines, Instagram sums up their position thus: 'We want
Instagram to continue to be an authentic and safe place for
inspiration and expression. Help us foster this community.
Post only your own photos and videos and always follow the
law. Respect everyone on Instagram, don't spam people or
post nudity' (Instagram 2018b). There are far more details
after that short summary, but in essence the description
reminds users that Instagram is a policed platform, and there
are rules to follow. Internet researcher Tarleton Gillespie
describes the Instagram guidelines as a positioning of the
platform as a community keeper, meaning that the Instagram
community is spoken about as a 'fragile community, one that
must be guarded so as to survive' (Gillespie 2018, p. 49). This
rationale leads to a number of different rules and forms of
content moderation, both algorithmically automated – where
algorithms detect and delete the most obvious forms of non-
permitted content such as explicit pornography – and manual,

where human moderators view and judge content explicitly reported by other Instagram users.

Initially the Instagram Community Guidelines explicitly banned all nudity, regardless of context, including any display of female nipples. However, after a number of Instagram users publicly reported their accounts being shut down for showing breast-feeding photos, Instagram eventually responded to strong community sentiment that this activity should not be positioned as sexual or worthy of banning (Grossman 2015). The community outcry over the hypocrisy of removing, amongst others, many images of breastfeeding mothers, saw Instagram and Facebook revise their guidelines to create exceptions to this rule (Locatelli 2017). As such, Instagram's updated Community Guidelines show a more contextually aware approach to the visibility of nipples on the platform:

> We know that there are times when people might want to share nude images that are artistic or creative in nature, but for a variety of reasons, we don't allow nudity on Instagram. This includes photos, videos, and some digitally-created content that show sexual intercourse, genitals, and close-ups of fully-nude buttocks. It also includes some photos of female nipples, but photos of post-mastectomy scarring and women actively breastfeeding are allowed. Nudity in photos of paintings and sculptures is OK, too. (Instagram 2018b)

This tempering of the guidelines serves as a reminder that guidelines are constantly being revised, as are the ways that human moderators judge flagged content, and this process can often be perceived as responding to potential bad publicity (such as the media outcry around breastfeeding photos being removed) rather than necessarily internally driven reviews of what the singular, imagined Instagram community actually want (Gillespie 2018). The constant revision of the Community Guidelines also reflects the potential arbitrariness of the moderation process, in terms of the reporting options available to users, the feedback they are given after a report, and questions about the consistency of moderation decisions (Witt, Suzor & Huggins 2019).

Instagram, like many social media platforms, has also had real difficulty in managing content which valorizes and promotes eating disorders, which we refer to collectively as 'pro-ED', but is usually referred to by those who post and search for this material as 'pro-ana' (promoting anorexia) content (Gerrard 2018). The line between pro-ED material and more socially acceptable depictions of, and aspirations for, thinness, are blurred at best. As gender and media researcher Gemma Cobb (2017) argues, on many platforms pro-ED material is deliberately disguised as health motivation posts, aspirational (healthy) weight images or something else which is – in terms of culture promoted by the platform – socially acceptable. For several years, Instagram's Community Guidelines explicitly banned eating disorder accounts and content, stating they would remove 'any account found encouraging or urging users to embrace anorexia, bulimia, or other eating disorders' (quoted in Cobb 2017). While that absolute ban has been lifted, Instagram now provides warnings and resources rather than erasing all pro-ED material. Building on advice from health professionals, a new sub-section of Instagram's Help Centre called 'About Eating Disorders' (Instagram 2018a) provides suggestions on how to engage with people with eating disorders, and refers to explicit resources and services that can provide support.

While Instagram employs a mix of algorithmic filtering, hashtag bans (some permanent, some temporary), account removal and limiting content from search and explore, the policing of hashtags has received the most attention, but is also the easiest to do since this is where content has been explicitly labelled by the user posting it. Yet hashtag banning is far from perfect; when thin inspiration tags #thinspo and #thinspiration were blocked, for example, thinly veiled alternative spellings would quickly emerge such as #thynspiration or #thinspoooo (Cobb 2017). Also, when images are ambiguous (possibly about eating disorders, possibly not), often users will use many hashtags, disrupting the potential of a hashtag to clearly provide context and situate a post. So, a post might include #diet, #healthy, #gymlife and many other tags before also including #thinspo and #bonespo, confusing easy (and automated) banning and classification of images (Cobb 2017, p. 109). At the time of writing this chapter, for example, #bonespo returned a health warning before directing users to (a) Get Support, (b) See Posts Anyway or (c) cancel the search (see figure 1.2). And while #bonespo returns the health warning screen, the tag #bonespoo (with one extra o), which was suggested when searching for #bonespo, does not have a warning screen. However, top #bonespoo posts clearly include pro-ED content from accounts which have in their description the request 'Don't report, just block', showing these users have an active awareness of Instagram's policing of these images, and are trying to circumvent being deleted. Similarly, while hashtags for pro-ED are being banned and policed, other Instagram mechanisms actively achieve the opposite, using alternate signals to effectively assist users looking for pro-ED content (Gerrard 2018; Olszanowski 2014).

While Instagram has always publicly been a family friendly environment, the platform has a long history of being used to distribute all sorts of pornography and other adult material (Shah 2015). While many posts have been removed, accounts closed and hashtags banned (some permanently, others temporarily), Instagram has never been able to completely remove adult material from the platform. Indeed, the eggplant emoji hashtag # 🍆 has the dubious honour of being the first known emoji hashtag to be (temporarily) banned from Instagram searches, in large part due to the use of the hashtag to playfully indicate male genitals (Highfield 2018). In many ways, the increased privacy that direct messages and self-deleting stories offer may also provide new avenues for the sharing of nudity, pornography and other material that is simply not publicly visible and thus never flagged by users who see this

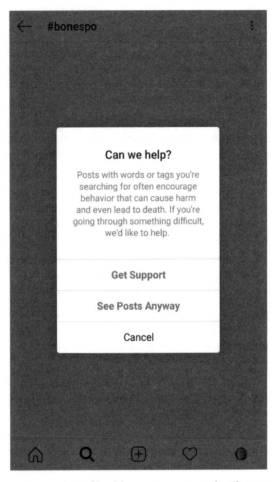

Figure 1.2. Screenshot of health warning returned with Instagram #bonespo search

as problematic. Instagram's algorithms similarly appear to do a much better job at automatically detecting nudity and pornography and removing it than other banned content (either directly, or triggering review by moderators) but even then the algorithms can be foiled by low resolution images and other visual elements that distort the digital footprint of nudity to fool an algorithm, but which is still clearly and obviously nudity to (human) viewers.

The development of communities also leads to norms within these groups, ideas of acceptable practice and conduct, which might work against what other users view as appropriate, or even against Instagram's own guidelines. As Tarleton Gillespie (2018, p. 197) argues, the way content is policed explains a lot about the power and politics behind a platform:

> Content moderation is such a complex sociotechnical undertaking that, all things considered, it's amazing that it works at all, and as well as it does. Even so, as a society we have once again handed over to private companies the power to set and enforce the boundaries of appropriate public speech for us. That is enormous cultural power held by a few deeply invested stakeholders, and it is being done behind closed doors, making it difficult for anyone else to inspect or challenge.

Instagram's insistence on describing their more than a billion users as a singular community, with one set of rules to govern that entire community, means that the diversity of users and specific contexts of communication and content sharing are often lost. While chapter 5 outlines some of the very diverse communities that flourish and connect on Instagram, the boundaries established by Instagram's content moderation and removal policies mean that other groups and other communities have either dived deeper into Instagram, beyond hashtags and public accounts, or have moved to other visual social media platforms altogether.

Stories and Snapchat

By the beginning of 2016, Instagram's biggest competitor in the visual social media landscape was Snapchat. Like Instagram, Snapchat's focus was on the app experience, but unlike Instagram, and almost every other social media platform at the time, Snapchat focused on content which disappeared. Snapchat's 'Snaps' were content which, after being viewed, were removed from the app. Snapchat can be understood as part of a new type of social media platform which is underpinned by the appeal of ephemerality, or the notion that communication in the form of photos, visuals and video is not permanent but can disappear either immediately or after 24 hours (Bayer et al. 2016). Ephemerality is a significant shift since previous understandings of social media positioned *permanence* of communication as one of their defining features (boyd & Ellison 2007). Snapchat had huge appeal to the lucrative teen market, and quickly challenged Instagram for the youth market. Indeed in 2013, Snapchat very publicly rejected an offer of US$3 billion from Facebook to buy the platform (Ask 2013), the same year that Snapchat introduced Stories, a new type of sharing where users can post images and video in (up to) ten-second chunks which can be viewed for 24 hours from their initial posting.

Communication scholar Oren Soffer (2016) argues that Snapchat's ephemerality is 'the counter-logic of new media information aggregation'. For Soffer, ephemeral applications return to an oral paradigm of communication, where the visual is now a disappearing utterance (thus more oral than textual in nature). This inability to store and archive the message (or 'Snap') changes the nature of the communication process. Or, as Professor of Digital Culture Jill Walker Rettberg (2018, p. 192) succinctly puts it, 'Snapchat is a conversation, not an archive.' Equally important, the ephemeral nature of this conversation means that more users tend to pay more focused attention to these exchanges as they know they're unable to return to them (Bayer et al. 2016). Thus, in Snapchat, Instagram had a competitor that was capturing both the conversation, and attention, of one of their most prized demographic groups.

While mainstream press reporting made Snapchat and sexting synonymous as soon as self-deleting social media began, almost all research has found that while sexting is certainly a minority use, the vast majority of Snapchat exchanges are far more mundane elements of everyday life, from jokes to cute kittens and beyond (Bayer et al. 2016; Roesner, Gill & Kohno 2014). However, the ephemeral or disappearing nature of Snapchat content was never as absolute as it appeared. Even when Snapchat was only Snaps (before the Stories function), it was still possible to capture a snap by taking a screenshot, and far from being a violation of privacy expectations (although clearly this would be the case in some contexts), often taking screenshots demonstrates the value of the Snap, showing the recipient valued it enough to go to more effort to capture and save it. In effect, screenshotting thus takes on a form of value and currency in seemingly ephemeral Snapchat exchanges (Handyside & Ringrose 2017). Given the popularity of Snapchat for everyday uses and communication, it is no surprise then that Instagram adapted the format for their own.

In August 2016, Instagram launched their own Stories format and gave the new communication tool pride of place, at the top of the Instagram app. At the time of the launch, Instagram CEO Kevin Systrom was perfectly happy to admit that Snapchat had pioneered the Stories format and had initially popularized it; Instagram was not reinventing the wheel, but rather adapting the already successful format and expanding it in new ways with Instagram's users. Systrom argued that Facebook invented newsfeed, Twitter invented hashtags and now Snapchat had invented Stories, but this was a format that Instagram and others could integrate and build on (Constine 2016). Before Stories launched, users were spending less and less time on Instagram; the more polished main Instagram feed meant many people were carefully choosing images, but posting rarely, and thus checking Instagram less often. Instagram Stories immediately turned that trend around, with users spending more time on the platform, and finding in Stories a space where they could post multiple times, sometimes many times, daily. Similarly, the fact that Stories disappeared after 24 hours meant users checked in more often, so they would not miss any important material from their friends and people they follow. In reflecting on the launch of Stories, Systrom emphasized that Stories created a space where people are much more comfortable sharing, discussing and playing with all the little moments of their everyday life which do not really fit into the (often more polished) main Instagram timeline (Constine 2018c).

By 2017, the growth of Stories on Instagram was the biggest driver for Instagram's overall success. The leaner Stories format was quickly expanded, to include options for Live Video, the inclusion of a range of filters – including the very prominent face filters popularized by Snapchat – as well as a range of other creative tools, including 'stickers' for text, for polls, for asking followers questions, and many other things. By the first anniversary of Stories on Instagram, there were 250 million Instagram users using Stories every single day, a number which was more than the total number of users on Snapchat at the same time. While Instagram did not, and did not claim to, invent the Stories format, the platform quickly became the most popular home for Stories. At the same time, the ephemeral, disappearing nature of Stories was dulled somewhat with the appearance of Stories Highlights, where users could gather a collection of themed Story segments and prominently display them on their main profile. Here, the balance between the ephemerality of communication and the performativity of the main Instagram profile seemingly allowed the best of both worlds for Instagram.

Stories not only became the research and development space for Instagram, where almost all new tools, integrations and changes were first rolled out, but Stories opened Instagram to other partnerships, either integrating messages from other platforms like Spotify to add what users are listening to, or deeper integrations where content and media from third parties were integrated into the Stories toolkit and experience. The inclusions of animated GIFs and music 'stickers' are two prominent examples of these strategic integrations and partnerships. The normalization of vertical video in Instagram (and other platform) Stories even led to the mid-2018 launch of IGTV – InstaGram TeleVision – both as a standalone app, and integrated into the main Instagram app, which initially supported video of up to sixty minutes. Whether vertical video has as much appeal as Stories remains to be seen, but IGTV is just one more example of terrain Instagram has explored thanks to the Stories format. IGTV has also allowed Instagram quietly to explore streaming video in part to combat newer platforms like Twitch that attract more and more viewers.

GIF Stickers
While GIFs (short animated images) have a much longer history than Instagram, having been very popular on the early web, they were for a time quite uncommon online, only to have had a major resurgence with the popularity of reaction GIFs, both standalone, on tumblr, and, significantly, embedded into many popular platforms, including Twitter and Facebook (Highfield & Leaver 2016; Miltner & Highfield 2017). While not encoded in the GIF format, the aesthetic norms of GIFs are evident in Instagram's Boomerang app (and Boomerang button in Stories), which captures a very short video clip which is then looped backwards and forwards. However, by late January 2018 it was clear that GIFs were an important expressive form that Instagram had not yet capitalized on, so the platform released GIF Stickers for Stories, allowing GIFs to be added to and overlaid on Instagram Stories. Like Snapchat, Instagram partnered with the company Giphy to deliver a moderated library of GIFs to Instagram users. The addition of GIF Stickers, like the Stories format itself, was clearly aimed at keeping teens and younger users on Instagram, ensuring they have the full visual social media suite of tools to express themselves.

The integration of GIFs on Instagram also shows one of the challenges in integrating third-party services and content. Just a month after the stickers were launched, Instagram quickly removed all GIFs from their platform after a highly offensive and racist GIF was found, shared and then decried on social media (Constine 2018e). A few weeks later the GIF Sticker returned to Instagram, but only after some very careful media in which Giphy took complete responsibility for the racist GIF slipping onto Instagram (and Snapchat), and promised such content would never make it through to the carefully moderated library that Giphy provides to third parties, including Instagram (Welch 2018). Giphy's tightened moderation appears to have worked, with no notable complaints since this one incident, but this example does serve as a reminder that Instagram includes content from a range of sources and other companies and platforms, so that decisions about content are not just exercises in moderating users and their media, but also decisions about what other material to draw onto Instagram, and what to avoid. All of these decisions shape the experience and use of Instagram as a platform.

Music Stickers

The official integration of music into Instagram came relatively late given the enormous success of Musical.ly, which eclipsed Snapchat's number of users in 2017 and was purchased by and integrated into TikTok (or douyin in China) in 2018 (Price 2018). TikTok allows teens to lip sync and perform to fifteen-second clips from various songs and audio sources. The affordances and limitations of the platform shaped these performances; recordings could be done in slow or fast time, but no extra audio and no other text or visual elements (emoji or gifs) could be added. This led to a rich, vibrant shared lexicon of hand signs and gestural meaning which tended to add emphasis and depth to performances (Rettberg 2017). Thus, when Instagram added Song Stickers to Instagram Stories in mid-2018, the stickers completely replaced any audio from the story, in keeping with the norms teens and others had learnt and brought with them from using Musical.ly/TikTok/douyin.

Moreover, Instagram's initial release of the Music Stickers happened just weeks before Musical.ly's purchase by TikTok and the Musical.ly app was removed (with users forcibly migrated to TikTok), a perfect time to capture some of those Musical.ly users (or 'musers') who felt alienated by the forced transition to a new service (Spangler 2018). As with Giphy and GIFs, though, integrating music into Stories is a complicated balance of technical and legal issues. Initially Music Stickers were only released in Australia, New Zealand, France, Germany, Sweden, the UK and the US, under the umbrella licensing deal Facebook struck with a range of music corporations including Universal Music, Sony Music and Warner Music as well as a number of independent licensing agencies (Dredge 2018). Instagram users in other countries not covered by this deal initially saw a label indicating music is not available in their region (as discussed in chapter 3). Overall, though, the integration of music, GIFs, and other content into Stories, with little fanfare, shows the ongoing importance of Stories as the format and area where Instagram's changes, growth and development are most tightly focused.

A Business Model

When Facebook purchased Instagram for US$1 billion, it is worth remembering that at that time Instagram had not made a single cent in profit. The platform was very popular and growing rapidly, but there was no existing business model in place. While Facebook clearly had their eye on monetization from the beginning, Instagram only began experimenting with official advertisements in October 2013, and then only in the United States. Every advertisement featured a prominent 'Sponsored' notification (as official advertisements still do), but were relatively rare in the main feed. While the platform was slow and careful in rolling out advertising more widely, by September 2015 the Instagram advertising tools were made available to anyone who wanted to use them, for advertising across the entire platform. As Instagram became more and more popular for advertisers, the number of paid messages in the main feed reached as high as one in four or five, but the gradual roll out meant that people became acclimatized slowly to the change, and no significant resistance or protest was registered. As Instagram Stories increased in popularity, specific advertising tools were released for Stories, with Shopping Stickers rolling out in 2018, as well as direct sales links also in 2018, allowing Instagram users to make purchases without leaving the platform at all.

Somewhat more controversially, though, Instagram also became home for a less official economy in the form of sponsored, promoted and paid messages delivered by Influencers. While the Influencer economy is explored in far more detail in chapter 4, it is still worth noting that the difficulty in balancing communication with commerce is most evident when examining Influencer practices. Initially, Influencers rarely declared when their content was paid sponsorship, which led to a range of controversies. In most cases, national advertising standards were unclear as to whether existing rules required Influencers to declare when posts were paid advertising, but over the last few years these rules have tightened significantly. In June 2017 Instagram tried to defuse this tension by giving Influencers (and all business accounts) a tool to declare that specific posts were 'Paid Partnership With' the specific brand or company. While this and other changes are important, finding the right balance between official advertising, the economy of Influencers, and a platform premised on authentic sharing and personal communication, remains an ongoing challenge.

The Departure of Instagram Founders Kevin Systrom and Mike Krieger

In October 2018, Kevin Systrom and Mike Krieger both officially stepped down from their roles heading Instagram.

While this was done quietly, with polite congratulations and thanks from a range of people, including Mark Zuckerberg, it nevertheless marked a huge shift for Instagram itself, and for the relationship between it and its parent company, Facebook. In interviews following his departure, Systrom was diplomatically quiet on the details, but did concede that 'No one ever leaves a job because everything's awesome', which was widely interpreted to mean the tensions around keeping Instagram independent were too much as Mark Zuckerberg wrestled more and more control away from Systrom and Krieger (Wagner 2018). A cover story for *Wired* magazine in April 2019 claimed that Mark Zuckerberg had been threatened by Instagram and Kevin Systrom's success, and Systrom's obvious appeal to the media. More than that, Zuckerberg had deliberately made it harder for traffic to flow from the main Facebook app to Instagram after he learnt that users were 'leaking' away from Facebook to Instagram (Thompson & Vogelstein 2019). Systrom was replaced by Adam Mosseri who was previously the Head of Newsfeed at Facebook, suggesting that Instagram's direction, and Facebook's, were going to be much more closely tied in the coming years. However Mosseri's first six months at Instagram were rocky ones, with revelations about the depth of Instagram as a site of political interference in US elections coming to light, a major scandal in the UK relating to self-harm content on Instagram after the suicide of British teenager Molly Russell, and news of Zuckerberg's plans to redevelop all the core Facebook apps to integrate messaging across Facebook, Instagram and Whatsapp.

Political Interference in the US
In the wake of the 2016 Presidential elections in the US, it became apparent that both Facebook and Twitter had been utilized by Russian-based groups to manipulate public sentiment about the American elections both through traditional posts as well as paid advertising. Most notable of the groups

investigated and named was the Russian-based Internet Research Agency (IRA). Perhaps less well known is the fact that Instagram was also an avenue through which the IRA delivered political messaging and electoral interference. Moreover, far from ending with President Trump's election, research released in 2018 showed that not only that Instagram continued to be a conduit for political manipulation, but that after the interference on Facebook and Twitter was made public, the focus of the IRA's activity shifted specifically, and in largest proportion, to Instagram (DiResta et al. 2018; Howard et al. 2018).

What was most notable about the IRA Instagram accounts is that they did not begin as political accounts, but rather built a distinct and reliable network through what appeared to be legitimate content, before periodically integrating explicitly political material which usually favoured then-candidate Donald Trump and denounced Democratic candidate Hilary Clinton. Of 133 IRA Instagram accounts mapped in a New Knowledge report (DiResta et al. 2018), the largest account, @blackstagram__ had over 300,000 followers, with their content receiving more than 27 million likes. The aim of this account appears to have been to sow distrust and discord amongst black communities and convince them that voting for any candidate was a waste of their time. Moreover, many of the most effective Instagram posts were memes of various kinds, some recognizable, some using the images of the presidential candidates, but all clearly conveying a political payload. Some IRA accounts went as far as to sell merchandise, both as a fundraising effort for their own messaging campaigns but also, crucially, as a means to gather both clearer personal data (name, exact address, credit card details) and as a marker of clear political leaning, as the purchasing of political merchandise is a very direct marker of political allegiance.

In 2017 when Facebook admitted they had detected and shut down a raft of IRA accounts on Facebook, they also, more quietly, acknowledged a further 170 IRA Instagram accounts had just been detected and removed (Isaac & Wakabayashi 2017). Notably, while less in overall volume, the IRA posts on Instagram appear to have been the most effective, on average provoking the largest measurable reactions in terms of likes and comments (DiResta et al. 2018; Howard et al. 2018). For Instagram, Facebook and all large online platforms, the question of political manipulation remains an ongoing and important challenge. Balancing the Silicon Valley ideology underpinning Facebook and Instagram, while operating across the globe, and attempting not to upset countries, citizens and political systems with differing, at times divergent, needs, is no small issue. Indeed, Facebook commented that most IRA content on their platforms, including on Instagram, did not obviously violate any of their policies, which is why the content persisted (Isaac & Wakabayashi 2017). Whether this material violated US laws, or whether new laws will come into place in the US or elsewhere, is also a topic of considerable debate.

It is clear and undeniable that Instagram is a space for political discussion, political debate and, to date at least, political manipulation. The fact that the IRA went to so much effort to utilize Instagram shows their belief in the value of the social ties that exist between Instagram users. Targeting Instagram confirms that Instagram matters as a realm of taste, politics and cultural knowledge, something explored in more detail in chapter 5. How Instagram, Facebook and others respond to the more explicit political uses, and misuses, of their platforms may well colour how much trust, and use, these platforms enjoy in years to come.

Molly Russell's Suicide and Self-Harm Images on Instagram
As noted earlier, for several years, Instagram's Community Guidelines explicitly banned a range of content, stating 'any account found encouraging or urging users to ... cut, harm themselves, or commit suicide will result in a disabled account without warning' (quoted in Cobb 2017). Research on the

impact of Instagram and other social media on mental health, self-harm and youth suicide emphasizes social media as an amplifier, but whether this is positive or negative depends as much on the user and context as anything else (Seabrook, Kern & Rickard 2016). Notably, even amongst calls to ban any mention of suicide or self-harm on large social media platforms, there is evidence that these are very effective platforms for suicide prevention messaging, and while depression, anxiety and social media are linked at times, there is no clear causation from one to the other (Robinson, Bailey & Byrne 2017).

In 2017, British teenager Molly Russell tragically took her own life. In early 2019, Molly Russell's father very publicly and articulately argued that Instagram 'helped kill my daughter' after it was found she had been following a number of accounts that displayed and romanticized self-harm and suicide (Crawford 2019). In the wake of Molly Russell's death, UK Health Secretary Matt Hancock very publicly called for social media companies to do more in removing self-harm and suicide content, linking increasing levels of teen self-harm and suicide with the rise of social media (Savage 2019). Instagram was singled out in particular as not doing enough to police the content children could access. After initially responding with a piece in *The Independent* promising to do more (Mosseri 2019a), new Instagram head Adam Mosseri had to elevate the platform's response further in the next few days, promising that it will 'not allow any graphic images of self-harm, such as cutting on Instagram', and 'will continue to remove it when reported', even if this new commitment still relies on users reporting this content before it can be found and removed (Mosseri 2019b). At the same time, parent company Facebook made public statements reiterating that their approach to self-harm and suicide images was informed by experts across the globe, and that balancing removal with allowing inspirational stories of overcoming issues was a difficult one as many of the latter images are shown to help and support people suffering from mental health issues (Davis 2019). To try and ensure Instagram's efforts were taken seriously, Mosseri met with the UK Health Secretary in an attempt to defuse the clearly political desire to more heavily regulate Instagram and other social media platforms (Lomas 2019). Yet, whether Instagram and Facebook can meaningfully police or deal with self-harm content remains to be seen.

Instagram by Facebook
In early 2019, Mark Zuckerberg's plans to completely redesign the back end of his core properties Messenger, Facebook, Instagram and WhatsApp to integrate messaging across all four (Hern 2019) showed the clearest signs that the 2012 commitment to keep Instagram and Facebook functionally separate was all but forgotten. While Systrom and Krieger fought hard to ensure Instagram was thought of, and seen, as a separate platform, Adam Mosseri's tenure as Instagram's Head shows no such commitment. Yet even as Zuckerberg's integration plans were being discussed in the media, German regulators effectively put up the first major roadblock as they attempted to enact a law that would prevent sharing data between the various services Facebook owns without much more explicit user consent being sought (Kraus 2019; White, Bodoni & Nicola 2019).

While the technical integration of elements of Facebook, Instagram and other Facebook apps and platforms is likely to happen in some form or other, whether this paints Instagram as more like Facebook in the public eye, or not, remains to be seen. Even as Facebook's reputation took a battering in 2018, its profits did not, so either way, Instagram and Facebook are here to stay. Perhaps tellingly, though, in Facebook's first 2019 earnings report, the company noted they would be moving away from giving user statistics for each platform or service they own, instead reporting grouped 'Facebook family metrics' in the future, noting there were 2.7 billion Facebook family users by the end of 2018 (Constine 2019).

This subtle change clearly shows that Facebook expects its biggest growth to come from the other platforms it owns, including Instagram, not the Facebook platform by itself. In 2018 Facebook introduced a menu item in Instagram called 'Open Facebook', and then doubled down on this decision in 2019 when they confirmed that a future update would add the text 'Instagram by Facebook' in the Instagram menu. These are further indications of the importance of Instagram to Facebook's current and future commercial success.

Conclusion

This chapter has mapped some of the bigger changes and challenges Instagram has faced since it was released in October 2010. The platform's initial competition and growth, being purchased by Facebook, changing the way it works with third-party apps, beating Snapchat at its own game by rolling out Stories, and using Stories to reinvigorate growth while diversifying the tools inside Stories, are all a big part of what makes Instagram what it is today. Yet the challenges, as Systrom and Krieger left and Adam Mosseri took over, show there is still a lot of change ahead, and the shape of Instagram more tightly under Mark Zuckerberg's control may look quite different in years to come. Most importantly, this chapter shows that Instagram is constantly changing, both in and of itself, and as part of a broader visual social media landscape, and those changes need to be kept in mind in order to understand what Instagram is, where it has come from, and where it is likely headed.

CHAPTER TWO

Aesthetics

Introduction: The Visuality of Instagram

In its earliest forms, Instagram was just one of several mobile apps doing similar things: offering a retro take on mobile phone photography, letting users capture or edit images that would appear like, for example, photos from Polaroid cameras or lo-fi film cameras like the Holga. The aesthetic appeal of such imagery, with washed-out colours, heavy vignetting, and even simulated physical artefacts like film borders and scratches, was also apparent in how Instagram presented itself, alongside competitors like Hipstamatic. Over the subsequent years, though, the retro-specific aesthetic was minimized in comparison with the broader visual opportunities and possibilities of Instagram, as its user base grew and the uses of the platform expanded. Commercial accounts advertising and selling their products through the platform, for example, may have considerably less desire to make their content seem like it was from the 1970s. What has developed instead is a much broader sense of Instagram aesthetics, that take in both the functions and affordances of the platform, and the tropes and practices developed by its users (and, at times, directed by Instagram). Mobile photography researcher Elisa Serafinelli (2018) argues that 'the extensive use of Instagram represents the foundation of a new mobile visualities aesthetic' (p. 8), representing not just the platform but the devices and practices involved, and in this chapter and chapter 3's coverage of ecologies, these ideas will be explored further.

New media theorist Lev Manovich (2017) treats Instagram's visual aesthetics as key to the platform's appeal and rationale, arguing that 'if Google is an information retrieval service, Twitter is for news and links exchange, Facebook is for social communication, and Flickr is for image archiving, Instagram is for *aesthetic visual communication*' (p. 41). Yet none of these platforms are solely used for the purposes Manovich describes, nor are, arguably, these aims the dominant ones for the users, developers or stakeholders involved. Furthermore, when we talk about aesthetics and Instagram, too, what are we referring to? What is the Instagram aesthetic? Is there even a singular Instagram aesthetic, and how is this different to those of other platforms, devices or digital cultures? Is it the contrast between colours, the visual presentation of shapes and lines, the filters available, the physical parameters dictating the appearance of the content? Is it the genres of content apparent across the cumulative profiles of Instagram users, the tropes and clichés that have developed over time? Do the same aesthetics apply to selfies or food porn or the assorted animals of Instagram, or to disappearing Instagram Stories and to more permanent posts?

This chapter explores the content, practices and users of Instagram, covering different aspects of Instagram aesthetics. Three key ideas are featured here: visual aesthetics, including genres and tropes of content and visual normalization; user practices and norms; and audiences and motivations for Instagram use. The analysis and discussion in this chapter leads into ideas developed further in later chapters, including Instagram economies. In addition, the chapter concludes by reflecting on how the aesthetics of Instagram (whether promoted by the platform or perceived by users) do not happen in a vacuum: planned and unintended uses develop out of multiple contexts, including the visual and the mobile. Media and technology scholars Martin Gibbs et al. (2015) have noted that 'each social media platform comes to have its own unique combination of styles, grammars, and logics, which can be considered as constituting a "platform vernacular" (p. 257); the platform-specific twist apparent on Instagram, though, is still similar to – yet distinct from – practices, content, and cultures witnessed elsewhere.

Instagram's Foundational Visualities

Underpinning Instagram's aesthetics and functionalities, especially early on in its development, is a digital reimagining of photographic traditions. Despite the app's iconography, Instagram is not synonymous with photography in many ways: like other digital forms of photography, the technical processes involved here do not require film or chemical development, and the content posted to Instagram is not solely 'photographic'. Yet the myriad visual forms presented on Instagram accounts all contribute to the presentation of experiences, identities, communication and more that were examined within the practice of photography.

In *On Photography*, essayist Susan Sontag (2005) argued that 'what photography supplies is not only a record of the past but a new way of dealing with the present'; while photography was from its initial development a technology for recording and saving memories, digital culture scholar José van Dijck (2008) argues that it 'always also served as an instrument of communication and as a means of sharing experience' (p. 59). Photography (eventually) enabled engagement with what is happening in the moment – and changing how that is experienced – particularly with the provision of cameras which were affordable and accessible to many, and even more so with the development of digital cameras and, later, cameraphones which meant that the capacity for capturing images was extended. Rather than being limited to the number of exposures available on photographic film – and not being able to check the success of any image prior to development – digital photography meant that images were restricted by the capacity of the storage medium used. Digital photography

Figure 2.1. Selfie sticks warning sign, Kyoto train station, June 2016

could also be seen as more disposable than film, in the sense that several photographs could be taken of the same scene and then the best picked and the rest deleted (or left to the individual's archive, until more space was required). Such developments further integrated photography into everyday settings, to the ubiquity studied by sociologist Martin Hand (2012). This has also led to resistance and pushback against how taking pictures has become realized, whether it is the shaming directed at selfie cultures (see Tiidenberg 2018 for more), bans on particular types of photography at events and cultural institutions, or, as in figure 2.1, signage directed at the perils of selfie sticks.

These practices are associated in particular with the use of smartphones as photographic devices, enabling capture, storage, editing and sharing, all in one. In their study of the use of the iPhone for photography, communication scholars Megan

Halpern and Lee Humphreys argue that 'the practices surrounding iphoneography represent important moves in the sociology of visual media' (2016, p. 63): creating photographic art on the iPhone, and distributing it on the networked spaces connected through the same device, means that the visual and the everyday, the mobile and the now are heavily intertwined, available to anyone with the same technology. Any moment could potentially be deemed worthy of capturing and sharing. Posting to Instagram is just one of the ways this happens, with everyday experiences routinely presented through digital media in text, image and other updates. As new media scholar José van Dijck (2008) argues, 'the tendency to fuse photography with daily experience and communication is part of a broader cultural transformation that involves individualization and intensification of experience' (p. 62). Instagram offers a further means for these multiple photographic functions of memory, communication and experience, framed in different ways than previously available yet still recognizable.

In the preface to *Mediated Memories in the Digital Age*, van Dijck (2007) reflects on her personal archival journey – and dilemmas – experienced after purchasing a digital camera. In particular, she highlights the impact of digitization of both practice (photography) and media (scanning physical photos, for instance). More than a decade later, writing in 2018, the technology may have changed – while many people may still use a camera (digital or otherwise), for others the smartphone has replaced this, offering similar functionality without requiring a second device – but the questions around mediation and memory remain. Van Dijck asks about how we choose what to make mediated memories of, how we do this, and what is the relationship 'between media technologies and our habits and rituals of remembrance' (2007, p. xii). These questions are complicated in various ways by Instagram, as will be seen later in this chapter, but they are also implicated by the aesthetics and cultures of the platform. Not all photographs or videos captured by an individual get posted to their Instagram account; not even everything opened in the app and edited as a potential post gets published. There is a selectiveness apparent in the profile. The parameters of this selectivity will vary between users, but the choices made around what and how we post to Instagram highlight how for many, the platform is not an exhaustive technology for 'storage and retrieval' (2007, p. xii).

However, despite the visual identity promoted by Instagram, the app is not just a space for photography, even if such content is prevalent. Regardless of what users are sharing, whether photos, videos, drawings, memes or other forms of visual content, though, what is posted to Instagram form both the visual culture of the platform, and are part of the broader visual cultures in which users are situated. The visual, in its myriad forms, is critical to Instagram, to how accounts present themselves and their content, and to how this is interpreted and responded to by others. This is not specific to Instagram, of course; in *Ways of Seeing*, art critic John Berger and his co-authors (2008) noted that 'we never just look at one thing; we are always looking at the relation between things and ourselves'. In other words, it is not just about what is posted, but what it represents to each of us individually, too.

In the context of digital communication, social media and digital culture researchers Katrin Tiidenberg and Edgar Gómez Cruz (2015) argue that 'images play an important role in how we experience being in the world and increasingly, due to the ubiquity of online interaction, how we "shape" our world' (p. 79). What visual content we choose to share – whether on Instagram or elsewhere – has meaning because of its form, its context, and our communicative intentions, and these vary between individuals. This is aided by the surrounding contextual information, be it captions, hashtags, profile information, comments or other annotations; just as semiotician and philosopher Roland Barthes (1977) noted about press photography, so Instagram posts are also not isolated structures but appear in concert with other visual and text-based information (p. 16). The visual alone offers some – but not all – detail for interpreting meaning. Writing about memes, media scholar Ryan Milner (2016) notes that these 'carry complex layers of meaning, which embed multiple modes of communication ... multiple communicative modes intertwine into a single message' (pp. 24–5), and the visual more broadly affords this same potential (see also Highfield & Leaver 2016). For the aesthetics of Instagram, though, the visual is of paramount importance: it determines how (and what) content is shared, how communication takes place on the platform, and shapes interactive possibilities. Building on social semioticians Gunther Kress and Theo van Leeuwen (2006), who claim that 'visual structures ... point to particular interpretations of experience and forms of social interaction' (p. 2), the following sections explore how Instagram's aesthetics are implicated within the experiences, communication and interaction happening in this space.

Instagram's Visual Identity

Before considering the aesthetics presented and promoted by Instagram users, though, it is pertinent to examine the visuality put forward by the platform itself, and its evolution over time. From its iconography to its general appearance, Instagram's own aesthetics provide insight into its identity and aims; in the following section, a visual walkthrough of the Instagram app based on the iPhone versions of Instagram (up to version 63.0; September 2018) is undertaken (see Light, Burgess & Duguay 2018), encompassing visual elements presented in the feed and the profile, the story, the post and the filters. Building on the historical examination of Instagram by semiotic technology researcher Søren Vigild Poulsen (2018), this examination highlights the aesthetics of normalization encouraged on the platform, ahead of the later discussion of the tropes, genres and cultural practices surrounding Instagram content.

As chapter 1 highlighted, Instagram was originally an iPhone-only app: accessible only on a subset of the total smartphone market, without a web version, among various camera and photo-sharing apps and other platforms. From its earliest versions, though, Instagram's visual identity has called back to familiar – and retro – forms of photography, even when the connection between the app and physical photographic acts is diminished. Its iconography acts as a photographic referent (Barthes 1977, p. 24), aesthetically symbolizing physical, retro cameras and photographs without being either. Over time, this has become more abstract – yet still recognizable as both symbolizing a camera *and* Instagram's previous icons – as part of a common, simplistic visual identity across Instagram's stable of apps. In its beginnings, though, the referential aesthetics of the platform were more explicit.

As at August 2018, there have been three Instagram icons which together depict an increasingly abstract reference to photography and a particular generation of camera. The first Instagram icon, used in testing until the official launch in 2010, featured a stylized version of a Polaroid OneStep instant camera, designed by co-founder Kevin Systrom, with custom 'Instagram' logo on the body; ostensibly, this was chosen because Systrom 'really just liked the idea of having a retro camera stand for Instagram' (in D'Onfro 2013). When that icon was found to be a potential trademark violation (and, in Systrom's words, 'had nothing to do with Instagram'), though, a redesigned version kept the vintage camera vibe without being too specific in its referentiality. This second icon, designed by Cole Rise, kept some elements of the original – the rainbow stripe, a small nameplate (reduced to just 'Insta') – while taking inspiration from 1950s cameras (Pachal 2016). Bar some minor redesigns, this remained the app's icon until 2016, when it was replaced in a full-scale overhaul of Instagram's visual identity.

Instagram's 2016 redesign saw a reimagining of the visual aesthetics of the app itself, as well as a suite of new, consistent iconography for Instagram and its associated apps Layout, Hyperlapse and Boomerang (see chapter 3 for more on these). The new Instagram icon kept the general shape of the stylized camera complete with allusions to a viewfinder and lens, but all detail was removed to render the icon as simply an arrangement of two circles and a rounded square, backed by a red-yellow-purple-blue gradient. Based on internal research, Instagram's designers found the camera-specific elements of the logo – viewfinder and lens – were commonly recognized as defining aspects of the icon itself. Taking the form of an abstract camera, rather than an explicitly retro icon, the new logo attempted to overcome concerns that (for the platform) 'the Instagram icon and design was beginning to feel, well ... not reflective of the community' (Ian 2016). The community, though, was not as impressed with the new icon as Instagram was; as with many major redesigns on platforms like Facebook and Twitter, Instagram's update met with immediate resistance, voiced in headlines like 'Instagram changed their logo and uhh... It's pretty bad' (Barna 2016), and 'Instagram's new logo is a travesty. Can we change it back? Please?' (Nudd 2016; see also Parkinson 2016).

Two years on, the icon had become generally accepted (Klara 2018), as with the overall simplified aesthetic put forward across the app. The abstract camera reflects Instagram's move away from the explicitly retro and the still photography of its initial version: not only is the icon less representative of *how* images are captured before publishing on Instagram, but also demonstrates how the type of new content pushed by the platform is less photographic in form. Live broadcasting, stories and Instagram TV are at the forefront of the platform's strategies in 2018, through augmented images, video and user engagement and interaction through in-post options, from shopping to voting in polls. Such approaches would be impossible on the cameras of the first Instagram logos, referents of an imagined photography long since replaced by the new possibilities for content, commerce and community on Instagram.

These same possibilities influenced the redesign of the entire Instagram app and its new visual structure in 2016; explaining the move to a simple, black and white appearance, it was argued that '[w]hile the icon is a colorful doorway into the Instagram app, once inside the app, we believe the color should come directly from the community's photos and videos' (Ian 2016). This simplified iconography and white space, without borders, offered a very different appeal to previous user interfaces. The earliest versions were characterized by blocky icons and a comparatively more cramped appearance, with blue and chrome bars and buttons across the top and bottom of the interface. Over time, the size of icons and buttons decreased, but, until the full redesign in 2016, they were still visually separated from the feed by appearing on blue or grey menu bars.

Smaller aesthetic tweaks had happened prior to the 2016 redesign. The typography of the Instagram logo was updated in 2013; in a precursor to the icon revamp three years later, the new script was described as connecting 'with the nostalgia that Instagram was built from' (Saturday 2013). The various options available to the user in the app had also been altered and reimagined, both structurally and visually. Whereas the early instances of the app in 2011 featured a menu of 'feed', 'popular', 'share', 'news' and 'profile' (complete with captions for the icons), transformations had seen 'news', which originally included Instagram's own news (Poulson 2018, p. 127), become a notifications feed, and 'popular' become 'explore'. This latter option had gone through multiple visual updates, from the 'popular' heart to a star, a compass rose, and then the more generic magnifying glass typically associated with search and related processes.

The changing meanings of different icons across Instagram's history is not just seen with the heart icon. Perhaps most tellingly with regard to the platform's user engagement strategies, the camera icon used as a gateway to adding new content became more abstract, in keeping with the general visual identity of the platform – indeed, at times it was stylized as the Instagram logo – to not being a camera at all in the current (as at September 2018) version. While that particular function was always the middle option in the bottom menu bar, by 2018 the 'new post' icon was instead a simple rounded square with a plus sign, offering consistency with other 'add' functions across the web. However, the camera has not been removed completely. In 2018's Instagram, a different camera icon can be seen in the top left of the interface: like swiping to the right, it launches the in-app camera, but this is not the camera for making a new post. Here, the focus is on new content for Stories, through the vertical full-frame camera, with all the related options of type posts, superzoom and more (examined in depth in the next sections). The same function is also accessed by the 'your story' icon, a rounded profile picture with a plus sign in a small blue circle, at the top of the feed; however, since the Stories display disappears as the user scrolls down their feed, the camera icon offers a (for now) permanent means of accessing this option.

The visual evolution of the Instagram app has taken place within wider trends in social media, too: see, for example, the move from square user icons to rounded ones, a format also seen on Facebook, Twitter and Snapchat, among others. What has also evolved alongside the platform's visual identity is what users could do with Instagram (and, occasionally, what they can no longer do). These underline changes suggested by Instagram's own visuals, regarding the types of content and interaction it encourages. From the initial square posts to the support for short videos, carousel posts containing multiple images, and then to Stories, with filters or without, Instagram content over time demonstrates the promoted – and at times normalized – aesthetics of the platform.

Instagram's Evolving Aesthetics of Normalization

Square Times

The aesthetics of an Instagram post offers a further demonstration of how the Instagram of 2018 is far different from the Instagram of 2010, in appearance, functionality and practices. One of the early defining visual aspects of the app was the square dimensions for posted images: limiting users to that shape, forcing cropping of rectangular images and encouraging either taking photos within the app or using the 'square' option on the smartphone camera. These aesthetic constraints saw Instagram described by artist and feminist scholar Magdalena Olszanowski (2015) as 'the 1x1 common': in examining the networked image and how hashtags facilitated communicative and affective exchanges between women on Instagram, a consistent element, varyingly deployed, was the square.

As with many elements of early Instagram, the square had its analogue in an older, somewhat fetishized photographic culture: Polaroids, instant-printed photographs with plenty of white space under the square image to annotate if so desired. The space for captions, hashtags, likes and comments underneath the Instagram image in its own way acted as the digital realization of these annotations; this is perhaps most clearly seen in the physical Instagram frames adopted by museums, zoos and various other public institutions, with square openings for poses and group photos, where the frame provides a much-enlarged version of a Polaroid film paper.

Early Instagram posts were also notably low in resolution, offering square renderings of scenes in less detail than might be captured by the native smartphone cameras of the time (particularly when also filtered using the in-app options; see below). While not necessarily desired by all users, working with these various aesthetic constraints reflected their inclusion within the 'platform vernacular' (Gibbs et al. 2015) of Instagram; in their study of graffiti and street art on the platform, cultural researchers Lachlan MacDowall and Poppy de Souza (2018) note that while murals and similar pieces are not well-suited to square framings, 'this restriction has also prompted innovative responses that sometimes directly address these conditions of constraint' (p. 8). This included appropriating other functionalities as they developed, such as the fifteen-second video options introduced in 2013, use of collaging tools to include multiple images in one square (see chapter 3), or posting multiple, individual images that will together form a 3×3 grid in the user's profile (p. 8).

Such strategies demonstrate user-developed workarounds with the limitations of Instagram: as late as August 2015, all image and video content were only able to be published with square dimensions, while the carousel option allowing multiple images or videos as a group in a single post did not appear until February 2017. Even Instagram-approved support for combining several images into a single square collage only happened in March 2015 with the release of the Layout app; prior to that, third-party apps were required to make such content. The opening up of the constraints since 2015, though, has meant a shift away from the initial aesthetics privileged by Instagram: being able to post non-square portrait or landscape content has meant that the 1x1 image is not necessarily such a key part of the Instagram vernacular. Furthermore, while the horizontal, landscape image remains mostly prominent in the feed and the profiles of Instagram users, elsewhere on the platform the vertical and portrait orientation is taking precedence.

If the square dimensions of early Instagram posts demonstrate one form of aesthetic normalization by the platform, this is still one that affected the shape of the content, but not the content itself. For the actual posts themselves and the visuals depicted within, Instagram offered other aesthetic possibilities, even more defining elements of the platform (especially pre-2016) and a further realization of its promoted retro, vintage ideals: filters.

The Aesthetics of Filters

Inkwell, Nashville, Sierra, Toaster, Ashby, Gingham, Rise, Aden, Moon ... The repertoire of filters available to Instagram users features names evoking the San Francisco Bay Area, places, people and animals important to the designers and developers at Instagram, and particular moods and aesthetics. Offering pre-fabricated templates for reimagining images, Instagram filters helped to normalize notions of editing and touching up content before posting, and reduced the amount of artistic and technical ability required to make images appear these ways. Indeed, Katrin Tiidenberg (2018) suggests that 'Instagram was arguably the application that mainstreamed (at least in the Western context) the idea that editing is, or should be, a default action prior to posting an image to social media' (p. 56). As the functionality around filters developed, too, users could also easily adjust the brightness and contrast, highlights and shadows, warmth and saturation, and other settings for their images before publishing (initially, filters only offered on/off options, rather than variable levels). Rather than posting a photograph as-is, taking some care over presentation and appearance was encouraged. Such thinking might reflect particular aesthetic aims, in keeping with other visual styles and artistic movements, for example adjusting the contrast or saturation of an image to bring out particular colours. It can also reflect a general acceptance that simply taking a photograph is not the end of the process – and, indeed, a recognition of how an image could be improved or have greater visual appeal through editing.

Beyond the general possibilities of editing images, though, Instagram's filters also reflected the retro aesthetics somewhat prevalent within the app. Where the early logos drew upon cameras from the 1970s and 1980s, rather than any current photographic devices, so several of the featured filters were highly reminiscent of Polaroid photos and their ilk, mimicking 'the washed-out, dreamy aesthetic and mood of analogue photography, as well as the hyper-saturated contrast of super-8 moving image film' (MacDowell & de Souza 2018, p. 8). The vintage visuals evoked here abet what visual scholar Gil Bartholeyns (2014) describes as 'self-induced nostalgia' (p. 55), where 'the cult of the referent is being replaced by the cult of the reference, reference to an iconography that, in its form, is typical of memory' (p. 65): it is not enough to invoke a particular mood or idea, but to make specific connections, explicit links to the past (see also the late 2010s trend of 1980s nostalgia-inviting popular culture, riffing on these aesthetics, such as the Netflix shows *Stranger Things* and *GLOW*).

The aesthetics of nostalgia promoted by Instagram filters was not original to the app, though; as Instagram emerged, rival apps like Hipstamatic, Retro Camera, FxCamera, and more offered digital emulations of disposable cameras, with a particular vintage appeal within iphoneography (see Halpern & Humphreys 2016). These recreations of film photography went so far as to simulate the artefacts and blemishes typical of the physical material: scratches, residue, film edges and borders, and the like (as seen in figure 2.2).

Several early Instagram filters also offered these specific vintage references; not just allowing users to make their photos appear washed-out, over-exposed or desaturated, in a visually appealing manner, but creating the artifice that they were old-school slides or film photographs; the present, 'projected back into the past', as Bartholeyns suggests (2014, p. 66). Filters like Nashville added borders and edges to images (as seen in figure 2.3), sometimes explicitly referring back to these past photographic objects, with the added result of making it easier to identify which filter(s) had been used for a particular post.

A key difference between Instagram and its rivals, though, was that the retro aesthetic became highly editable: there was not just a range of filters to choose from, but Instagram users could also edit the results, initially around colour and focus, and from 2014 through more advanced settings such as brightness or contrast (Poulsen 2018). Unlike the disposable camera-emulating apps of 2012 (and, indeed, of 2018 – see chapter 3),

Figure 2.2. Scene from western Austria, July 2012, as captured using Retro Camera for Android (author archive)

which attempted to recreate point-and-click-and-hope photography, Instagram promoted filters as a gateway to new aesthetic possibilities with which the user could still do some tinkering.

While filters set Instagram apart, it was also easy to overdo the filtering when posting photos (and later on videos too). Social media linguist Michele Zappavigna (2016) suggests that in addition to vintage aesthetics, filtering had a social function: 'rendering more poignant the present moment, in particular the banal, everyday present moment' (p. 286). The visual stakes of any image can be heightened by strategic filter use, transforming the mundane into a more dramatic or emotional scene purely by adjusting colours and shadows.

Figure 2.3. 'Temporary placement object'; Perth train station, April 2014 (author archive)

The possibilities, and resulting filtered aesthetic, became so prominent though that actively resisting it became a badge of honour: the #nofilter hashtag demonstrated that an image had not been edited, but was in fact impressive – or authentic (for whatever value of 'authentic' you might want to interpret) – in its own right. The non-use of filters meant pushing back against the overly familiar visual styles of X-Pro II and its ilk, where what made them special had become common and tired; as Jill Walker Rettberg (2014) has argued, 'Instagram-style filters may make our selfies and photos of our everyday life seem unfamiliar, but the filter itself is repeated so often that the defamiliarization effect wears off and becomes a cliché' (p. 26).

Instagram filters thus offered different aesthetics of normalization. By making vintage styles available to users through a repertoire of off-the-shelf options, removing the need for additional software or technical literacy, the platform encouraged different visual representations of the familiar and the mundane, as well as the unusual and the extraordinary. Yet the popularity of these approaches reduced their impact: even if individuals might use filters sparingly, the cumulative impact of 1977 and Valencia-enhanced images meant that these became normalized. To set scenes apart, to give them new visual appeal, filtering was no longer enough – or, perhaps, was already too much.

Filtering had other, possibly unforeseen, effects, too. The aesthetics of filters and their impact on images' colouring and appearance, for instance, may have been encouraged as a fun and different way of engaging with image sharing. The racial dimensions of image filtering, though, also belied the imagined user base (or real development team) for these features; this applies not just to the initial filters on Instagram, but to the face filters and other effects of Stories.

By August 2018, Instagram had 40 filters available to users for their posts (not counting 'normal'), listed in table 2.1; these included filters that had originated as video-only options and later been adapted for images too. Several filters previously available had also been removed; these are listed in table 2.2. The nomenclature for the filters variously reflects subjects like the Bay Area origins of Instagram (including Reyes, Dogpatch, Clarendon and Perpetua), and the pets of developers and investors (Juno, Toaster); the names may take inspiration from the aesthetics of particular subjects (Crema, Hefe), or from photographic traditions and approaches (Lo-Fi), evoking specific moods or feelings for the people naming them.

However, although filters were a further defining element of Instagram and its platform vernacular (see MacDowell & de Souza 2018, pp. 7–9), the repository has been stable for

Table 2.1. List of Instagram filters (as at August 2018)

Name	Year introduced
1977	2010†
Aden	2014
Amaro	2011
Ashby*	2013
Brannan	2011
Brooklyn*	2013
Charmes*	2013
Clarendon*	2013
Crema	2014
Dogpatch*	2013
Earlybird	2010†
Gingham*	2013
Ginza*	2013
Hefe	2011
Helena*	2013
Hudson	2011
Inkwell	2010†
Juno	2015
Kelvin (formerly *Lord Kelvin*)	2010†
Lark	2015
Lo-Fi (formerly *Lomo-Fi*)	2010†
Ludwig	2014
Maven*	2013
Mayfair	2012
Moon*	2013
Nashville	2010†
Perpetua	2014
Reyes	2015
Rise	2011
Sierra	2012
Skyline*	2013
Slumber	2014
Stinson*	2013
Sutro	2010
Toaster	2010
Valencia	2011
Vesper*	2013
Walden	2011
Willow	2012
X-Pro II	2010†

* Originally video-only filters (2013), later expanded to all posted content.
† Part of the original filter set.

Table 2.2. List of defunct Instagram filters (as at August 2018)		
Name	Date introduced	Date removed
Apollo	2010†	2011
Gotham	2010†	2011
Lily	2010†	2010
	2010†	
Poprocket	2010†	2010, but reinstated in 2011; removed again in 2011

† Part of the original filter set.

several years. The most recent filters were introduced in April 2015 with the release of Lark, Reyes and Juno. Despite claiming at the time that 'we plan to bring you additional [filters] more regularly going forward' (Instagram 2015), the following three years saw Instagram's focus move further from the standard post, towards other forms of filters and engagement. In this way, the visuality of filters reflects Instagram's evolving relationship with its early aesthetics and aims: from the explicit retromania of the early logos and filters, to a more abstract iconography and lack of further development of the features that helped bring it initial popularity.

Telling Instagram Stories and the New Aesthetics of Normalization

When talking about Instagram's own aesthetics, the tale is heavily intertwined within the platform's development and corporate strategies. Many of the early defining visual features of Instagram have either been removed or neglected, left as they are for now but without any apparent interest in expanding their options. Instead, the Instagram story since 2015 is dominated by exactly that, and this is the case for the aesthetics of the platform too.

As explored in chapter 1, the August 2016 launch of Instagram Stories was essentially a response to the popularity of Snapchat, with its own ephemeral Stories feature, particularly amongst younger social media users. Stories have very different dimensions to the posts on an Instagram feed: the vertical display means there is no place here for the square (not without a lot of empty space surrounding it). It also reflects a push towards viewing content natively on a mobile device, as opposed to the landscape orientation of laptops, monitors, and tablets, in recognition of what makes sense for the capturing device. Whereas tech blogs of the late 2000s tried to convince people to turn their phone sideways when recording videos to make their presentation on YouTube, Facebook and the like more appealing (Chen 2010), Stories and IGTV have promoted the vertical format as default. While the commercial success of IGTV in particular remains to be seen late in 2018, Instagram's commitment to a vertical visual aesthetic here demonstrates a clear shift from the established norms of presenting video, part of a rupturing of visual paradigms (K. Ryan 2018).

Stories, both on Snapchat and on Instagram, promoted sharing content in the moment, as it happened, including directly with friends. This approach offers a sharp contrast to common beliefs about the Instagram feed: while not a universal ideal, there is a general view for many users that what gets posted to Instagram is curated, chosen for its interest (aesthetic or otherwise), and represents selected aspects of the user's experiences. Particularly as cultural norms developed around the platform, the idea of posting every little thing that happened in a day to Instagram was not one that would meet with widespread approval (either to the user posting or the people following them). With Stories, though, the built-in disposability of the format means that there is no need to be concerned with whether or not a particular post should be posted to a user's profile permanently. Here, the user is encouraged to post in the now – rediscovering one meaning of the *insta* of Instagram in the process – whether by sharing live content (introduced to all users in 2017) or by publishing photos, videos and other posts to their individual story.

The aesthetic differences between Stories and Instagram posts are apparent in the options available to users. The ephemerality of Stories is coupled with various 'fun' features that push various types of post. The likes of X-Pro II, Hefe and the other filters are not included here; while there are built-in photo filters accessed by swiping left or right, all named after global cities from Paris and Lagos to Jakarta and Oslo, these are not the most prominent options given to users. Instead, the most visually promoted filters available are more akin to the frivolous and irreverent visuals seen on Snapchat. Through facial recognition and tracking, a rabbit's ears and nose, or a dog's, or a cat's, can be rendered onto the individual seen through the camera, or their appearance could be augmented by sunglasses, make-up, over-sized mouth, and more. These seemingly cute and silly filters and masks have plenty to offer the platform (and associated stakeholders), as users grant them access through the camera and creates a further case of normalization: that of facial recognition technologies in everyday life (see Stark 2018). For the user, outside of any queries about surveillance and similar concerns, though, the filters offer an outlet for a different kind of visual than might be featured in their individual feed.

Stories are not just visual, either; the different post types include type posts, offering their own aesthetics for presenting quotes, thoughts and other content that has no image or video (or does not require one). With four different type templates – modern, neon, typewriter and strong (see figure 2.4) – instead of multiple typeface options or customization, the user is restricted to a limited aesthetic palette, as with Facebook's type posts. The various templates also suggest more muted aesthetic inspirations: they evoke moods and settings, rather than the overt retro stylings of the early Instagram filters. Directly working with characters (whether numerals, letters, symbols or emoji) in content is also not something supported within the standard Instagram post, where to publish a text-heavy, quote-laden image first requires that visual to

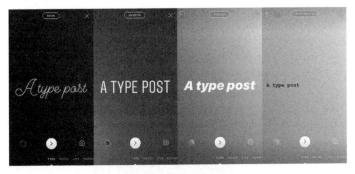

Figure 2.4. Type post templates (screenshots, 1 August 2018)

be created through another app or program. Instead, Stories offers various aesthetic possibilities unavailable elsewhere on the platform.

Other options available – as Story post types – include 'superzooms', where a scene is punctuated by various zoom effects, whether 'dramatic' (staggered, jerky zoom), 'beats' (zooming in and out and changing colour in quick time), or 'fire', featuring a border of animated flames. Different types of retro aesthetics are promoted here, too: among the growing stable of Stories effects, RetroFilm offers a scrolling roll of film, with overlaid artefacts, while B&W Film does similar but in monochrome, and VCR brings the appearance of videotape recordings. Stories is also the only place within the Instagram app where Boomerang clips can be created in-app; for equivalent posts on a user's feed, they have to be brought in from Boomerang itself, or created in Stories, saved and re-posted. Further video posts are supported through the 'rewind' and 'hands-free' options. Stories also demonstrates, though, the staggered release of various features and functionalities: music posts are – as at September 2018 – available in certain markets (including the USA and Australia), but not others (such as the Netherlands), as shown in figure 2.5.

The Story posted in figure 2.5, in addition to not being experienced equally by all users, demonstrates further aesthetic

Figure 2.5. Screenshot of Instagram story (with music) as viewed in the Netherlands in July 2018 (where music remains unavailable as of early 2019). Screenshot by TH of story posted by TL for @polityinstabook

characteristics of the format. Instagram encourages the augmentation of Stories with text and emoji, providing captions or remarks or feelings that might contextualize the post. These serve as the equivalents of captions and comments on a standard Instagram post. But the potential annotation of a Story goes far beyond simple text strings; there are numerous stickers that can be added on top of an image or video to provide location, time or temperature information, for instance, and there is the opportunity to tag other accounts through @mentions, or to include hashtags. Instagram also has a whole gallery of banners and images which play into the vernacular of younger users – 'lit', 'it me', 'yasss' and more – at the same time potentially downplaying the sociocultural origins of these terms, particularly from African American Vernacular English and among LGBTQ communities (Blay 2015). Further options are also introduced to select contexts, available only temporarily: in November 2018, for instance, Instagram introduced stickers for users to display their participation in the US midterm elections, along with a 'We Voted' story collecting stories featuring Instagram's 'I Voted' sticker (Instagram 2018d). Such features also reflect Instagram's recognition of the use of popular social media for participating within political contexts (see Highfield 2016); as will be seen later in chapter 5, visually engaging with the political (or politics-adjacent) takes additional forms on Instagram.

Story annotation options also allow for interaction in ways not supported elsewhere in the app. Users can create in-post polls, prompt questions from their followers, or feature an approval/response slider featuring the heart-eyes emoji in their Stories. Meanwhile, since January 2018, users have also been able to add GIFs – sourced from the Giphy repository – as additional stickers in their Stories. The cumulative aesthetic effect of much of these options, though, whether GIFs or superzooms or face filters, is a different kind of retro throwback to the initial Instagram visual nostalgia – especially when combined in a single post. When making use of these various features, Stories present a version of the kitschy visuals of early websites, resplendent in animated GIFs (see Eppink 2014; Miltner & Highfield 2017), and the clutter and busyness of MySpace profiles, harkening back to a particular digital aesthetic. In this sense, it is another form of vintage, with roots in movements like 'internet ugly' (Douglas 2014), and the deliberately over-the-top and clashing visuals of platforms like Blingee.

Through its various functionalities and features, Stories demonstrate different aesthetics of normalization for Instagram. Offering different ways of vernacular, creative expression, including emoji- and GIF-annotations and live content, has meant that the Stories aesthetic has also turned up as a storytelling device in other media – perhaps most prominently in the Stories-inspired first episode of *Broad City*'s fifth season in January 2019. The push towards vertical content as standard, meanwhile, which has extended into IGTV (see chapter 3), is a major change in how the platform has encouraged user content to develop and the aesthetics pushed within the app. What is also clear, though, is the different aesthetic possibilities within Stories and posts, and changing views towards how both elements are used by users and supported by Instagram. The platform culture, which saw Stories become a way of posting content that was shareworthy but not perhaps deserving of permanence on the profile, also brings with it different aesthetic ideals of what makes a publishable story versus an Instagram post; yet even the idea of Stories as ephemeral is complicated by the platform, its archival options, and the ability to share others' Stories. So far, though, this discussion has focused primarily on the platformed aesthetics of Instagram; the flipside to the Instagram aesthetic is that which emerges from user practices, norms, tropes and their application of the platform's affordances in ways that are both encouraged and unexpected.

Instagram's Platform Vernaculars and Practices

In their definition of platform vernaculars, Gibbs et al. (2015) note that each platform, however popular or niche, has its own specific mix of 'styles, grammars, and logics', which contribute to what is possible here, through the affordances provided, adapted and appropriated (p. 257). They also highlight, though, that 'the vernacular of a platform is also shaped by the mediated practices and communicative habits of users' (p. 257): it is not something which is solely directed by the platform, but which is negotiated through user-led practices and platform-enabled options and reactions, dynamically evolving. While the development team behind a platform may have a particular use in mind, that does not restrict the creation of new, emergent practices which employ the technical and communicative possibilities of the platform outside of what is prescribed within their initial design (see, for example, the 'off-label' uses of hook-up apps studied by Albury & Byron 2016).

In the remainder of this chapter, we explore Instagram's platform vernacular and how it encourages and fosters the development of visual genres and forms, whether native to the platform, adapted from elsewhere on social media, or crossing platforms. These includes the tropes and clichés of Instagram, including the subversive emerging from the hackneyed, in order to examine what sets images – and other visual content – posted here apart from other platforms. After all, the likes of selfies and memes are not Instagram-specific, and Instagram is not the only platform where users can share visual content. The idea of 'doing it for the gram', though, reflecting the creation of situations for their insta-grammability rather than the experience and the inspirational or aspirational aesthetics of visual content performed for an audience, underlines the predominance of Instagram over other spaces for this type of content.

The phrase 'do it for the gram' was featured on Urban Dictionary in October 2013 ('do it for the gram' n.d.), and it has been used in articles, blog posts and other writing about Instagram, both seriously and ironically, in the years since (receiving greater attention after 2015). As we elaborate on in chapter 7, while initially associated with younger users and their Instagram-related slang, it could also be argued that the mainstream awareness of the phrase means that its usage (and any measure of 'cool' here) has changed: indeed, the fact that early 2000s singer Craig David released a song called 'For The Gram' in 2017 – sample lyrics 'We do it for the Insta' / We do it for the 'Gram... When she's done takin' pictures / Don't forget to hashtag' – would suggest as much. At play here, then, is the aesthetics of Instagram, its visual vernacular, coupled with the communicative reality of the platform, be it presenting visuals for the intent of particular reactions, or the social sharing opportunities of posting.

As with prior photo-sharing networks and platforms like Flickr, Instagram fosters communities around aesthetics and practices of photography. In her research with photographers, Elisa Serafinelli (2017) argues that the platform's 'visualities introduce an additional layer of connectivity and mediality' (p. 109) for Instagram users: the shared visuals act as a social connector, and as an inspiration or catalyst for physical meets. Aesthetic communities also develop around particular visual styles and genres, from minimalism to brutalist architecture, around sharing art and documenting creative practice. Such communities may be extensions of pre-existing networks on Facebook, Twitter and more, but they may also involve new connections and content not shared elsewhere.

The production and sharing of visual content on social media platforms, including Instagram, involves many different subjects, themes and styles. In an in-depth dive through a single user's feed and their representation of motherhood through content posted to Instagram, Zappavigna (2016) suggests that social photography in these contexts had led to the creation of multiple visual genres, referring back to established photographic and artistic forms: the mediated portrait, the mediated still life and the mediated landscape (on the latter, see also Saethre-McGuirk 2018). The act of mediation in these forms is not just the adaptation for mobile apps, in content captured through smartphone cameras. There is a social function here, where mediated portraits and still-life content 'invite ambient viewers to approach the image as if they were sharing in the photographer's subjective experience and are activated by the discourse of self inherent in social media' (p. 289). Taking a semiotic approach to Instagram imagery, Zappavigna notes the subjectivity of the photographer in posted content, where the visual choices they make in framing and styling images lead to inferences and assumptions that can be made by the viewer, based on the norms of this type of photography; for example, the point-of-view photo featuring legs which presumably belong to the person taking the photo, allowing where the 'ambient viewer shares the perspective of the photographer' (p. 277). While there are multiple ways the photographer might be invoked within a given image, implicitly or explicitly, there is one type of content which offers 'the most obvious instances where the photographer's subjectivity is inscribed in the image' (p. 283): the selfie.

Selfies are both object and gesture (Senft & Baym 2015): not just a photograph, but a practice demonstrating multiple meanings, interpretations, and relationships between creator and audience. At a most basic level, a selfie is a self-portrait photograph of the individual, usually captured using the front-facing camera on a smartphone, often with some intent of sharing behind it (see, e.g., San Cornelio & Roig 2018). A standard distinction is that a selfie is taken by the person in the photo, rather than being a photo of them taken by someone else. However, the definition of selfie has become contested and jumbled, such that it is also used to just refer to a picture of an individual regardless of its provenance. There are also many genres and sub-categories of selfie, sometimes taking the '-ie' prefix; from the group selfie (occasionally dubbed an 'usie' or 'wefie') to the 'shoefie' (a photo looking down at the floor or ground, with the individual's shoes in frame; Pearson 2018) to the 'shelfie' (a photo of the individual's shelves, showcasing books or games, for example, as self-representation), among many others. The selfie, in its myriad forms, is not unique to Instagram, and it is not our intent here to unpack selfies in depth (instead, see Tiidenberg 2018); however, the prominence of the selfie as genre on Instagram – over 366 million posts tagged with #selfie as at November 2018 – means that it is important to explore as part of the aesthetics and vernacular of the platform.

The popularity, and general visibility, of the selfie on Instagram inspired early large-scale academic explorations of the platform. The *SelfieCity* project, for example, gathered self-ies with geolocation data from specific global cities, in order to quantitatively analyse selfie patterns around the world (Manovich et al. 2014). Applying big data methods to the collection and examination of selfies from Bangkok, Berlin, Moscow, New York City and São Paulo, the researchers iden-tified specific demographics of selfie-takers and selfie styles (see also Losh 2015); this extended to expressions and poses in the posted images, offering 'average smile scores' and head tilt angles for each city. However, such analyses, while dem-onstrating the computational possibilities of studying large datasets of visual material, by necessity also lose contextual information about, for instance, the how and why of the selfie.

More qualitative work has explored the motivations behind selfie-taking and -sharing, by Influencers (Abidin 2016), celebrities (Deller & Tilton 2015), young people (Albury 2015), pregnant women (Tiidenberg 2015), breastfeeding mothers (Locatelli 2017), and LGBTQ-identifying individuals (Duguay 2016; Wargo 2017), among many other examples. Rather than being narcissistic or frivolous, selfies are important for representation and visibility, promoting personal views and identity, and countering dominant narratives; as internet researchers Teresa Senft and Nancy Baym (2015) note, '[a]ny time anyone uses a selfie to take a stand against racist, classist, misogynist, homophobic, ageist, or ableist views of what a worthwhile representation is, or should be, issues of political power are clearly at stake' (p. 1597). For Influencers, mean-while, the apparent disposability of the selfie, its seemingly inconsequential nature, masks the amount of labour that goes into it, and the commercial motivations underpinning it (Abidin 2016).

Selfies form part of the wider aesthetic presentation of the self as practised on Instagram and other platforms. These may reflect different aims, different levels of seeking out responses and attention. The deployment of 'thirst traps', focusing on the attractiveness of the subject as strategy for likes (such as through shirtless poses or revealing outfits), pushing sexiness or flirting, reflect the thirst of the posting user for attention; prevalent on Vine prior to its shuttering in 2016 (Duguay 2017), for instance, thirst traps appear on Instagram in posts and Stories, by celebrities, Influencers and other users alike (Isador 2017; Safronova 2017). Whether used to seek validation, give an ego boost or feel confident, or indeed providing a visual hook to a current event or topic (Lorenz 2018c), their aesthetic appeal is key to getting their audience to engage.

As forms like the group selfie highlight, a selfie need not feature just the individual; 'felfies', for instance, are selfies by farmers alongside livestock or machinery (Burgess, Galloway & Sauter 2015), while 'pelfies' describe the recurring genre of selfies with pets. Of course, an animal need not be in a selfie in order to appear on Instagram, and pet-related hashtags are particularly popular in terms of the sheer number of posts featuring them: in August 2018, #petsofinstagram had been used in 20,631,175 posts, while #instapet featured in over 18 million posts, and #instapets over 5 million. The numbers grow with slightly more specificity, too, when focusing on the particular species of pet. While 'cat photography has come to play a large role in the visual economy of the internet' (Harper 2016; cf. Meese 2014; Miltner 2014), dogs rule on Instagram in the popularity of related hashtags (this might also be reflective of a general digital trend towards the more 'wholesome' innocence of dogs; Drill 2017). The #dogsofinstagram featured in just under 110 million posts, compared to the 86 million uses of #catsofinstagram. For some animals, a level of celebrity arrives; the Cincinnati Zoo Instagram account, for example, while also promoting other animals and topics, dedicates a lot of content to Fiona the hippopotamus, born prematurely in 2017 and who attracted global fame through the zoo's #teamfiona social media promotion (Dionne 2017; Syme 2017). In Crimea, a stray cat on a bridge construction site was given the name Mostik and became the mascot of the project (Horton 2018). Given his own Instagram account to showcase his own activity around the site (@cat_the_most) alongside the official bridgework account (@krymsky_bridge), the cat's celebrity status (over 45,000 followers by November 2018) inevitably also saw Mostik merchandise available for purchase.

Pets and other animals also appear within content shared on Instagram as social visuals, part of the performance and presentation of experiences both mundane and extraordinary. Animals might be company when watching television at home, for example, and so would appear within any documentation of this experience. This could be as part of a 'social TV' engagement, wherein the watching of a particular programme is also accompanied by participating with social media discussions about it (Bredl et al. 2013); among Australian viewers of the Eurovision Song Contest, for instance, pets from cats to dogs to rabbits made appearances in Instagram posts tagged with the hashtag promoted by the contest broadcaster (Highfield 2017). This was not the sole type of experience documented on Instagram around Eurovision, though: images and videos of parties, explicit engagement with broadcast content, and other demonstrations of the physical activity of watching television (solo or with friends and family), allow users to provide evidence and context for their own social experiences (as opposed to the recurring engagement promoted by live-tweeting television shows, for instance).

This approach to the recording and sharing of events is seen across other contexts, too; from ultrasounds and sonograms during pregnancy to funerals (as examined in chapter 6), Instagram content tagged with relevant hashtags demonstrates how the visual is used for 'sharing and communicating significant social experiences' (Leaver & Highfield 2018). While negative attention has accompanied the idea of taking selfies at funerals, content tagged with #funeral often reflects more the social experience of the event, from attire to family to reflective commentary and imagery, more than any seemingly vain and disrespectful actions (Gibbs et al. 2015). The visual aesthetics of this documentation takes in styles ranging from collages of the journeys to this point – for instance, birth collages depicting key moments from ultrasound to newborn (Leaver 2015) – to carousel posts with multiple images, and quotes and artistic, non-photo imagery.

Individual hashtags overall provide their own tropes and aesthetics, too. Different aesthetics apply to different tropes; the same rules do not apply to all content. Indeed, in some cases it is the aesthetics *within* the visual rather than (or at least as well as) the aesthetics *of* the visual which make the trope. Images posted as part of #ThrowbackThursday (#tbt) or #FlashbackFriday (#fbf) share less a common aesthetic between images, but instead a common marker for presenting prior experiences, younger selves and reminiscences. The popularity of 'Throwback Thursday' as a trope, using Thursday as an opportunity to delve into past content, is also seen on other platforms as user-led and platform-directed initiatives; Spotify, for instance, has an official #ThrowbackThursday playlist updated weekly.

Scrolling through #tbt content, what is of interest is the aesthetics within the chosen images – dated fashions, portraits of the user as a child, long-gone places, and so on – and the accompanying stories in the captions and comments. The trope is less uniformly visual than the presentation of food or flatlays, for example, yet such content adds layers to the lives and personae presented on Instagram. In her study of socially mediated memory and self/media accounting, Humphreys argues that for #tbt posts on Instagram, 'the aesthetic contracts and awkward poses become reconciled with our contemporary understandings of who we are in socially meaningful ways' (Humphreys 2018, p. 111). The self depicted on Instagram is predominantly that coinciding with the time active on the platform; new content is posted, rather than delves back into the individual's personal archives. The collected posts of a single user, then, represent a temporally specific snapshot, in addition to the curatorial choices made in deciding what to post. For new followers or friends who have not known the user for a long time, #tbt and similar content offers an opportunity to see a different side to the poster, adding perspective and familiarity.

In her examples, Humphreys looks at the act of presenting older – often physical – photographs, not hiding the reality of being a photo (or post) of a photo. Even when a #tbt post does not feature the user's hold on a physical photograph being captured, though, the deliberately historical lookback of the hashtag is one which seemingly goes against much of Instagram's rationale: rather than being an instantaneous depiction of what is happening in the moment, a #tbt post is explicitly out of sync with the current events in a user's feed. Humphreys suggests that '#tbt shows that the poster knows they are violating the norms of presentism on social media' (Humphreys 2018, p. 111); similarly, it could be argued that any such norms on the part of the platform have long since been complicated by Instagram's own temporal strategies (see chapter 3).

How experiences get presented on Instagram has also led to numerous tropes, templates and clichés, as common, normalized and expected aesthetics: muted pastel palettes and washed-out backgrounds; flatlay still lifes, personal items painstakingly arranged for best visual appeal; point-of-view perspectives of beaches and pools, gazing over the individual's legs at the water; food porn of latte art, brunches and dinners (Taylor & Keating 2018); mid-air jumping group shots; the 'follow me', hand-holding travel photograph style popularized by Murad and Nataly Osmann (Johnson 2016). Such aesthetics engrain their inspirational and affective appeal: the visual representation of space and experience becomes aspirational, both for recreating the look and for obtaining that feeling. Locations become recognized for their aesthetic potential, promoted by travel bloggers and Influencers, to the point of cliché (Bogle 2016). Such aesthetics can go beyond aspirational to ostentatious, glorifying particular lifestyles, glamourizing excess, and highlighting social inequalities, such as the 'rich kids of Instagram'. However, the apparent attraction of life carefully presented for Instagram can lead to feelings of inadequacy and jealousy among others; in Tiidenberg's (2018) research, 'participants described Instagram as an app that demands a lot of effort and tight self-control, which is occasionally depressing because of comparison with, and the envy of, strangers' beautiful lives' (p. 57).

The impact of Instagram content on an individual depends on factors like the accounts they follow and their reasons for using the app, though. The development of communities on the platform has led to expected and specialized aesthetics which reflect the support and inspiration of such groups; the aspirational visuals promoted are about demystification and accessibility, rather than pretension. Health and wellness communities, for example, use Instagram to promote particular lifestyles, share weight loss journeys and visualize ways of being; in their study of clean eating on the platform, sociologists Stephanie Alice Baker and Michael J. Walsh (2018) note that '[a]dopting a healthy diet on Instagram was depicted not only as an individual choice but as a means of collective membership into a community with other like-minded individuals' (p. 4564). Within these communities, aesthetic and communicative approaches are used in common with practices seen elsewhere on the platform and across social media; following the inspiration of Influencers and vloggers, for example, clean-eating Instagram accounts 'used the platform to brand themselves as lifestyle icons and devotees'. Content posted to Instagram becomes just one part of the social media strategy promoted here, from sponsored posts to external websites, podcasts and other material shared on additional sites ('link in bio'), commodifying communities and practices in the process, something we discuss in detail in chapter 4.

Since Instagram supports emoji hashtags (unlike, at the time of writing, rival platforms like Twitter), this has encouraged further aesthetic developments through the use of multiple emoji in hashtagged sequences to denote themes (whether safe for work or not), and this also includes the combination of emoji and text within a single hashtag (for more, see Highfield 2018). There are aesthetic considerations around the presentation of hashtags, as well. Despite serving a structural role in terms of being searchable and annotative, filling a caption with numerous hashtags does not always provide a clean or ideal appearance; Instagram users will then hide the hashtags by either featuring them below the rest of the caption, several lines down, so that they will be cut off when seen in a user's feed, or by putting them in a separate comment. Here, the platform vernacular comes up against, and develops in response to, the visual aesthetics of Instagram: cultural practices around hashtagging mean that the use of the feature may be necessary, but (especially when using dozens of hashtags) their own appearance is less appealing, whether to the posting user or their followers. The workaround of hiding hashtags is a vernacular practice that then allows the user to maintain a cleaner profile, in keeping with the platform's own promoted aesthetic.

Conclusion

This chapter tracked the aesthetic development of Instagram, across its own platformed identity, through the functions and affordances of the app, and through the vernaculars and styles promoted by its users. Such approaches, tropes and genres have not arisen solely because of Instagram, though: the aesthetics of the platform comes out of various contextual and historical factors, from earlier digital capabilities and social networking sites, to the evolution of mobile technologies and the visual cultures and formats supported on social media. In the following chapter, we move from the Instagram aesthetic to the Instagram ecology, exploring how these factors have shaped the Instagram app – and its own stable of apps, including Hyperlapse, Boomerang and Layout – as well as the wider landscape of visual apps and platforms around it.

CHAPTER THREE

Ecologies

Regardless of the aesthetic choices made for any Instagram post or story, there are three key situational aspects that hold true (as at 2018) for each and every post: the mobile, the social and the visual. New content is posted to Instagram through the mobile app – even if viewing through a browser, the web interface still does not allow for new uploads to a profile. In order to post to a profile, content also needs to be published, to be shared, as a social act; even if the audience who can see the post is just the contributing user, there is an act of sharing that is required to add content to Instagram (see also John 2017, pp. 120–1). Finally, new content requires a visual element – whether it is a photo, an illustration, a quote or rendered text, a video, or a text-oriented story, the presentation of this content is still predicated on the visual; there is no option to post a caption without a visual element.

These aspects highlight the importance of the mobile, social and visual to Instagram. The particular combination of these three elements also distinguishes Instagram from various apps and platforms which offer different approaches to some, or all, of these. However, Instagram is also just one in a long line of web-based and mobile sites and platforms which utilize these elements as a way of pushing user engagement, encouraging social communication, or promoting particular content types. In this chapter, we explore Instagram as part of a wider visual social media ecology, encompassing apps and platforms which both pre- and post-date Instagram's launch. In exploring this extended ecology of visual and mobile media and apps, we investigate those elements which are part of

Instagram's own brand, as well as its rivals. The platform is also placed in a continuum of web-based services for personal photography and image-sharing, such as Flickr, and within the development of apps and mobile media, from camphones to locative media such as Foursquare, which have contributed to Instagram's development and popularity.

The Visual, Mobile and Locative before Instagram

In the previous chapter, we examined how Instagram's visual identity and aesthetics were grounded in references to older forms of visual communication, most notably decades-old photographic technology. At a functional level, though, Instagram evolved from, and has responded to, numerous precursors and rivals that offered internet users opportunities to share and explore visual content.

The early photographic focus of Instagram noted in chapter 2, for example, was far from the first time that users could digitally post and socially share their photos. The likes of Shutterfly (1999), Snapfish (2000), deviantART (2000), Picasa (2002, bought by Google in 2004), Photobucket (2003), and ImageShack (2003) offered image-hosting at a time when personal server space was scarce, expensive or technically prohibitive. Some services were more generic, supporting images in general, but others had a more outright photo-centric outlook, complete with photo-oriented products such as photobooks and other printed material. Flickr's launch in 2004, meanwhile, extended web-based support for photography, bringing in Web 2.0 principles, user-generated content, tagging, groups, and Creative Commons licensing to provide a platform promoting and supporting photographers around the world.

As Web 2.0 morphed into social networking and social media, encouraging the centralizing of content on the likes of Facebook, new visual platforms and repositories developed;

even if the visual was not the dominant component, as in the case of tumblr (launched in 2007), the platform's support for visual formats meant that it played a key role in developing user practices and communities. Imgur (2009) provided a centralized repository for visual content shared on reddit, while yfrog (run by Photobucket) and Twitpic were among the services hosting visual content shared in tweets before Twitter supported it locally. The popularity of these platforms also led to numerous commercial developments: both Flickr (in 2005) and tumblr (in 2013) were bought by Yahoo!, for instance. These also inspired competitor strategies, with Ipernity (launched in 2007) changing its interface in 2013 to directly appeal to disillusioned Flickr users in the wake of the latter's redesign and strategic development.

As with Instagram, these platforms offered different forms of engagement with the visual; the visual cultures developing around meme-heavy sites like 4chan, and reddit, for instance, which eventually bled into the memes shared on Facebook, Twitter and more, demonstrate different visual styles as well as varying norms and practices on each site (Milner 2016; Phillips 2015; Phillips & Milner 2017; Shifman 2014). The animated GIF, a file format previously associated with the early web, experienced a resurgence through use on reddit and tumblr, eventually becoming supported on major social media and generating its own economy (Kanai 2015a, 2015b; Miltner & Highfield 2017). As visual content developed, and capabilities on platforms improved for hosting, embedding and sharing content, so the visual moved across the social media ecology, changing their form, their meaning, their intent, as they crossed contexts and cultures (Gries 2015).

The visual ecology is partly shaped by the shift in digital architecture towards profiles and sharing, and the capabilities of the technology at the time (and the deprecation of others); these are not just technical at the level of the platforms though. The desired uses and applications of digital media are also reflective of the move from standalone digital cameras to cameraphones and smartphones, as technology becomes multi-purpose and the need for peripherals declines. Already in 2005, researchers were noting that 'cameraphones will soon be the dominant platform for low end consumer digital imaging' (Van House et al. 2005). However, cameraphones were not without their logistical limitations, including 'getting media off device; finding and managing media assets; and sharing media' (Davis et al. 2005, p. 2). As the resolution and quality of the cameras improved, though, as part of the general technological improvement of mobile devices, so camera-enabled phones became more commonplace, making photography ubiquitous within the everyday (Cook & Garduño Freeman 2011). Cameraphone practices and cultures developed, along with the digital platforms promoting photographic works (Garduño Freeman 2010), as personal photography became accessible in both technology and opportunity (Larsen 2008; Nightingale 2007; Van House 2011).

The advent of the smartphone, and especially the iPhone, developed this further; as Halpern and Humphreys (2016) note, 'the ability of the [iPhone] to share images on the Internet or via email, makes it a significantly faster, more convenient tool for distributing photography than traditional cameraphones … smartphone app capabilities make it not only a means of photo taking and photo sharing, but also a means of photo editing' (pp. 62–3). The rise of 'iphoneography' – 'a community of people who use the iPhone and its various photo apps to create, edit, and distribute photographic art' (p. 63) – not only reflected the technological capabilities of the iPhone's built-in camera (used in Apple's own marketing materials) but also the opportunities provided through the range of photography-related mobile apps. Using Apple's own camera app was not the only option. Different apps were subsequently launched which did various photographic things, including the likes of Hipstamatic and other retro camera apps discussed in chapter 2. Cumulatively, the iPhone and other smartphones enabled a merging of the various steps in photography into one device, where it is 'possible to control the whole process, not only of image production and distribution of those images (like any mobile phone) but also the possibility of processing those images, in the same device, to obtain different results' (Gómez Cruz & Meyer 2012, p. 216).

What is also important here is that the capacity to record visually is coupled with the mobility of the device – taking a photograph, or a video, is always an option when the phone is available. The constant presence of the camera within the mobile, the endless possibilities for creating images, for communicating, in hand, pocket or bag, reflects what sociocultural anthropologist Heather Horst (2016) describes as 'mobile intimacies', as individuals use and respond to the materiality of a device (p. 162). These also highlight the communicative affordances of mobile devices identified by communication and technology researcher Andrew Schrock (2015) – portability, availability, locatability and multimediality – which are critical not just for enabling mobile photography in general, but in how Instagram is used and promotes itself.

As outlined in chapter 1, Instagram's earliest form was a location-based app and Foursquare-competitor, not as Instagram but as Burbn. The main success of the app, though, was in the photo-sharing elements rather than checking-in, and prompted a redevelopment of the app (Garber 2014). Its locative origins, though, reflect the ongoing importance of location information to mobile media, from checking in to places through Foursquare and its rivals, to using mobile devices to mediate experiences, offer recommendations, give directions or tailor gaming (Frith 2015; Wilken & Goggin 2015). Even if the explicit locative framing of Instagram is no longer apparent, too, this aspect of mobile media is still implicated in how the platform engages with location both through content and through the device's geodata and permissions given by the user (Mitchell & Highfield 2017).

The evolution of the social, the mobile, the visual and the locative within digital media provides the overlapping contexts for Instagram. The growth and popularity of the platform, outlined in chapter 1, has led to its integration into practices across contexts, from being part of the mediation and presentation of the political (Kasra 2017; Larsson 2017; Liebhart & Bernhardt 2017), to the branded experiences of events and places (Carah & Angus 2018; Thelander & Cassinger 2017), and the provision of journalistic news and information (Alper 2014; Borges-Rey 2015; Maares & Hanusch 2018). Such integration means that Instagram is a particularly prominent example of visual participation and engagement through digital media; for the participants in Tiidenberg's (2018) research, Instagram was seen 'as synonymous with "posting images on social media"' (p. 58). In the following section, we examine how such developments and practices, both on the platform and among rivals, have led to Instagram developing its own ecology over time. This provides the user with functionalities and apps that allow them to do more with both their content and the platform. Building off the previous chapter's exploration of post and feed, we turn our focus to how Instagram has evolved in new directions, complicating previous practices and capabilities on the platform while responding to its competitors.

The Instagram Ecology

Prior to 2013, Instagram was essentially just the app – officially, anyway. You could post photos, like, comment, but that was about it (as noted in chapters 1 and 2). Instagram's evolution, though, has brought in additional abilities and standalone apps which do more than just post images. These variously represent responses to rival apps offering different functionality (such as layout options), to competitors doing other things with the mobile and the visual (the direct copying of Snapchat with Stories), and to popular forms of visual content (including GIFs and Vines).

The first major addition to the Instagram ecology was an

extension to the app itself: Instagram Direct. Introduced in December 2013, it offered private messaging between accounts that followed one another. The private image-sharing and chat enabled here was the first step away from the public-facing (of sorts) communication that was previously the only option: if you wanted to leave a comment on a post, it could not be shared privately, although its visibility would also depend on whether or not the accounts in question were public.

The publicness or privacy of communication through the Instagram app was also complicated by the introduction of Stories in August 2016. As discussed in chapters 1 and 2, Stories offers different types of post, with their own aesthetics, to the standard Instagram post, but the function also offers the selective audience and directed content also seen with Snapchat; Stories can be posted to 'your Story', but can also be sent to specific users without all the users following the account seeing it (Stories can also be hidden from selected users). Like Snapchat, Instagram Stories are designed to be ephemeral (see also Ekman 2015; Verstraete 2016): they disappear after 24 hours, unless otherwise pinned to the account's profile (a feature added later). This further complicates the experience of Instagram, how content is presented, and the decision-making behind it. Not being a separate element of Instagram, Stories are promoted at the top of the app above all other content in a feed, highlighting their short lifespan and advised necessity of viewing. The advent of Stories though was also a disruption in the Instagram ecology: a recognition of the value of impermanent content, of user practices that do not privilege an exhaustive archive of everything posted, and of realizing the different intentions behind Stories and feeds.

In noting how Instagram's introduction of Stories seemed 'to run counter to its precious spirit – a betrayal of all the careful curation and perfect visuals', Casey Johnston (2016), writing in *The New Yorker*, also argued that 'the app's introduction of an expiring highlight reel is ... a response to a demand:

on an Internet that always remembers, we are fighting for places we can go to forget'. Any change to the app's ecology is both a response to changing practices and aims – of users, of platforms, of other stakeholders – and an opportunity for new and emerging applications, whether intended by developers or otherwise. In the case of Stories, as Johnston notes, the introduction of Stories did not just demonstrate Instagram and Facebook attempting to implement functionalities from a popular rival. It was also illustrative of tight curatorial practices among younger Instagram users, who regularly delete content and manage their profiles.

Stories was not Instagram's first attempt at introducing ephemerality to both content and messaging, though. Two years earlier, in July 2014, the first standalone app beyond Instagram was launched: Bolt. Offering more than the private messaging of Direct introduced less than a year previously, Bolt let users send images and videos to one another which would – once again, like Snapchat messages – then disappear after reading (Hamburger 2014). As a first addition to the Instagram ecology, Bolt was a very tentative step. It was first only made available in New Zealand, South Africa and Singapore, with a gradual rollout intended across markets. However, although Bolt made it to Australia the following month (Brooker 2014), the app was quietly discontinued before it was launched in the US or Europe.

With Bolt's failure, any attempt at copying Snapchat through peripheral apps was seemingly renounced. Instead, the subsequent apps which were globally released by Instagram focused on singular image- and video-based functionalities that were fed back into Instagram or Facebook in order for users to share content. Each of the three apps provided users with opportunities that could not be realized within Instagram itself – but which, crucially, were possible in non-Instagram apps. Hyperlapse, launched in August 2014, allows users to record time-lapse videos, save them to their device, and share them on Facebook or Instagram. With just two record modes ('hyperlapse' and 'selfielapse'), depending on which camera on the smartphone is being used, and the only edit option being to determine the speed of the time-lapse, the app offers little in terms of functionality. The same holds for Layout (released in March 2015) and Boomerang (October 2015), the next Instagram apps. Prior to Layout's release, Instagram users had to make use of third-party apps in order to create collages and combine multiple images into a single one – something that was particularly critical before carousel posts, enabling as many as 10 images or videos in one post, were introduced in 2017. Accessible through Instagram when preparing a new post as well as launchable independently, Layout provides templates for as many as nine images in a single collage, with some minor editing options; any individual image edits (such as contrast and saturation), though, need to happen before making the collage, as once imported into Instagram, only the collage as a whole is affected by filters and adjustments. Other apps allow for more presentation options and editability; for basic arrangements of multiple images, though, and with direct integration into Instagram, Layout gives users access to a popular function promoting convenience over creativity.

While Hyperlapse and Layout are predicated upon functions and options previously featured in rival apps, Boomerang is perhaps the most unique of the apps presented 'by Instagram'. Like Hyperlapse, Boomerang has two capture modes depending on the camera used: 'boomerang' and 'selfieboom'. In either mode, the app records a short, one-second sequence of images that then plays forwards and backwards in a loop. The resulting Boomerang can be shared to Instagram and Facebook, but there is no editing option within the app (nor is there any option to not loop – if you do not want this type of video, you would not be using Boomerang). Aesthetic changes can be made in Instagram, but Boomerang is solely for recording these loops. The exception comes through using Boomerang functionality within Stories, where face filters can also be overlaid while recording.

Despite being quite different to the other apps, Boomerang offers Instagram's own take on looping visual media and affective expression. In their silent loops, Boomerangs are similar to animated GIFs, but rather than being intertextual demonstrations of affect, Boomerangs are intended to be created by the user, through recording new scenes. Similar options are offered by apps like GiphyCam, which uses the smartphone camera to record loops which can be overlaid with artistic and kitschy filters and effects, and by the photo editing app VSCO's DSCO functionality (previously its own standalone app). At the time of launch, too, Boomerang offered Instagram and Facebook's own responses to the cultures and applications of Vine. Owned by Twitter, Vine allowed users to post videos of up to six seconds in length which then loop infinitely. These loops included audio, though, and this led to numerous creative approaches to using Vine, from music to comedy to other forms of vernacular expression. In particular, it became a space for Black creativity and youth culture (Hughes 2016; Romano 2016), flourishing in finding new ways to employ the platform and creating its own (micro)celebrities (Cushing 2015), but this was not enough to stop Twitter discontinuing Vine in late 2016.

In all of these cases, Hyperlapse, Layout and Boomerang, the Instagram ecology is firmly focused on the mobile: the apps are accessible purely as apps, and without any profile or feed of their own. Privileging the mobile is a common strategy for Instagram. Even though web profiles were enabled in 2012, allowing user content to be seen through a browser, the platform has not introduced any functionality to post to Instagram through the web interface. Only with the introduction of the most recent Instagram-adjacent app, Instagram TV (IGTV), has this become a necessity: longer videos, which for verified users could be as long as an hour, *have* to be uploaded from a computer. It is possible to explore Instagram content through instagram.com, to login and view stories and respond to follower requests. As at November 2018, though, the encouraged way to post new content to Instagram remains through the app itself. Changes to this may be dependent on the fortunes of IGTV, in encouraging take-up and in competing with YouTube and creator culture. Available both through Instagram and as its own app, IGTV is a marked change from the previous standalone Instagram apps and their single functions, and from the in-app-only presence of Stories. How successful it will be in expanding – as well as disrupting – Instagram's own ecology, though, is unclear at the time of writing.

Situating Instagram

The Instagram ecology is not just the apps and functions available to users; it offers a sense of situation, too, spatially and temporally, which varies across Instagram. However, the dominant promoted use of Instagram as positioned around sharing in the moment, wherever the user happens to be, is complicated by other realizations of the spatio-temporal on the platform. While visual mobile communication in its various forms allows for mediated presence, connecting individuals in and across space and time (Villi 2015; Villi & Stocchetti 2011), this is implemented, encouraged, and also challenged by Instagram in various ways.

Given the locative origins of Burbn, the spatial has long been an important consideration for the platform, and this has extended into the experience of space and place *for* Instagram users. Location information remains one of the only means that users can search for content on Instagram (the others including hashtags and user names); if you wanted to find posts about Paris, for instance, searching for 'paris' would give relevant hashtag suggestions (#paris and the like), accounts with user names containing 'paris', and popular locations pertaining to 'Paris'. The success of a location search and the relevance of the posts found, though, is reliant on users tagging the location in their post, and the level of specificity (and accuracy) provided in their choice of tag. Locations can be cities and neighbourhoods, but also landmarks and businesses; this becomes a form of check-in, of sorts, with a public geotagged post linked to that particular location.

In the absence of keyword search functionality, location information is a valuable hook for exploring content on Instagram; geographic metadata forms an important basis for much of the initial large-scale analysis of Instagram content, from the temporal rhythms of posts from Tel Aviv (Hochman & Manovich 2013) to the *SelfieCity* project, where selfies were identified within a much larger dataset of posts made from chosen cities (Manovich et al. 2014). How Instagram represents this, though, has changed somewhat over time. While searching for places and tagging locations remains an option, the individual user cannot see on their profile where they have tagged posts; photo maps, which did visualize the geographic distribution of a user's tagged images, were removed by the platform in 2016 (Hinchliffe, 2016).

Even if not represented cartographically on a profile, though, the experience of space has been remediated through the cultures, practices and visual aesthetics of Instagram and other platforms. As noted in chapter 2, and explored further in chapter 7, particularly vibrant and appealing locations become Instagram-worthy. As we argue in chapter 7, physical space becomes set up for the purposes of smartphone photography, selfies and social sharing. Locations become interlinked with brands on Instagram, as events and experiences become opportunities for further mediation of commercial content (Carah & Angus 2018) and as locations *become* branded through deliberate visual representation strategies (Thelander & Cassinger 2017) and slogans through hashtags like #thisisqueensland or #justanotherdayinwa.

At the same time, the apparent ubiquity of recording such experiences through smartphones, 'changing how we frame and experience nature' (Saethre-McGuirk 2018), has also led to concerns over the impact of this practice; this includes the apparent overlooking of the physical reality of a location, with people putting themselves in dangerous situations while seeking to take photos, at times resulting in death (Maddox 2017). The appropriateness of such practices has also been questioned, both with visual social media and with other forms of locative media. Content (especially selfies) posted from Holocaust memorials and the sites of concentration camps, for example, raise questions about the experience of such places, where collective trauma and memory are so prominent, with regard to respect, commemoration and appropriateness (see Zalewska 2017).

The Experience of Instagram Time

Just as the spatial experience promoted by Instagram is changing, so the Insta of the platform is also perhaps becoming a misnomer. While the mobile and the now were key attributes setting Instagram apart from other social media and previous photo-sharing apps, Serafinelli argues that 'the practice of photosharing on Instagram does not really follow the basic principle of the platform, which is the instantaneity of sharing' (2018, p. 62). Her study of photographers' use of the platform demonstrated 'a particular effort in the planning for photosharing ... The most common strategies can be summed up as a good quality of photography, particularity and unconventionality of scenarios, creativity of the visual composition and images able to convey emotions and feeling' (p. 62). These aesthetic and communicative ideals override temporal pressures; for Serafinelli's participants, posting in the moment is less important than the quality of the content shared.

The temporality of Instagram is further complicated by how content is presented on the platform. Posts in a user's feed are temporally positioned in relation to the current moment: they were posted '4 minutes ago', '7 hours ago', '2 days ago', '1 week ago', and so on. While each post's metadata includes the time and date of publication, such information is not visible to the user through the app's interface; the '[x time] ago' description is eventually replaced with a specific date, but no other time-related data is made available. This also applies to other elements of a post: comments, for instance, feature a brief indicator of how long ago they were posted, but only up to the week level of detail (so you saw '2w' for two weeks, '114w' for 114 weeks, or '240w' for 240 weeks ago), although posts now transition to an actual date at some point. The decay in temporal resolution over time means that the clearest information about a post's appearance accompanies one that is only seconds or minutes old; as the hours and days pass, when it was posted becomes less discernible.

Of course, reconstructing the timeline of an Instagram feed is also a futile activity in the sense that it seeks to create something that the platform itself did not provide: since 2016, the feed of content posted by the accounts a user follows has been algorithmically ordered, rather than a reverse-chronological, linear ordering. The move to an algorithmic feed is in keeping with other social media, including Facebook and Twitter, where content and users deemed to be most relevant or of most interest (based on previous engagement) is given prominence over metrics of recency, for instance. In addition to disrupting users' understanding of the linearity of the feed (Crook 2016; Turton 2016) – and knowing if they'd seen everything or when they'd reached the end of the new content – Instagram's decision to introduce an algorithmic feed had other, unforeseen results. Previously, if an individual chose to not go on Instagram on a particular day, they would reasonably expect to not see that content after the fact unless they went scrolling down the feed. If they wanted to avoid dates of personal significance or associated with intense feelings and memories, for instance, that was straightforward. However, with the algorithmic feed, not going on the app on the relevant day does not mean the content will not show up: for instance, as Gizmodo contributor Lindsey Adler found, not looking at Instagram on Mother's Day does not stop related content, algorithmically determined as important or relevant, showing up when you eventually do go on the app (Adler 2017).

Unlike Facebook or Twitter, though, there is no option on Instagram to select a chronological feed or to recreate one through various settings and searches. Critiques and backlash to the algorithmic feed led to changes by the platform in order to promote more recent content (Constine 2018a). However, while Instagram provided some overview of how the algorithmic feed worked (Constine 2018b), the determination of interest and relevance was unclear. An exploratory analysis in June 2018 examined the make-up of the feed having not opened the app for a week. Of the first 111 posts (including ads), their temporal origins ranged from '45 minutes ago' to '1 week ago', but without any apparent logic to their appearance: a post made '8 hours ago', one of the seven most recent posts in the sample, appeared as the 104th post in the feed – 50 posts after one dating from over a week previously (54th in the feed). The distribution of users, too, was limited: only 25% of the total users followed were represented in the posts, despite a reasonable expectation that more users had posted at least once during the period. Replicating this experience is implausible, though: not only is the algorithmic feed different for each user, but closing and re-opening the app brought a new selection of unseen content to the top of the feed, featuring different accounts and temporal distributions.

As a means to potentially overcome the vagaries of the algorithmic feed and the uncertainty of having seen everything, Instagram introduced an indicator in mid-2018 to let users know that 'you're all caught up' (figure 3.1), that you had now seen all the content posted by the accounts you follow over the last few days.

Content here, though, is just what is posted to users' accounts, visible through the feed; the fleeting existence of Stories, for instance, is a separate temporal concern, as is the 'live' functionality available here. Multiple temporalities exist alongside one another on Instagram (as on other

You're All Caught Up

You've seen all new posts from the past 2 days.

Figure 3.1. 'You're all caught up' message. Screenshot, 3 July 2018

platforms), with varying levels of visibility and permanence. They offer different ways of engaging with the platform, for being notified about updates, and for monitoring user activity. These strategies reflect what Weltevrede, Helmond & Gerlitz (2014) describe as the 'politics of real time', where 'social media platforms invest in a multiplicity of real-time features, which explicitly offer different paces, rhythms, and durations of content engagement to cater to the interests of their multiple cooperating partners' (p. 145). Competing interests are at play here for the platform: the push for more engagement with content (and advertisers), but also acknowledgement of responsibility for how the platform is used; the 'you're caught up' indicator was introduced as part of a new support strategy to help users 'better control their experience' (Ranadive & Ginsberg 2018), which included tools and metrics to manage the time an individual spent on Instagram and Facebook.

The contrasting times featured within Instagram content – archival photos posted on #tbt, emulated styles of older photographic forms, and so on – as well as the encouragement to post and to share what we are doing, as we are doing it, reflect how 'we use time-based media as a way of both recording and relieving our anxiety over time itself' (Mirzoeff 2015, p. 26). Instagram offers an additional way of mediating memory, of 'changing our inscription and remembrance of lived experience' (van Dijck 2007, p. xii). This might be temporary, an experience shared in the moment and gone 24 hours later, or something that is posted more permanently to a profile, but the choice is made to document and publish. Similar choices are made with posting out-of-sync with experiences (#latergram); regardless of any cultural norms or platform incentives on how to engage with Instagram, there is no requirement to post in any one way. As Serafinelli's participants noted, '[t]here is interest in sharing visual information even if disconnected by the principle of "here and now"' (2018, p. 62). The diversity of account types, of interests and purposes represented in the use of Instagram, mean that describing it as purely a photo-sharing app is an extremely reductive – and incorrect – generalization.

The Broader Instagram Ecology

The influence of the temporal is not just found in Instagram's own architecture and presentation. As noted in chapter 2, it is aesthetic and aspirational, in the retro stylings of posts and the tropes of #tbt, among others. They demonstrate how, as visual culture theorist Nicholas Mirzoeff (2015) notes, 'modern visual media are time-based … Today, digital media are always time-stamped as part of their metadata, even if that time is not visibly recorded in the image' (p. 26). Such temporal concerns and aesthetics are found – and challenged – in the extended ecology of apps and functionalities beyond Instagram itself, offering new potentialities unsupported by Instagram itself. These are the boundaries of the Instagram ecology; some apps will integrate Instagram connectivity to make their output more easily shareable, while others will offer options which Instagram currently does not, but which provide new aesthetic and content opportunities. In early 2018, for example, the app Huji Cam received attention, aided by its adoption by celebrities, for its particular brand of visual nostalgia. Appearing like a disposable camera on the smartphone screen, with a small viewfinder and film iconography to denote the 'developing' time of photos, Huji Cam is explicitly referential in form and description ('press the shutter when you are ready to face 1998'). Visual touches like lens flare and time-stamps on the

Figure 3.2. Example photograph taken with Huji Cam –
Amsterdam, 17 September 2018 (styled as 1998)

photographs, mimicking the aesthetics of 1990s disposable
cameras, further blur the lines between the simulated and the
real: demonstrating inauthentic retro styles but (potentially)
accurate temporal information (see figure 3.2).

Huji Cam is a throwback to the likes of Hipstamatic and
RetroCam, the predecessors and rivals to Instagram when it
launched, and it is not alone in doing so in 2018; retro photography, complete with disposable camera aesthetics, are
featured in apps like Kamon and 1888. While these deliberately offer the opportunity to do less with your photos than
Instagram, other apps go the other way. For example, although
filters are somewhat synonymous with Instagram, there
is only so much that can be done using the in-app options,
working with preset styles. Beyond Instagram itself, there are
a wealth of image-editing options which are used as part of
the process of making visuals Insta-ready, offering some very
different approaches to touching up and reimagining images.

Apps like VSCO (described in a 2013 *FastCompany* head-line as the 'anti-Instagram') offer finer tuning in the editing and filtering of images before they got posted to Instagram; while these apps also have their own communities, the cross-posting and pre-processing of content eventually destined for Instagram is well-established. The different aims and cultures of use of these apps may be apparent here; the photography (and apparent higher quality photography) angle of VSCO versus the many functions of Instagram, including commerce and celebrity.

The many apps at the edges of the Instagram ecology also reflect different social, visual and technical cultures, among others, where the initial uses and awareness of these may be distinctly different from what happens when the wider Instagram user base intervenes. One of the most notable cases of this was the app Meitu XiuXiu (or Meitu Pic). Launched in 2013, Meitu XiuXiu was initially a Chinese-language app that offered extensive photo-editing functionalities. These were not just in touching up the levels of an image overall, but in adjusting the appearance of individuals in the photo, allowing for beautifying tweaks and retouching to faces, eyes, skin tone and more (demonstrated in figure 3.3). With these editing capabilities, the app and others offering similar possibilities

Figure 3.3. Selfie by TH in Amsterdam (March 2018), with various levels of Meitu filter applied

became commonplace among influencers in Singapore and elsewhere in east Asia, 'where the tasteful editing or "shopping" of selfies is neither shamed nor scorned but celebrated and rewarded' (Abidin 2017c). However, when the app suddenly received attention from predominantly white, English-speaking sources in January 2017, these normal and established uses of Meitu XiuXiu were overlooked in place of memetic othering, focusing on the exotic and different over the app's actual practices and cultures.

Other apps take different approaches to image-editing, automating the process even further. In June 2016, for example, an app named Prisma appeared in the Apple App Store. Prisma took the filter application model that had become normalized on Instagram. However, rather than evoking moods or aesthetics through the new renderings of images like Instagram's own filters, Prisma's filters made more extreme changes to an image's appearance while evoking explicit references to different artistic styles and works. Moving beyond the retro photography aesthetics of Instagram, Prisma instead allowed users to very easily see what their photos would look like if presented as Japanese woodblock prints, Degas-esque impressionist paintings, or pen-drawn line art, among others.

Using a neural network approach that algorithmically renders the user's image in the chosen style, Prisma filters were not filters in the same way as Instagram's; instead, the deep learning technique meant that the selected image was reproduced following the example of the original artwork inspiring the filter. These included reimaginings of specific artworks and artists; for example, the 'Wave' filter draws from Hokusai's *The Great Wave Off Kanagawa*, 'The Scream' from the painting of the same name by Edvard Munch, and 'We Can Do It' the J. Howard Miller poster from the Second World War. 'Roy', meanwhile, is based on the work of Roy Liechtenstein (with *Go for Baroque* as its icon), and 'Mondrian' revisits the abstract, geometric art of Piet Mondrian (see figure 3.4). Other filters apply more stylistic inspiration, from rendering images

Figure 3.4. Sample output from Prisma, using 'Mondrian' style; based on original selfie by TH seen in figure 3.3

as mosaics, impressionistic paintings, manga art, or ink and pencil sketches. Some further editing is also possible after running a filter on a given image, adjusting settings including brightness, contrast, vibrancy and saturation. Since Prisma's original release and popularity, its stable of filters has grown, with daily releases, only briefly accessible, and additional filters available for purchase.

When Prisma launched, part of its initial success was attributed to the ability for users to share their creations directly to Instagram (Lomas 2016). The artistic potential offered by the app meant that it presented a very different opportunity to Instagram in making images visually appealing and unique, setting Prisma-created posts apart from the by-now humdrum likes of X-Pro II and Valencia. Without the links to platforms already popularly used, though, the attention given to Prisma might not have been as extensive – although users could still screenshot and post even if easy sharing was not set up. Rather than trying to create a new social network around the emerging platform, making the connection to the established social media ecology for content sharing meant that apps like Prisma had less functionality to worry about developing, but also could harness practices already commonplace among users. Applying different artistic styles to content has since been adopted in different contexts on Instagram, though: within the numerous effects offered in Stories, the entire visual appearance of the scene can be reimaged using the style of comic book art, a 16-bit rendering, watercolours, or a charcoal sketch, among many others.

Similar to Instagram and retro visual aesthetics, Prisma did not originate the algorithmic mixing and rendering of two images or visual styles, but offered a streamlined version of something that was receiving increased attention. The original research behind the deep learning style transfer approach (Gatys, Ecker & Bethge 2015) led to numerous technical implementations like Prisma, including the DeepArt website created by the original researchers. Rather than the limited palette of artistic styles offered by Prisma, DeepArt allows users to designate a source image and a style image which is to be applied. The greater creative potential here has seen effective style transfers for incongruous imagery, and unexpected aesthetic delights, such as dinosaurs made of flowers (Rodley 2017). The attention given to the approach in general, too, has seen this type of artificial intelligence-aided visual transfer implemented elsewhere, from Google-led projects to Facebook video filters (Vincent 2016). This had meant that, as with many apps that offer a singular function, Prisma's initial popularity saw a great flurry of interest, but not extended growth or usage. A paid subscription model was later introduced, for users who wished to use high-definition images and get access to more styles, as well as pushing user content to Prisma's own feed – in a display sharing aesthetic similarities with Instagram – but the app also remains (as at November 2018) free to use in its base form. In this regard, Prisma demonstrates what Bratton (2016) refers to as the 'generative entrenchment' of an app like Instagram: the size of Instagram's user base and established practices and patterns of use, as well as the backing of Facebook, mean that it is in a better position to add new functionalities, including those inspired by competing apps, than a new app or platform operating in a similar space.

For other apps and platforms that overlap with Instagram with regard to functionality, practice or content, for instance, one strategy has been to provide services which improve the Instagram experience of users, rather than directly competing. The graphic design platform Canva, which offers templates for print and web design formats along with extensive graphic and textual resources, includes dozens of designs for Instagram posts among its social graphic options. Apps like Over and Unfold, meanwhile, focus on providing templates for Stories on Instagram and Facebook, bringing further aesthetic possibilities here that contrast distinctly with those promoted in Instagram's own story options (see chapter 2). Just as Instagram introduced apps like Layout in response to competitors offering functions that it did not, the ongoing development of new affordances and functionalities for the app, from post to story, mean that the ecosystem of Instagram-adjacent apps has also continued to grow.

Instagram's boundaries also impact upon how content shared on the platform spreads across other social media. The sudden use of Meitu XiuXiu (for English-speaking users) or Prisma, for instance, was a practice that spread rather than a single image, as users created their own variations on what others had already posted. Despite the cultural associations of Instagram with content types like selfies, such images which have taken on global prominence on social media do not necessarily originate with the platform; the infamous group selfie from the 2014 Academy Awards ceremony, for instance, was posted on Ellen DeGeneres's Twitter account. Indeed, just because Instagram is a highly visual platform does not mean that visual content is spread easily or more efficiently here. The lack of a built-in regram function, or similar *public* sharing tool, limits the potential for boosting content visibility, unlike the 'share' option on Facebook or retweeting on Twitter. In Pearce et al. (2018)'s study of visual content pertaining to climate change on multiple platforms, for instance, the authors conclude that 'although Instagram is seen as the more visual platform, it appears that images circulate more readily on Twitter' (p. 12). As with other functionalities not provided by Instagram itself, regramming as practice is dependent on third-party apps or manual screenshotting, and comes with its own etiquette and norms of how to post someone else's content (Pardes 2018; for more on screenshots as cultural practice, see Frosh 2019). These are both streamlined and complicated by Instagram's introduction of posting others' content into your own Stories, though, which provides attribution plus the user's own optional commentary, but which also only provides the function for temporary posting.

The lack of regram functionality, and its take-up in other forms, also notes how a shadow economy of practices has emerged to subvert the limitations of the platform. Instagram users exercise ad hoc workarounds, including manual screenshots and reposts, the use of third-party apps, and utilizing a host of unofficial spin-off apps that allow users to curate and archive various posts for their own use. This shadow economy extends to the commerce of buying followers and likes on Instagram, whether bots or actual users, in attempts to cultivate visibility of an account and its content, and to similar strategies employed here like spamming and hooking into popular existing hashtags.

The wider platform and app ecology further define Instagram's boundaries. Directing users beyond Instagram is limited by the platform's support for linking; external hyperlinks do not work in captions and comments, so are often placed in the user's bio field instead. The inter-platform relationship also affects how content can travel across platforms. Due to Facebook's ownership of Instagram, cross-posting between the two is a different consideration than publishing Instagram content to Twitter, for instance. While it is still possible, a tweet containing an Instagram link will not display the image or video; instead, the user has to follow the link back to Instagram to view the content. Even though a cross- or multi-platform social media engagement strategy might promote the use of all of these platforms, with a common hashtag (such as with social television; see Highfield 2017), the actual experience of cross-posting content to each is not equal. At times, Instagram also has geographical boundaries. Various features have been rolled out in limited release, determined by location, as seen in testing out apps like Bolt, as discussed earlier in this chapter, as well as for copyright and licensing reasons; as noted in chapter 2, the option to add music to Stories is currently only available in some countries. There are also local differences based on language and regional differences; the impersonal 'likes' in English become 'j'aime' (lit: 'I like's) in French and 'vind-ik-leuks' (lit: 'I like this'es) in Dutch, for instance.

Conclusion

The Instagram ecology discussed in this chapter establishes what is possible and encouraged by the platform, and how it emerged from the visual, social and mobile contexts (and continues to develop in response to popular trends and practices); what is still to be seen, though, is how these opportunities are actually used by Instagram users. In the following chapter, this is explored with particular focus on Instagram economies, and the harnessing of the platform for commercial purposes by individuals and brands alike.

CHAPTER FOUR

Economies

In earlier chapters, we mapped out the early histories of Instagram to ascertain that the platform did not start out with commercial intentions or uses. This has since changed; as we wrote this book in 2018–19: Facebook Inc. has introduced native advertisements on Instagram where app-sponsored posts are interspersed with those from accounts that we follow and flicks between Instagram Stories are also consistently interrupted by in-app sponsored Stories. However, the earliest sightings of commercial activity on Instagram were not initiated by the app, but were instead orchestrated by networks of users who saw the potential to monetize their critical mass of followers by personally integrating sponsored messages into their Instagram posts. This chapter traces this early history of economies on Instagram by focusing on social media Influencers and their vernacular practice of generating advertorials and sponsored content before Instagram introduced in-app advertisements.

It is March 2012. Prior to returning to Singapore for a second leg of fieldwork, one of our authors is Skyping a Singaporean Influencer to learn more about their background before meeting in person. At one point, Carrie talks us through the plethora of social media platforms she actively uses for work and leisure, and mentions 'Instagram': 'And there's this newish app, sort of – Instagram. Have you heard of it?' The author shakes their head and makes a joke that perhaps it is true that everything moves slower in Australia, where we were living at the time of the interview. Carrie continues: 'So, I don't have an account yet, but some of my [Influencer] friends already do and I know what it looks like. It's basically like Twitter but instead of text, it's for your photos.' The author queries Carrie to ask if and when she would take up the new app. She laments that these 'new kids on the block' are a dime a dozen, and that like many of her peers, she is growing fatigued of learning the terrain of yet another new app, investing new content on it, only to have it fade into obscurity just as rapidly as it had emerged:

> I think I will try it soon … seems like a faster way to share photos with my readers rather than, you know, upload all these pics on my blog one by one. But ultimately I will use it if more people [as prospective followers] use it lah, if not, [there's] no point just posting for nobody to see.

Shortly after we spoke, Carrie took to using Instagram to post finely curated images of her everyday life as a teenager. In a matter of weeks, it already seemed commonplace for her and other Influencers to publish sponsored posts for various clients. By December 2012 when the author had gone to Singapore to visit Influencer agencies, managers were talking us through the slide decks they use to pitch Influencers' portfolios to prospective clients, and highlighted that several Influencers were already beginning to turn down 'deals' due to a 'backlog for months' of posts already scheduled for contracted clients. One particular manager, Sarah, from a mid-sized Influencer agency tells us:

> These days I don't even have to really promote [Instagram to clients] anymore. A few months ago I still had to explain what this app was, but now all [the clients] want is Instagram, Instagram. They are not interested in Twitter, blogs, so much any more. You know la, new things [are] shiny things, everyone just wants to try [Instagram for sponsored content] even if they don't know how to use it.

As both Carrie and Sarah point out, the swift uptake and incorporation of Instagram into Influencers' repertoire of sponsored content occurred seamlessly because there was a strong traction among a core group of Influencers, a core group of followers, and a core group of clients simultaneously – a combination that is usually a rarity as many new apps face inertia in accumulating faith among users that they are not just a fad but are sustainable and will have retention ('new kids on the block'); that there will be sufficient interest among the general population of ordinary social media users such that Influencers are willing to build up their portfolios for a willing audience ('if more people use it'); and that there is already a pre-existing experiential vocabulary from which users can learn to navigate the new app with proximate knowledge of already established ones ('basically like Twitter'). As the interest in Instagram from all three groups – Influencers, followers and clients – coincided, the demand for sponsored content on the app rose ('backlog for months') and created a sense of exclusivity that added a layer of allure onto the app.

In this chapter, we consider how social media Influencers commercialized Instagram into a marketplace, their social and cultural strategies for driving up client demand on the app and engaging followers, some vernacular strategies for gaming savvy Instagram use in the midst of changes in the platform over the years, and some challenges that have emerged as Instagram became an ecology of economies.

Reappropriating Instagram

Historically, from the perspective of its creators, the intended use of Instagram did not seem to consider the potential for individual users to reappropriate the platform for commercial intents. Instagram's philosophy, as listed on its FAQ (Instagram 2016a) page reads:

> What is Instagram? Instagram is a fun and quirky way to share your life with friends through a series of pictures. Snap a photo with your mobile phone, then choose a filter to transform the image into a memory to keep around forever. We're building Instagram to allow you to experience moments

in your friends' lives through pictures as they happen. We imagine a world more connected through photos.

From this, it has been noted (Abidin 2016, p. 7) that Instagram (1) positions itself as cultivating a 'networked intimacy' by referring to its users collectively as 'friends' rather than 'followers' and 'followings'; (2) intends for users to navigate the app via 'mobile phones' with inbuilt cameras while on the move; (3) views users' collection of 'moments' as keepsakes; and (4) desires to capture happenings spontaneously 'as they happen'. However, Influencers have repurposed much of this rhetoric, gamifying some affordances of Instagram to the extent that an economy of Instagram commerce has emerged.

Firstly, despite the rhetoric of friendship in Instagram's philosophy, Influencers intentionally curate high follower-to-following ratios, with a large number of unknown users subscribing to them while themselves following only a small pool of users such as personal friends, fellow Influencers, and elite followers. As such, the dominance of commercial displays and exchanges on Instagram has resulted in a shift from its promised *networked intimacy* towards a '*networked public*' (boyd 2013), wherein users such as Influencers were not primarily sharing content for small, intimate, groups of friends, but instead publishing content in the persona of a public figure for an imagined, unseen audience.

Secondly, despite the expectancy of Instagram as a mobile phone app, Influencers integrate various devices in their production of images in order to outdo each other and generate better feeds. At the time of writing, the posting of content on Instagram is still limited to mobile phone, unlike other popular social media such as Twitter and Facebook that allow users to post from a variety of personal electronic devices. Thus, to improve the quality of their content, a common practice is for Influencers to snap high-resolution photographs using high-end digital cameras, transfer the images to a computer on which the photos undergo intensive editing, then transfer the finished product to mobile phones via data storage platforms such as Dropbox or Google Drive so that they can be published on the mobile app – there were intricate digital literacies being exchanged among Influencers around how best to maintain the quality and resolution of an image between device and platform transfers. As such, the originally intended *accessibility* of Instagram has been moving towards professionalization, and the *barriers to entry* for curating an account of normative standards is increasing.

Thirdly, despite being touted as a platform to collect memories, Influencers are utilizing Instagram as a digital repository of advertorials and self-branded images, in which followers may scroll through an account to locate purchasing information or use the Influencers' projected lifestyles as a referent. Rather than marking memories through images, Influencers are instead posing, grooming and constructing idealized versions of their 'best life' to cultivate a sense of future-oriented aspiration rather than past-oriented nostalgia. As such, the main use of Instagram is no longer centred on *archiving keepsakes*, but instead primed for *circulating and amplifying content* for maximum visibility and reach.

Lastly, despite the prospect of using Instagram spontaneously, Influencers are scheduling their posts, designing their feeds and timing their posts in order to optimize publicity and visibility among followers (Abidin 2014). They often curate dedicated and highly personalized hashtags as a repository to display original content to followers or solicit their participation in a dialogue. As such, the original spirit of *spontaneity* behind the app has been foregone for an *intentional and effortful programming and scheduling of content*, in which feelings of spontaneity, naturalism and authenticity have become staged practices (MacCannell 1973) and performances in and of themselves, with an established aesthetic vocabulary of disclosures to convey a carefully calibrated amateurism (Abidin 2017d).

Influencers on Instagram

Conceptually, scholars have studied forms of celebrity on the internet as a practice of 'microcelebrity' (Senft 2008; Marwick 2013), wherein some prolific internet users manage to cultivate a niche audience who are loyal to them through the savvy use of digital media affordances. Coined in the late-2000s, the 'micro' in 'microcelebrity' was defined in opposition to mainstream celebrities from the traditional entertainment industry in terms of the scale of their fame and the depth of followers' engagements with them: (1) whereas the scale of a global film star's celebrity is fairly wide in that many people around the world would have heard of them, the popularity of a microcelebrity is usually a lot smaller and thus 'micro' in measure; but (2) whereas the depth of a global film star's celebrity is fairly shallow in that not much is known about their personal lives off-screen unless audiences specifically indulge in the derogatory shadow economies of tabloids and paparazzi cultures, it is the norm for microcelebrities to engage in extensive disclosures of their personal lives as lived in order to draw in audiences, such that the depth of (albeit smaller) public audience's knowledge of them is rather deep and invested in the 'micro' details of everyday life (Abidin 2018a).

However, many forms of internet celebrity do not actually intentionally court online fame or practise microcelebrity. Think about the parent who shares funny home videos of their child to their small audience on social media, only to have it reshared beyond their intentions to the extent of virality; think about the person whose compromising facial expression or posture in a photograph has instigated so much humour and interest that they unwittingly become the 'face' of a meme without their control; think about the eyewitness who is interviewed on the street by a news network whose casual quip (usually in African American Vernacular English) is suddenly spliced and reposted on the network's social media and shared widely among the general internet population without their permission (see Abidin 2018a). These are people who have become internet celebrities but who do not actively pursue microcelebrity, whereas the reverse is true for Influencers.

Internet celebrities are 'media formats' (that is, any person, creature, item, icon or anything at all that can be converted into images or texts on a digital screen) who have 'high visibility' online regardless of the reasons behind or routes towards their prominence – such as 'fame or infamy, positive or negative attention, talent and skill or otherwise, and whether it be sustained or transient, intentional or happenstance, monetized or not' – and whose celebrity and fame is 'native to the internet' in that their rise to prominence first occurs on digital platforms (as opposed to already established celebrities from the mainstream entertainment industries who occasionally use social media as a complementary tool to connect with their fans) (Abidin 2018a, pp. 15–16).

The wide spectrum of internet celebrities can thus include figures such as Influencers, the faces of memes, and the persons who (happen to) star in viral social media posts whether celebratory or shaming (see Abidin 2018a). But the epitome of internet celebrities is the figure of the Influencer, for whom four additional criteria apply: Influencers usually engage with positive self-branding strategies (as opposed to playing with notions of shame and scandal); manage a public visibility that is sustained and stable (as opposed to being briefly viral or transient); groom followers to consume their content aspirationally (as opposed to accumulating hate-watchers or audiences who tune in only with the desire to watch them fail or to gawk at them); and can parlay their high internet visibility into an income that is lucrative enough for a full-time career (Abidin 2018a). As a process, Influencers are an established and mature form of internet celebrity who intentionally engage in practices of microcelebrity; they usually begin as everyday, ordinary internet users who adopt techniques of relatability coherently in the textual and visual narrations of their lifestyles across multiple digital states, to accumulate a following whom they then monetize through advertorials (Abidin 2015b). Thus, while everyone has the potential to be an internet celebrity, and while everyone is performing microcelebrity to some extent by virtue of using social media, only an elite group of users are able to strategically become Influencers.

On Instagram, Influencers are usually identified through a high-follower to low-following ratio; a sparing use of validity metrics such as 'likes', 'comments' and 'views'; the presence of advertorials; and more recently, the switch from a personal account to a business account, which allows for additional features such as a 'contact' button, the use of the 'paid partnership' stamp, the ability to hide followers' options to comment on specific posts, and more thorough metric tracking in the backend.

Primacy of Instagram Selfies

Any casual user of Instagram will soon notice the primacy of selfies or the 'face' on Influencers' Instagram feeds, as opposed to feeds of professional photographers who focus on scenery or those of shops who focus on their products. After all, Influencers are in the business of cultivating a brand image based on their appearances and everyday lifestyles, to be used as a canvas for embedding sponsored messages. But above and beyond this, the efficacy of Influencers' Instagram selfies is more strategic.

Influencers may often post selfies while holding a sponsored product or experiencing a sponsored service, to convey to followers that they have themselves personally experienced the product or service. These product placement selfies are meant to be a mark of *experiential authority*, implying that Influencers are not indiscriminately promoting every sponsored product/service, but have actually taken the time and effort to try it out themselves before making an honest recommendation. These product placement selfies also serve as a further authenticating device that Influencers have personally crafted their posts and messages, as opposed to simply using a stock image provided by a client or duplicating an image from elsewhere (Abidin 2016).

Influencers also post product placement selfies as a way to express their copyright and ownership over the image, especially since many prominent Instagram Influencers regularly experience plagiarism or identity theft. In a session in which we were allowed to witness Influencer Jeanette photograph herself with a new line of beauty products, she tells us in jest that 'nobody will wanna steal this photo with my big face on it'. This sentiment was echoed by Influencer Jane, who lamented over lunch that her earliest images on Instagram have been 'stolen by lazy Influencers' who just 'copy and paste' instead of producing their own advertorial images. She tells us that these days she will try her best to incorporate her face into every advertorial to deter plagiarism and theft, and jokes 'if they [competitors] really wanna steal then they have to make the effort to photoshop my face [out]'. Thus, Influencers' Instagram selfies are not a mere matter of vanity but crucial *markers of ownership* over the sponsored post. A particularly memorable quip which best encapsulates this idea was a conversation one of us had with Influencer Belinda over ice cream. She told us that if not for her presence in every Instagram image – at times even a mere hand with her distinctive manicure or jewellery – her Instagram posts could pass off as 'just a postcard': templatable, replicable and stereotypical.

Finally, at times Influencers may selectively post selfies with other people whose faces are intended as the 'product' to showcase an Influencers' social networks and status. In the same way that fans of public figures may like to capture and share images of their interactions – i.e. the time a president held you up as a baby, the time you ran into a television star in the store – lower-ranked Influencers are prone to posting Instagram selfies with more popular Influencers as a strategy for upward social mobility (the reverse is unusual, unless a mentoring relationship or favour to boost content is at play).

Further, between competing groups of Influencers, some are fond of posting selfies of their 'clique' in which the subtext of who is excluded and absent from the photos is more valued that the actual group selfie. Influencers sometimes utilize these photo ops to declare their allegiance to a particular social circle, announce their new entry or recent departure from another social circle, or as petty 'sub-grams' (posting Instagram content about a person without overtly mentioning them, usually for gossip or criticism) for followers to speculate over the inclusion of unlikely faces or exclusion of the usual suspects in the group. Such human product placement selfies serve as a *network surfacing* strategy for Influencers to indicate their social capital and standing within their own local and regional communities.

Finstagrams

As mentioned in chapter 1, in August 2017 Instagram introduced a new function allowing users to link and log into multiple accounts which can be toggled by tapping on one's username on the profile page (figure 1.1). Prior to this, users who owned multiple accounts had to manually log in and out of each specific one. For many Influencers, this meant a constant switching across their Influencer profiles: their corporate profiles for their fashion, cosmetics or miscellaneous businesses; their 'personal account' that published less pristine images but was still open to the public who could follow them for more 'unfiltered' content; and their actual private accounts, if they had one. But this new function to toggle across multiple profiles was to ease this inconvenience.

Instagram's latest project seemed intended to drive up their consumer base by encouraging users to create multiple accounts (Kircher 2017). In relation to economies of Instagram accounts, there are three main takeaways.

Firstly, Instagram's multiple account prompt borrows from the discourse of Finstagrams. By now encouraging multiple accounts through their new affordances and direction prompts, Instagram is bringing into officialdom the practice of Finstagramming. Finstagrams – 'Fake Instagrams', as opposed to Rinstagrams or Real instagrams – have long been prolific among young users (see chapter 1). Of the dozens of popular media articles reporting on Finstas, there seem to be three emergent themes:

- Finstas allow young users to construct continuums of privacy by segregating their audiences. For instance, Finstas are where young people 'hide their real lives from the prying eyes of parents and teachers' (Kircher 2015), or curate an 'employable social media front' (Duffy 2017).
- Finstas allow users the freedom to curate several digital personae without the need for brand coherence. Young people may use Finstas to post 'random streams of screenshots, memes and ugly selfies' (Gil 2017), and dump content that is not congruent with their primary account so as to 'protect [their] personal Instabrand' (Harman 2015). In other words, this is 'splintering as self-preservation' (Safronova 2015).
- Finstas are a backlash against the picture-perfect pristine ecology of Instagram normativity, undoubtedly popularized by social media Influencers. Such separate, distinct and unlinked accounts thus allow them to escape 'the pressure to create a beautifully curated Instagram account' (Jean 2016), rebel against the 'overly stylized content shared by celebs and so-called influencers' (Shah 2017), and expose the 'artifice of normal social media' (Luckhurst 2017).

Multiple Instagram accounts are thus an overt signifier to young users that what once began as a subculture of subversive use has now moved into the mainstream, and has become co-opted, promoted and monetized by the platform itself.

Secondly, as iterated in chapter 1, Instagram's multiple account prompt contradicts its parent company Facebook's single account policy and real name policy (Facebook 2018a). Where parent company Facebook is adamant and imposing about the singularity and coherence of its consumers' digital personae, it encourages its app Instagram to diverge and splinter at the opposite end of the singular-identity spectrum by encouraging users to play with self-presentation and selective audiencing. On Instagram, however, the primary motivation for the network appears to be less the archival of membership and more the generation of digital content, no doubt stimulated by the free labour of its users. While Instagram does not legally own any content posted, its terms of use grants them the 'non-exclusive, fully paid and royalty-free, transferable, sub-licensable, worldwide license to use the content that you post on or through the Service' (Instagram 2018e).

Thirdly, Instagram's multiple account prompt verifies the rise of 'calibrated amateurism' (Abidin 2017d). In its drop-down bar prompt, Instagram's strategically worded key phrases 'different side', 'private account' and 'close group' suggest that users have long been practising strategies of self-presentation on digital media, in spite of its 'authenticity rhetoric' on parent company and platform Facebook. It supports the need for scholarship on digital identity to go beyond simplistic dichotomies that the 'online' is 'fake' and the 'offline' more 'authentic', given that all self-presentation in digital and physical spaces is curated. In fact, in the age of picture-perfect, luxury-oriented, hyper-feminine Instagram Influencers who have dominated the Instagram economy thus far, authenticity has become less of a static quality and more of a performative ecology and parasocial strategy with its own bona fide genre and self-presentation elements. One of the authors has studied the rise of such performative authenticity as 'calibrated amateurism', which we define as a 'practice and aesthetic in which actors in an attention economy labour specifically over crafting contrived authenticity that portrays the raw aesthetic of an amateur, whether or not they really are amateurs by status or practice, by relying on the performance ecology of appropriate platforms, affordances, tools, cultural vernacular, and social capital' (Abidin 2017d).

Calibrated amateurism is a modern adaptation of sociologist Erving Goffman's (1956) theory of scheduling and human ecology researcher Dean MacCannell's (1973) theory of staged authenticity. Goffman argues that on stage as in everyday life, performers may engage in 'scheduling' (1956, p. 84) to segregate different audiences from each other. This is so that only one aspect of a persona is presented as required. Performers may also obscure the 'routine character' of their act and stress its spontaneity so as to foster the impression that this act is unique and specially tailored to whoever is watching (1956, pp. 31–2). In this space, there may be some 'informalit[ies]' and 'limitations' in 'decorum', which Goffman defines as 'the way in which the performer comports himself while in visual or aural range of the audience but not necessarily engaged in talk with them' (1956, p. 67). However, this 'backstage' is seldom as spontaneous as it postures to be but is instead a deliberate effort to manufacture a 'back region'. MacCannell studied tourist settings in similar back regions and describes tourists' pursuit of authenticity as complicit in the actual manufacturing of a backstage that does not exist. He writes that

> [j]ust having a back region generates the belief that there is something more than meets the eye; even where no secrets are actually kept, back regions are still the places where it is popularly believed the secrets are ... An unexplored aspect of back regions is how their mere existence, and the possibility of their violation, functions to sustain the commonsense polarity of social life into what is taken to be intimate and 'real' and what is thought to be 'show'. (MacCannell 1973, p. 591)

Combining these two classical theories for a contemporary digital phenomenon, internet users today also partake in deliberately curated and intentionally public forms of back-channeling through Finstas, Rinstas, and multiple Instas. Multiple accounts encourage followers and viewers to engage in cross-platform hopping, watching and matching. They imply that we all have backstages and hidden secrets on display on parallel platforms, if only our audience knows where to look and how to find these Easter eggs. Thus emerges a new game in the attention economy, where the pursuit is no longer some semblance of authentic disclosure, but a competitive investigation into and comparison of the different strands of selfhood that a single user may put out on multiple platforms through multiple usernames promoting multiple personae.

Visual Genres of Influencer Advertising on Instagram

In December 2016, 400 Influencers including mainstream celebrities with large followings on social media (Levin 2017) were paid to promote the Fyre Festival to take place in the Bahamas in April 2017. Accordingly, 'thousands of tickets' were successfully sold through Instagram Influencer-based marketing (White & Krol 2017) for this 'opulent music week-end' (Coscarelli & Ryzik 2017), with tickets costing up to US$250,000 (Karp 2017). However, during the actual event, the amenities, entertainment and activities that were previously advertised as a highly Instagrammable event were not delivered, and attendees had to be evacuated and eventually refunded.

Among the several legal repercussions, a group of Influencers were being sued for being involved in 'the widespread and uniform dissemination of the false promise' (Flanagan 2017), and for the fact that they were 'promot[ing] products without disclosing whether they are profiting or benefitting from doing so' (Flanagan 2017). In other words, these Influencers were engaging in *astroturfing*, or the orchestrated promotion of sponsored messages in the guise of unsolicited, non-commercial casualness, and without any indication or disclosure that these sentiments and messages are in fact calculated campaigns.

Although the practice of disclosing sponsored engagements and paid partnerships had long been instituted formally and established informally in several Influencer ecologies around the world such as Singapore and Sweden, it was during the

Fyre Festival fiasco that mass awareness around the questionable ethics of astroturfing and techniques of disclosure became more widespread in the US. The Federal Trade Commission (FTC), which oversees consumer welfare in the US, stated that '[a]nyone using their fame to promote products was now required to disclose a "material connection" between the endorser and the marketer of a product' (Richardson 2017).

However, back in the early 2010s, several ecologies of Influencers in Southeast Asia were already voluntarily engaging in the practice of disclosing their sponsored content by 'marking advertorials'. A pastiche of 'advertisement' and 'editorial', advertorials are highly personalized opinion-editorials (Abidin 2015b) with the main aim of marketing a message to viewers, and as such were initially more intentionally persuasive than rationally objective in their presentation of information. Advertorials are thought to be more effective than dispassionate and clinical advertisements as they usually incorporate the Influencers' honest perspectives from having experienced the service and product first-hand themselves. Instagram advertorials may be sold as a single post or series of posts, and their earliest iterations saw Influencers such as @ xiaxue promoting packages to clients via announcements on Instagram posts as such:

> FOR 1 WEEK ONLY! Special promotional price of $SGD600 for Instagram Ads! [3 screaming face smiley emoji] Blogshop owners can now feature their items (clothes, shoes, accessories or bags) on a sponsored Outfit of the Day post on my Instagram to 262,000 followers (and 161k followers on twitter). Hurry, it won't be this crazy price for long! Send your enquiries to xiaxue@gmail.com. [yellow heart emoji] Terms and condition apply. (Not a blogshop owner but also interested in advertising? Other questions? Do drop me an email)–@xiaxue

At this time, many pioneer and early-generation Influencers were voluntarily marking their advertorials to signal their commercial engagements and set themselves apart from aspirational Influencers – the latter of whom were producing (equally pristine) content for free or 'exposure dollars', to build up their portfolios and in the hope of being spotted by potential sponsors. It was only later on that Influencer agencies and clients formalized the use of sponsored campaign hashtags to aggregate content, and to safeguard themselves against accusations of deception. In this section, we review some of the earliest advertorial marketing strategies pioneered by Influencers in Singapore since 2012. These visual vocabularies constituted a cultural repertoire of advertorials through which Influencers carefully balanced the clear disclosure of sponsored content (whether voluntary, obligatory to clients or regulatory by law) against the maintenance of a 'clean' outlook (i.e. avoiding hashtag spamming, keyword jamming) and aesthetic (i.e. avoiding coming across as too commercial, too hard-sell) of their feeds.

Influencers produce Instagram advertorials in a myriad of ways, although some of these are more palatable, less overtly commercial, and come off as more relatable to followers. In this section, we suggest a continuum of commercial captures detailing how different Influencers disclose (or not) their paid practices. Derived from a close coding of Instagram screengrabs, the seven main styles – Promos, Small markers, Multi-Influencer campaigns, Shout outs and tags, Relative others, Lifestyle showcase, and The Instagram aesthetic – progress on a spectrum from most overt to most covert advertorial disclosures. Strategies tending towards 'the Instagram aesthetic' were deemed to be most effective, believable and relatable. In this section, we present the continuum of advertorial disclosures currently in practice on Instagram, their nuanced implications for Instagram Influencers and sponsors, and Influencers' strategies in selecting specific formats for specific advertorials.

Firstly, 'promos' are the conspicuous posting of promotional material. This is the least preferred by Influencers, as the captions are usually long and blatantly commercial, but are likely the most preferred by clients, because the vital information is displayed most overtly to followers. An Influencer may be featured prominently adorning the product or experiencing the service being marketed, alongside a straightforward caption that presents all the advertiser information in one glance. Most often, Influencers would post pictures of themselves holding a product or at the venue of an establishment at which they are receiving a service. They may redirect followers to their client's digital estates or brick-and-mortar stores. Further, some Influencers announce discount codes at the end of their captions while others overtly promote contests and giveaways. But perhaps the most naturalized of these noticeable promos would be when Influencers are photographed using the product, especially if it is in the aesthetic of a 'how to' tutorial, such as in the case of @ongxavier's collaboration with skincare brand Nivea (figure 4.1).

Secondly, Influencers may use 'small markers' placed within the Instagram caption to signpost advertorials. Popular conventions include '{AD}', '-sp' denoting 'sponsored post', 'c/o' denoting 'courtesy of', or obvious markers such as '#sponsored'.

Thirdly, 'multi-influencer campaigns' are when a select group of Influencers (usually from the same Influencer agency or company) are tasked to promote a brand or product on their individual Instagram streams within a designated period of time while using a dedicated hashtag. In this case, it is possible for each Influencer to be hired to post only one Instagram advertorial, while the hashtag stream maximizes its publicity and returns when followers are exposed to a larger collection of similar content on the campaign hashtag. For instance, Samsung's #SAMSUNGS5LTE campaign that was marketed by Influencers in Singapore reveal a diverse visual vocabulary of advertorials on its hashtag stream: Selfies with products, products in a flatlay of other items, products in Outfit Of The Day (OOTD) shots, among others. The ad campaign is also likely to remain in the imaginary of Instagram followers for

786 likes   15w

ongxavier Nivea Men Oil Control Mud Serum
Foam // now you can Unclog pores, Remove
oil and Hydrate skin with just one bottle; 3 in
1 products are the best for lazy guys like me
// Loving the refreshing; menthol feeling //
#NIVEAmensg

Figure 4.1. Instagram ad by @ongxavier demonstrating how he
uses Nivea products in his cleansing routine. Reproduced with
permission from @ongxavier

a longer period of time; as followers of Influencers are likely
to follow personalities within the same genre, social group or
clique, these Instagram ads will algorithmically surface more
often on the followers' feeds over the designated campaign

Figure 4.2. Artist impression of two Influencers who have tagged their accommodation and travel sponsor in their Instagram ad. Art provided by mistercrow.

period, unlike one-off advertorials. As Instagram changed its algorithm in its later years, its recommendation algorithm further enhanced the efficiency of this strategy, which is also known in the industry as a 'campaign blast'.

Fourthly, Influencers often receive freebies or exclusive services and experiences in exchange for 'shout-outs'. Shout-outs are public thanks and acknowledgements meant to direct followers' attention to the sponsors. Monetary compensation may or may not be involved depending on the contract negotiated. For Influencers, these credits may come in many forms, such as including sponsor's Instagram handle, featuring the brand's official hashtag, or 'tagging' the brand's official Instagram account as a user in the photo (figure 4.2). The last method of tagging is the 'cleanest' or 'least crowded' of the three, since

Instagram users have to tap on the image for the tags to be revealed. The purpose of these tags is to offer the possibility of redirecting follower traffic to the sponsors' Instagram feeds.

Fifthly, some Influencers attempt to naturalize their ads by composing their post with mentions of 'relative others'. With reference to a child, parent or partner, they may muse or quip about a product being used or an experience being shared. Before she had her own children, Influencer @bongqiuqiu would often post personal (non-sponsored) pictures of her niece (who has her dedicated hashtag) engaging in daily activities. Curiously, this was at times interspersed with pictures of her niece holding onto sponsored branded products. At first glance, this might seem like any other adorable toddler picture which the Influencer often posts. However, reading the caption with sponsor hashtags, tags and campaign information reveal these to be sponsored advertiser contents (figure 4.3).

In a similar vein, veteran Influencer @beatricesays usually gives followers little insights into her family life, such as their plans for festive occasions or events like birthdays and Mother's Day. Some of these activities include 'girls' day out' recounts of trips to spas, eateries and retail boutiques with her mother. Yet, on closer inspection, several of these posts, while naturalized into diary-speak, are in fact a series of sponsored posts as evidenced by the content of the caption. In order for these not to come off has being too hard-sell, in the following example the Influencer is observed spreading out at least three sponsored posts for luxury handbag brand Coach across eight weeks, and mentions her mother in two of the captions:

> Whoop! Thought mummykins should also get a Valentine gift & so I shopped [wink smiley face emoji] Shall keep the surprise in the box & can't wait to pass it to her on St. Valentine's Day! #coach #coachsg #withlovefromnew york–@beatricesays

> A little late but here's what I've picked from @coach (had a hard time deciding) for mummykins on valentine's day & she loves it! [red heart emoji] Thank you @coachsg for gifting

Figure 4.3. Artist impression of a young girl holding a burger from an internationally renowned fast food chain. Art provided by mistercrow.

us both & for helping to put a big smile on my mommy dearest. She says a big thank you! :)–@beatricesays

A joyous gift from @coach this Christmas! [red heart emoji] Love how classic this #boroughbag is & the @coachnewyork stories campaign is also fronted by one of my favourite international models [. . .]–@beatricesays

Perhaps the most convincing of these 'relative others' genre of advertorials are when Influencers market wares that are coherent with a newly entered life stage. At the time of this data gathering between 2013 and 2014, Influencers @belluspuera and @jaynetham were newlyweds whose relationships and weddings were catalogued on social media across several platforms. They have been known to muse about married life as young 20-something-year-old women. Both have also referenced their husbands in their 'naturalized' Instagram posts. @belluspuera's recount comes in the form of 'recommendations' to followers regarding home appliances, while @jaynetham appears to hashtag and promote the 'christmas gift' from her husband:

'Thought I should share that Fred & I have been in the pink of health of late, with the help of this guy! It has been purifying & humidifying the air we sleep in, keeping all airborne diseases at bay with its plasmacluster ion technology. Not only that, it helps to remove odours whenever we hold cookouts at home! #cannotlivewithout #livinginsharplife at Home' – @belluspuera, caption for a picture of an air purifier, set behind a bunny soft toy sitting on a stack of books–@belluspuera

'Best Christmas gift ever!!! Vernon and I got the latest Samsung Galaxy Note Edge and as the name states, the unique curved Edge screen lets me access my frequently used apps and while in lock mode, I can personalize it with my own handwriting! And guess what? It takes great selfies too! Pretty awesome eh? #SamsungMobileSG #GALAXYNoteEdgeSG' – @jaynetham, caption of a picture of a mobile phone with the homepage featuring an image of the influencer, her partner, and their pet dog–@jaynetham

Sixthly, at times a single Influencer may be engaged for a long-term campaign over a designated period we term a 'lifestyle showcase'. This approach requires more persona curation and thought from Influencers as it is paramount that they maintain the congruence of their social media persona and the aesthetic of their Instagram feeds while weaving in advertorials and discreet sponsor hashtags. An Influencer usually has great flexibility in choosing which of their posts and publication genres to utilize as long as the visual narrative can be fed back to the sponsored content. For instance, a holiday snap of an Influencer idling leisurely on the beach can, in the captions, be related to the purchase of premium insurance that one may enjoy alongside a luxury lifestyle, although these

Figure 4.4. Instagram ad by @collettemiles demonstrating how she takes photographs with the Samsung product. Reproduced with permission from @collettemiles

two conceptual ideas are not directly related to each other. In the following series of three posts, Influencer @collettemiles is variously photographed taking a photograph with her new Samsung phone (figure 4.4), placing her Samsung phone in her flatlay (figure 4.5), and slotting her Samsung tablet into a

Figure 4.5. Instagram ad by @collettemiles featuring the Samsung product in her flatlay of essential items. Reproduced with permission from @collettemiles

handbag before leaving home (figure 4.6). These were three posts from a larger collection that featured the Influencer and her lifestyle choices in situ, and how seamlessly her new (sponsored) Samsung products integrated with her established routines and added to her quality of life.

176 likes

collettemiles I never leave home without my Samsung #GalaxyTabS. It weighs less than 300g and is as thick as 5 credit cards. Its Super AMOLED display is out of this world,

Figure 4.6. Instagram ad by @collettemiles featuring her slipping the Samsung product into her handbag. Reproduced with permission from @collettemiles

Finally, advertorials that appeal to 'the Instagram aesthetic' (see chapter 2) are the most naturalized and subtle because it is difficult to discern if the post is sponsored or merely submitting to the clickability of hegemonic Instagram tastes. The following six styles of 'the Instagram aesthetic' were most

popular among lifestyle Influencers in Singapore when this
genre first made its debut around 2013–14:

- *OOTDs (Outfit Of The Day)* are snapshots of an Influencer's
  outfits. While the acronym suggests that these captures are
  taken daily to document one's dressing, many Influencers
  have been known to organize photography sessions to
  document several different OOTDs at once before queueing the posts and selectively publishing them over the week
  or month. The convention for OOTDs is also to state the
  labels that one is wearing. Some OOTD fashionistas may
  also publish the price of the individual pieces of apparel for
  the convenience of followers who wish to make a similar
  purchase, or if this was specifically requested by a sponsor.
- *Flatlays* are a variation of OOTDs where Influencers photograph their outfits on a flat surface. Usually, only selected
  clothes are tagged, presumably those that are sponsored
  and deserving of publicity. Flatlays are less cumbersome as
  Influencers do not have to wear the outfit and scout for pre-
  sentable photography backdrops (figure 4.7).
- *Fashion spotlights* are when an Influencer usually features
  one fashion accessory that they are fond of. For instance,
  some Influencers are known to showcase their impressive
  collection of luxury handbags, while others display jewellery, caps or dresses. @jaynetham is an Influencer who
  regularly posted closeups of her collection of shoes around
  2013–15. However, in many of these posts spread out over
  months, she is observed to be tagging the same shoe company, '@pvs_sg'. Read in tandem with sparsely flattering
  captions and the occasional post that redirects followers
  to the same company's events and sales, this collection of
  posts is probably sponsored by the company tagged. Since
  the Influencer also posts (untagged) images of other shoes
  from her personal collection, it is not always obvious to
  her followers that some of these fashion spotlights are ads.
  In addition, unless the caption is earmarked with obvious

Figure 4.7. Artist impression of a fashion flatlay @beatricesays.
Art provided by mistercrow.

discount codes or promotional material, it is often ambiguous if the Influencer is simply showing off the label of her apparel (similar to that of the OOTD and flatlay), or advertising for a brand. This approach is effective as followers are unlikely to notice the commercial activity and perceive her feed as being hard-sell.

- *Make-up libraries* are a variation of the fashion spotlight focusing on cosmetics. Brands are selectively named, tagged or hashtagged to redirect follower traffic to sponsors, but the commerciality is dispersed as products are presented as makeup/DIY tutorials emphasizing Influencers' expertise.

- *Partying* is also popular on Instagram. Be they behind-the-scenes of dressing up, pre-party drinks, party shenanigans or post-party recounts, these posts are especially rampant during festive periods. Influencers have been known to post a series of images of themselves photographed at different parties (judging by their different outfits, hairdos, and backdrops) spread out over weeks, with the only continuity across the posts being a campaign hashtag such as '#GrantsWhiskeySG'. Apart from the hashtag, there were no other telling signs of 'sponsorship' such as client logos or mentions, thus ensuring that only a keen eye would be able to ascertain the nature of the advertorial.

- *Café hopping* is yet another common Instagram trope. In Singapore, the rising popularity of café hopping photography came about when brunch grew to become a trendy weekend past-time among young adults. News outlets have reported over 200 new cafés in 2014 alone, with listicles and 'best of' countdowns being common blog fodder among social media microcelebrities. Café hopping is a middle-class privilege afforded to those with spending power, and this alludes to the classed aesthetic and curation of taste among young adults on Instagram in Singapore. In the follow posts, @beatricesays mentions the local café, 'Strangers' Reunion' in her captions (figure 4.8) and geolocation tags (figure 4.9). As above, the posts (and a couple of others) were spread out across eight weeks. The variety of 'name-dropping methods', including hashtags and tagging the café's official Instagram account in the picture, contributed to obscuring the sponsored nature of the post.

Other Commercial and Advertorial Innovations

Cross-platform Traffic

Many Instagram Influencers often experiment with Instagram-stylized hashtags to redirect traffic from their Instagram feeds to their blogs. Some popular hashtags are: #ontheblog, #blogged, #blogupdated, #newblogpost (see Abidin 2014). This redirection of web traffic is

beatricesays
📍Klarra

xxx likes

beatricesays Glad that @klarra's private preview went well today. Had my daily dose of caffeine from @strangersreu's pop-up booth here [...]

Figure 4.8. Artist impression of an Instagram post promoting Strangers' Reunion in the captions tag by @beatricesays. Art provided by mistercrow.

especially important to sustain Influencers' incomes. While they debuted around 2005, many Influencers in Southeast Asia began facing a decrease in blog readership by mid-2013, when Instagram became the most popular social media app in the region. This was detrimental as blogs had been perceived to be more effective than Instagram in terms of selling power, because they allowed the space for lengthy, detailed advertorials. Many Influencers are focused on improving their Instagram posts in order to 'lure readers back' to their blog. These self-promotion hashtags, while appearing like creative wordplay, are in fact deliberate efforts to steer readership towards avenues that are more profitable for bloggers. Some Instagram Influencers may choose instead to omit hashtags and announce their new blogpost in their Instagram captions.

beatricesays
Strangers' Reunion

...

xxx likes
beatricesays

Figure 4.9. Artist impression of an Instagram post promoting Strangers' Reunion in the geolocation tag by @beatricesays. Art provided by mistercrow.

Instablogging

In acknowledgement of the declining blog viewership and the rising popularity of Instagram use, Influencer @xiaxue coined 'Instablogging' where short text-based pictorial posts are primed to replace blogging (figure 4.10). While her first mention of 'Instablogging' was made in June 2013, the Influencer has since stopped this practice and returned to aesthetically stylized selfies and photographs of her child; the practice has continued among oher subcultures of Instagram accounts. During this time, several other short-form blogging mobile apps became widely popular in Southeast Asia, such as mobile app Dayre that allowed users to blog text, upload simple images and use in-app stickers. As of the late 2010s, Influencers who desire to share long-form text on Instagram now do so verbosely in their captions.

Figure 4.10. Artist impression of @xiaxue's instablog post. Art provided by mistercrow.

Corporate Takeovers

Popular Instagram Influencers are sometimes invited to 'take over' official accounts of brands as part of advertising campaigns. In these 'takeovers', the Influencer posts from the brand's official Instagram account for a specified period of time. This strategy expands the reach of the brand to the Instagrammer's (usually larger) following, thus riding on the Influencers' social currency in order for viewership to circulate across Instagram accounts. Engaged Influencers usually channel their personal Instagram aesthetic while marketing the brand in the style of advertorials.

Private Commercial Accounts

Traditionally, Influencers on Instagram would set their accounts to 'public' mode, allowing anyone to chance upon their content without the need to subscribe via the 'follow' button, while enabling the Instagram algorithm to occasionally surface their posts on the 'discover' feeds. Historically among pioneer cohorts of Instagram Influencers, setting accounts to 'private' was a temporary measure for damage control in the midst of scandals and Influencer wars. This enabled them to curtail the onslaught of hate comments, prevent mere passers-by from screengrabbing their content, or control the influx of 'fake followers' purchased by others as sabotage. However, by early 2017, many Influencers and commercial Instagram accounts were beginning to privatize their accounts as a default, thus necessitating users to subscribe via the 'follow' button before being allowed to view the content.

One genre of these private commercial accounts that is popular around the world is Instagram meme feeds. Owners of Instagram meme accounts who aggregate content from various sites online rely on user submissions for content, or generate their content by reportedly making their accounts 'private' by default. As a strategy for growth hacking, such accounts regularly post content encouraging subscribers to 'tag a friend' in the comments, thus persuading this potential group of yet-to-subscribe users to 'follow' the meme account in order to view the post. To foster an impression of exclusivity and to exploit users' sense of 'FOMO' (fear of missing out), such private meme accounts have also been known to 'tease the possibility of going private, posting announcements in their page bios like, "Going private in the next 24 hours", to entice people to follow while they can' (Lorenz 2018a).

Other private commercial accounts on Instagram may focus on hawking wares. Singaporean chef Ahmad Zahid runs the private Instagram account @globalmatsoulkitchen on which he sells limited servings of Malay cuisine Biryani each week. Prepared in his home-based kitchen in small batches of twenty to thirty servings, he announces each 'drop' on a random schedule on Instagram, after which customers have to send him a text via WhatsApp to reserve a 'slot'. Chef Ahmad Zahid says he usually receives forty to fifty requests each time, and has to turn down many willing customers including a 'high-profile clientele' of 'local actresses, radio personalities, and other chefs' (Kreems 2018). The resulting sense of competition among his customer base adds to the allure of his business, and has encouraged more potential clients to follow his private account for a sneak peek into the mystique of bidding for a slot. Thus, while the nature of this Instagram content is not private or personal per se, and while the barriers of entry to subscriber membership are actually low, the shroud of secrecy and exclusivity around this otherwise mundane food offering generates feelings of enticement among users.

Techniques of Relatability

Following the early years of Instagram commerce, in which Influencers dominated the platform with images of the pretty, pristine and perfect, users were beginning to experience saturation fatigue and 'picture perfect' Influencers began to lose their allure as followers sought what they felt was more 'authentic' content and more 'relatable' public figures. This sentiment was fuelled by a series of slip-ups by several Influencers around the world who unwittingly emphasized the hyper-commercial and contrived nature of their posts. For instance, a slip-up by Influencer @xiaxue in mid-2014 gave unaware followers a sneak peek into how the industry works. The Influencer had earlier uploaded an advertorial for 'SkinnyMint' but forgot to delete a brief from her manager that read as follows:

> Hello Wendy! Here's your EDITED caption for skinny mint 2nd IG: Loving my SkinnyMint tea! The morning boost is supposed to make you less bloated, increase alertness, lessen cravings and snackings, and have anti anxiety properties! [...]–@xiaxue

A selection of comments from followers on the now-deleted post read:

> 'did you mean to put that first line omg…'
> 'Did you mean to put "hey wendy"'
> 'BUSTED.'
> 'She has an editor?'

Many Instagram followers reacted in disbelief and called her out for being 'careless' and 'lazy'. The original post was quickly removed and replaced with the shortened caption that omitted the backend exchange. A selection of comments from followers who were aware of the deleted post include:

> '[2 crying laugh face emoji I saw what you did :P]'
> 'hahahahahaha xD'
> 'That was too funny.'
> 'Eheheh i saw that'
> 'Oh my … The dangers of careless fame …'

But the damage had been done and for weeks after, the Influencer was accused of being careless in her content production, and lazy towards eager followers who expected more professionalism of her.

Pro Bono Work

With the increasing commercialism of Instagram posts, it also appeared that personal posts that feature products that are not sponsored deserve their own earmark. Influencer @ yankaykay, for instance, occasionally publishes posts on her social media feeds and blog about genuine experiences she has had with retail staff. She has Instagrammed good products from jewellery lines and food and beverage outlets, and blogged about great customer service from an electronics store. This unsolicited publicity is given as a measure of gratitude for the service she has received. In these posts, she explicitly tells followers that her intent is 'not sponsored', and that she is merely sharing the information out of goodwill. In one particular post, she clearly acknowledges the commerce of her Instagram feed, but clarifies that this post is not sponsored, albeit appearing as a favour to a friend:

> I'm trained as a model/blogger to pose/post for ads and I
> know what this looks like but this isn't an ad. Val is a friend
> and she treated me to my first Jolly Bee and now the entire
> house adores it. Really super love this. I've had one with
> every meal since my first order.

Commercial gains aside, some Instagram Influencers have
mobilized their followers for charitable causes by promoting
social causes and not-for-profit events pro bono, despite being
able to fetch up to thousands of dollars for their Instagram
advertorials. On Twitter, these Influencers often retweet (and
urge followers to retweet) public notices on missing persons,
pets and property. In another instance, @yankaykay relied on
the goodwill of her followers to search for a missing dog. In
the comments section, her followers are seen tagging other
users who live in the vicinity of where the dog was last seen.
The dog was found within the day thanks to crowd-sourcing.
In her follow-up 'thank you' post, she tells followers that
the man who found the dog contacted her via his girlfriend,
who follows @yankaykay and had seen the missing notice.
The Influencer also thanks a string of fellow Influencers for
reposting the missing notice on their accounts in order to tap
into their own followers' networks.

'Behind-the-Scenes' Posts

Some Influencers use Instagram to maintain intimacy with
their followers through revelations into the backend process
of their stylized Instagram shots. These have become a bona
fide genre of 'behind-the-scenes' shots that involving back-
channelling the usually hidden snippets and decision-making
when constructing the 'perfect' Instagram shot. In mid-2013,
Influencer @euniceannabel would often post Instagram posts
from behind-the-scenes at the photoshoots she is usually
engaged in. She also frequently shares snippets of her journey
as a rising star in the television and cinema industry. These
are a stark contrast to the more aesthetic #OOTD shots that
she usually posts, and serve to underscore her accessibility

Figure 4.11. Artist impression of @naomineo_ publicly demonstrating and captioning the behind-the-scenes of capturing a good hair flip in her Instagram post. Art provided by mistercrow.

to followers who model themselves after her gendered and classed scripts (Abidin 2016). Some Instagram Influencers are also candidly upfront about the staging and labour that goes on behind their seemingly effortless and aesthetically tasteful shots. In one example, @naomineo_ publishes a photo of her hair apparently waving in the wind. Her humorous caption acknowledges the backstage as such: 'It wasn't the wind. I had to flip my hair a zillion times to get it right lol' (figure 4.11). In a second image, she shows the process behind taking a gorgeous selfie with cushions in the background and good lighting, including a rather comprising posture in which she is balancing a light ring on her feet while lying on her back (figure 4.12).

The Downside of Commercial Attention

Imposters, Bots and Scam Accounts

Apart from their social and cultural capital, the Instagram estates of Influencers are certainly highly valuable given that they are lucrative grounds for pushing out various sponsored messages. Through the years, several prolific Instagram Influencers have experienced identity theft, and weeding out and warning followers against imposters have become regular

naomineo_

xxx likes
naomineo_

Figure 4.12. Artist impression of @naomineo_ publicly demonstrating and captioning the behind-the-scenes of capturing a good selfie lighting in her Instagram post. Art provided by mistercrow.

affairs. For instance, Influencer @euniceannabel has encountered imposters that use the handle @euniceannabel_ which closely resembles the original. Such imposters thus rely upon less well-informed users' lack of familiarity or potential typos to chance upon their content and contribute to their views. A warning from @euniceannabel to followers in an Instagram post reads as such:

> EVERYONE LISTEN UP. Someone has set up an account under my name. Make sure that you're following the right EuniceAnnabel and not that FAKE account. Whatever is posted or said on that account isn't real. And to that idiotic person, let me remind you that 'Imitation isn't the highest point of flattering [. . .]'–@euniceannabel

In other instances, some Instagram Influencers experience imposters who completely fashion brand-new identities online by using the published images and selfies of Influencers, as was the case experienced by Influencer @jamietyj. Such actions are opportunistic and exploitative in that several of these identity-theft imposters have gone on to brand themselves as Influencers and accepted paid work for maintaining their feeds. The identity-theft imposters do this by saving selfies of Influencers that do not visibly show any products, and reposting these selfies with new captions that contain sponsor messages, thus altering the intention and meaning of the Influencers' original posts. Like @euniceannabel above, @jamietyj has taken to Twitter to troubleshoot the issue in a series of posts:

> 'Wtf crazy Thai girl using my photos on IG and has the audacity to block me and my bf so we can't find her!!!'–@jamietyj

> 'Is there any way for me to report her for using my photos on IG??? :(((' –@jamietyj

> 'Yay @Instagram removed the imposter's account already. A for Efficiency! [two palms high five emoji]' –@jamietyj

Signposting these frauds is important as they may have the propensity to tarnish the web reputation and social currency of popular Instagrammers, especially among new followers who are not aware of the actual Instagrammer's handle.

The Instagram Purge

As sponsored content on Instagram exploded and being an Instagram Influencer became increasingly desirable, the value of an Instagram account became tightly pegged to one's follower count. In the wake of the rise of imposters, fake accounts and bots, in December 2014, the company made its first move towards eradicating artificial inflation by conducting the first of several 'purges', systematically deleting millions of accounts (Lee 2014; Parkinson 2014). Instagram

Figure 4.13. Lists of hashtags that Instagram users used to commiserate over the loss of followers during 'The Instagram Purge'. Screengrabs by author.

users across the world were upset at the sudden move and their drop in follower count, and turned to Instagram hashtags and memes to commiserate with others (figures 4.13, 4.14 and 4.15).

Ironically, the mass panic instigated by the purge was capitalized upon by the very accounts that Instagram had sought to weed out to begin with – spam accounts and bots swiftly struck back by pandering to hysterical fears that all accounts would eventually be deleted if not properly validated. Internet folklore began to form around the need to follow specific 'verifying' accounts in order to sustain one's own Instagram. Permutations of words bearing semblance to the key terms 'verification' and '2014' brought up a selection of Instagram chain mail with images of text posts that read:

Figure 4.14. Lists of hashtags that Instagram users used to commiserate over the loss of followers during 'The Instagram Purge'. Screengrabs by author.

> If you noticed a Decrease in the number of followers your account may be at risk of being deleted unless verified.
> 1. Follow @verifyingpage
> 2. Report our verification page
> 3. Tag us and Hashtag #verifyingpage

Similar meme posts were sighted from other now defunct accounts @verifying2014, @verifying20144, @verifying. accounts.2014, @verifying2014x, @verifyingigs. Within hours, Instagram responded to the proliferation of such folklore by deleting these new scam 'verifying' accounts en masse. But this only encouraged opportunistic scammers to start afresh across a variety of mutated hashtags (e.g. '#verifying', '#verifying2k14', and '#verifying2014x'), and the cycle of mass fear, the spread of folklore, user reactions, Instagram

Figure 4.15. Lists of hashtags that Instagram users used to commiserate over the loss of followers during 'The Instagram Purge'. Screengrabs by author.

deletions, and mass fear again, looped hundreds of times for the next fortnight or so.

Although almost all Influencers took a hit from 'The Great Instagram Purge of December 2014', some were able to renarrativize the humiliating experience by speaking to 'relative loss' and 'relative shame' as a recuperation device. Many Influencers started to voluntarily announce their 'drop counts', often ahead of followers questioning them, as a preemptive measure to signpost their integrity and honesty, and to reaffirm that 'small dips' as measured by the percentage of one's total following was 'completely normal' and attributed to inactive accounts rather than bought followers (Abidin 2018a, p. 80). Veteran Influencers who emerged relatively unscathed also used this opportunity to encourage their peers to rethink and preserve their work ethic. Captions on 'the morning after' by Instagram Influencers @yankaykay and @melodyyap:

> I saw @melodyyap's post on how @instagram has been deleting inactive/bot/bought accounts and realized the reason for the drop. To clarify, I've never bought any followers on any of my social media platforms. I'm guessing the drop is from inactive accounts. [...] To be completely honest though, I have been tempted to buy followers. It's SO competitive here and clients always look at numbers and this is where I earn a significant part of my income from. I'd be lying if I said numbers don't matter to me. BUT I'm super glad I didn't. Cos now I'm looking at these accounts that have 50k or more drops (I hear some people dropped 80–90%??) and I'm thinking how embarrassing it is for them. Lesson this Friday: Legit means legit. Lucky I stuck to my guns and couldn't bring myself to buy followers if not I will be HOW paiseh [embarrassed] now!–@yankaykay

> On a separate note, it's lovely to know that @instagram is finally doing something about the spam bot accounts. Mine saw a 2k dip, and I am really happy about it. Someone once said I bought followers & created a big hoo-ha about this on her Instagram – not that I have no argument, but I just couldn't be bothered. More so, I am having a good laugh at those who really bought followers & denied they did. The dip in numbers really tickles me, and with this, I wonder how much longer you can deny about your buying followers. Integrity is key. For everything in life.–@melodyyap

Optimizing Attention on Instagram

Instapods
As Instagram institutionalized the illegitimacy of bots and bought accounts, Influencer agencies, networks and consortiums around the world similarly denounced the use of artificial and automated inflation and amplification of content. The blackbox of how posts are selected for the 'Explore' or 'Discover' page remained, and the platform also no longer displayed posts in chronological order. Taken together, this

meant that Influencers were losing reach on their posts on the whole. New Instagram folklore began to circulate, informing Influencers that the reach of their post can be algorithmically amplified if it registered an adequate number of engagements within the first few minutes of being posted, or even instructing Influencers on how to opt out of these new algorithmic patterns. Yet all this speculation was ultimately based on guesswork and the trial-and-error of some Influencers and agencies.

Sandwiched between the new algorithmic changes on the platform and the mass institutionalization of industry rules and taboos against purchasing followers, likes and views, groups of Influencers began to form 'informal networks to amplify each others' content within secret circuits' (Abidin 2018a, p. 82) known as 'Instagram pods'. Like a family of dolphins, these unseen (à la dolphins underwater) groups of usually ten to twenty Influencers would communicate with each other in highly private and closed messaging groups (à la dolphins and echolocation frequencies) to mutually promote each other's posts. The less covert method is to promote each other's accounts and posts in one's own captions and posts, such that followers are exposed to cross-promotion. The more sophisticated method is to announce in the closed group when one is about to publish a post, so that pod members can immediately and systematically provide 'feedback' to the platform by liking and commenting on it within minutes of publishing (Thompson 2017a), in a bid to trigger the algorithmic blackbox to register their actions as 'organic' engagement and further amplify exposure on the content by prioritizing it on other followers' feeds.

Technically, Instagram pods are not in violation of the platform's terms of use or of the Influencer industry's guidelines. Operationally, Instagram pods are difficult to track and clamp down on as some savvy Influencers are now collaborating with others across agencies, genres, languages and target demographics, thus requiring a keen eye to spot corroborative patterns across several Influencers' posts and comments, as well as their commenting and liking activity (Abidin 2018a, p. 82). But ethically, Instagram pods ultimately go against the rhetoric of 'organic' engagements as their aim is to manipulate the algorithmic blackbox to work in their favour.

'Witching Hour'

Evidently, the visibility of Influencers on Instagram is no longer confined to the responses from their willing audiences, but also that of the ambivalent algorithm. In other words, the mechanics of generating and capturing attention on Instagram comprises both the human eye and the machine eye. Another way that Instagram Influencers have been gaming with the politics of algorithmic ranking is by purposefully assigning their content a truncated lifespan. Many Influencers and managers I have interviewed in Southeast Asia speak of a 'dead time', 'quiet slot' or 'witching hour' during which Influencers would avoid publishing content. Usually pegged between 0200hrs and 0600hrs when most social media users are asleep, any content posted during this time has a very short shelf life because it receives little to no engagement, thus stimulating the platforms' algorithms to deprioritize its importance until it is 'lost to the interweb'.

However, some Instagram Influencers or their saboteurs intentionally use 'witching hour' to push out contentious content (i.e. leaked nudes, gossip, hate, etc.) to drive up user engagement and push up their algorithmic rankings. These Influencers hold the hope that a handful of wakeful and hawk-eyed followers would spot their posts and take screengrabs for safekeeping – it is common practice among fervent followers to take screengrabs of content that they feel will be pulled from social media, either due to censorship by the platform or self-censorship by Influencers after backlash. There are also many fan- and hater-run accounts that repost these screengrabs, and serve as public archives for content that Influencers have deleted.

At the break of dawn, when the majority of followers are awake and resuming their regular consumption of social media feeds, Influencers would then delete the contentious content they had previously published during 'witching hour'. By this time, a small ring of followers would already be circulating screengrabs and trending reposts among a larger audience. Competing aggregate sites would also tout their content as 'exclusive' copies of 'now-deleted' garb. But now, in the absence of the original post, the larger base of followers would partake in 'detective work' and search through hashtags, repost sites, and discussion forums for more copies and angles of the deleted content. En masse, these user actions then trigger the platforms' algorithms to read keywords relating to the particular Influencer as 'popular' or 'trending', and surface the Influencer's digital estates and content more prominently.

Other 'Marketing' Folklore
One of the oldest pieces of Instagram folklore to emerge within the Influencer community is that the allocation of a verification mark or 'blue tick' allows users a 'prime spot' on Instagram's Discover section, and 'access to special features' (Flynn 2017). Instagram has not made public how to acquire verification as it apparently cannot be purchased or requested, but one news outlet reports that verification has to be 'granted through a form that is not publicly available, but is accessible to some people in the tech and media industries' (Flynn 2017). In fact, there exists an entire underground economy of middlemen and brokers including 'seasoned publicists', social media marketers, or people who reportedly work at Instagram who claim to be able to secure verification for a commission, costing anywhere between 'a bottle of wine' to US$15,000 (Flynn 2017).

Drawing on their experience and expertise, many Influencers who have pulled through Instagram's various algorithmic updates regularly produce 'how to' guides for success, with tutorials by Influencers such as 'Grow your

Instagram ORGANICALLY in 2018 (How to work WITH the Instagram algorithm)' (Perkins 2018) and 'The ultimate way to grow on Instagram | Hacking the IG algorithm with methods you've never used' (Brinker 2018). But in the age of algorithms, where users are attempting to break into the blackbox of Instagram and optimize the attention economy through 'backdoors', many already successful Influencers seem to suggest that perhaps brushing up on one's content and skillset is still key. Several of these are entertaining, self-mocking skits that reflexively parody stereotypes of the Influencer industry, such as Singaporean YouTube channel TreePotatoes' (2016) 'How to be an Instagrammer parody' that advises aspirants to put on makeup before taking photos, acquire and exploit an 'Instagram boyfriend', or befriend social media-famous peers to exploit their social capital. But these comedic skits also bear some testament to the skills required in the industry, such as location scouting, camera framing, photo-editing abilities and eloquence for captions. In fact, such practices have been called out as less of a skill and more of a commodity, as other tongue-in-cheek 'how to' guides suggest simply hiring a professional photographer, location scout and stylist while on holiday to generate Instagram content in a breeze (Adams 2018). Further, aspirants can now literally take up professional courses on Influencer literacies, such as a three-year degree in 'modelling and etiquette' provided by Yiwu Industrial and Commercial College near Shanghai, where classes include 'makeup modeling', 'public relations etiquette', 'merchandise display', and 'aesthetics cultivation' (Yang 2017).

Recent Guidelines and Ethics Regarding Instagram Commerce

As reviewed in this chapter, Influencers appropriate a variety of creative strategies to maintain their audience interest and loyalty. To obscure the commerciality of their Instagram advertorials, a repertoire of vernacular advertorial disclosures was used to signal their paid partnerships without sacrificing the visual aesthetics and coherence of their feeds. However, the transparency of advertorial disclosures is a tricky endeavour with no universal laws in place, although there are emerging guidelines in some industry circles and some basic rules within some national jurisdictions.

On the one hand, Influencers have the responsibility to differentiate between sponsored and personal posts, as the opinions of the former are expected to be more flattering and inflated. Ad disclosures thus signal to followers the need to receive the information at their own discretion, and signposts the responsibility of information accuracy as a shared endeavour between the Influencer and the client (see 'Fyre Festival' case earlier in the chapter).

On the other hand, Influencers whose streams are overtly lined up with ads (and ad disclosures) come off as being too 'hard-sell', and ad markers clutter and distract from the photographic aesthetic of Instagram photos. Those whose Instagram streams become overtly commercial run the risk of losing followers who no longer find them relatable (Hopkins & Thomas 2011, p. 145). At the intersection of these, some prominent cases of astroturfing have been noted in recent years, wherein Influencers who were obliged to disclose their paid engagements masked the commerciality of their posts entirely. This has resulted in a few exposés (Abidin & Ots 2016) and witch-hunts on social media in which Influencers were named and shamed for their lack of transparency.

In response to the rise of such incidents, Instagram introduced in-app markers enabling its advertising partners and Instagram Influencers to earmark advertorials through embedded geolocation tags and 'In partnership with' bylines, among others. Following this, and having realized the economic potential of the platform to channel and disseminate advertising messages, Instagram later updated its platform to allow paid partners to embed advertisements into user feeds (see chapter 1), thus changing its users' experience of and relationship with the app.

External to the Instagram platform, many nationally regulated Influencer industries now require Influencers to clearly signpost their sponsored content (Purtill 2017), publicly mark their relationship to a brand mentioned in their post (Federal Trade Commission 2017), declare their earnings and pay taxes (Elle 2018), and even be subjected to an audit of their follower status when asked (Geller 2018). Organizations such as Bestfluence (Damsfeld 2017) organize seminars and training sessions for agencies and Influencers to benchmark their best practices; agencies such as Relatable (Relatable 2019) can be hired to set up backend tracking of follower engagements to provide accountability between clients and Influencers; and platforms such as Social Blade (Social Blade 2019) now allow anyone to publicly track and evaluate the genuineness of Influencers' follower engagements across various social media platforms. As one of the primary platforms on which Influencers have historically honed their craft and groomed their commercial talent, the reactions and responses from each iteration of Instagram's platform update has critically shaped the landscape of Influencer commerce towards greater transparency and longevity.

Conclusion

In this chapter, we reviewed some of the key infrastructures, actors and practices surrounding vernacular economies on Instagram. Specifically, we surveyed how Instagram was reappropriated by social media Influencers via specific narrative devices including selfies, Finstagrams and a diverse cultural repertoire of advertorial vocabularies. We also interrogated some of the key commercial innovations pioneered by Influencers to improve their standing in the increasingly saturated Instagram economy, including strategies around cross-platform traffic, Instablogging, corporate takeovers and the rise of private commercial accounts. Alongside such professionalization of commercialism, Influencers are also honing and preserving their techniques of relatability, by engaging in pro bono work or intentionally making visible their back-channelling in order to cultivate intimacies and foster more stable relationships with their followers. But given the stiff competition among Instagram Influencers, the downside of commercial attention has given rise to imposters, bots and scam accounts, which were swiftly dealt with during the 'Instagram Purge'. Post-purge, Influencers have continued to attempt to optimize attention on Instagram in the 'age of algorithms', resorting to consortiums of Instapods, experimenting with 'witching hour' and playing with other 'marketing' folklore rumoured to boost their visibility and status such as verification black markets. In response to all of these grassroots activities, formal state and corporate guidelines and ethics regarding Instagram commerce have begun to emerge around the world. Although press coverage of Instagram may often disproportionately focus on the key money makers and Influencers, the platform also hosts an array of subcultural groups and practices that have shaped Instagram's culture over the years. In the following chapter, we survey some of the communities and cultures that have proliferated on the app.

CHAPTER FIVE

Cultures

As stated in chapter 4, Influencers are a dominant commercial culture on Instagram and form a significant population on the platform. However, there are several other types of communities and cultures that have proliferated on Instagram. Some of these groups may be organized around the public repository of hashtags, the more complex networks of mutual 'followers' and 'followings', or interest groups that are not otherwise so easily accessed by visible affordances and metrics on the platform's interface but require a level of in-group knowledge. Still other cultures of Instagram bleed from the digital to the physical, revealing ritualistic habits that Instagram users seem to be practising en masse in a bid to capture a moment 'for the 'gram'. In this chapter, we take a look at some of these distinct communities of culture on Instagram through case studies.

Subcultures on Instagram

Art and Photographers
Influencer and celebrity Instagram accounts aside, many prolific Instagram users maintain conscientiously crafted feeds that appeal to users by being thematically coherent and highly specialized in content. Often, these are artists, photographers and businesses who have come to develop their own brand and distinctive markers on Instagram. Some of these include @friendswithyou which is an account run by two artists who photoshop smileys onto inanimate objects; @roaminggnome in which a 'Travelocity Roaming Gnome' is photographed

around the world in various locations; @micahnotfound where an artist known as 'Micah404' catalogues his artwork which interconnect to form a single massive portrait upon endless scrolling; and @orhganic in which a photographer strategically publishes black-and-white images of various objects that come together to resemble other objects and architectural shapes when users scroll down his feed. Within each of these accounts and communities of users, individual images are self-contained, self-referential and rarely include signs and symbols denoting trending happenings or hashtags. The community within these groups are self-contained, expressing admiration or suggestions via the metrics of 'likes' and 'comments'.

Emergent Teen Uses

Some Instagram subcultures appear to be generational, with teenagers and young adults repurposing the app for niche humour or age-specific needs. Many teenagers have taken to purposefully maintaining a low post count on their platforms, with 25 posts being the golden number (Godlewski 2016). This involves the constant curation and deletion of photographs that these teenagers feel are least popular, where posts that 'don't get enough likes' are removed presumably to maintain the image of perpetual popularity (Godlewski 2016).

Other teenagers have pioneered a 'new meme format' specific to Instagram, in the form of @samepictureofX, with X being any mundane object. In this genre, the exact same photograph of a toaster (@samepictureofatoaster), brick (@samepictureofbrick), plunger (@samepicofplunger), nugget (@samepicofanuggetdaily), kumquat (@same.picture.of.kumquat), banana (@thesamephotoofbanana), or a particular celebrity (@samephotooftaylorswift) is reposted daily on an account (Lorenz 2018b). Still other accounts post one different image a day dedicated to themes including milkshakes (@daily.milkshakes), pancakes (@_dailypancakes), crisps (@dailycrisps), and hamsters (@daily_pics_of_hamsters)

(Lorenz 2018b). In a piece for *The Atlantic*, journalist Taylor Lorenz argues that such 'same-pic accounts' are a 'low-pressure way' for teenagers to 'express themselves' and go viral via 'absurdist humour' (Lorenz 2018b). Interviews by Lorenz with teenagers reveal that '[t]he fact that someone has devoted such an enormous amount of effort to maintaining something seemingly so meaningless is also part of the appeal' (Lorenz 2018b).

There also exists a subculture of dating practices on Instagram. In mid-2017, a trend took off in which Instagram was repurposed by young people as a dating app. Some users employed Instagram Stories to entice or 'thirst trap' potential partners (Safronova 2017), while others exchanged flirtatious Direct Messages from old friends and friends-of-friends who are likely to chance upon one's account (Thompson 2017b). Some of these Insta-flirts may be a result of users connecting their Instagram accounts to dating apps such as Tinder, in a phenomenon cumbersomely named 'Tindstagramming' (Murdoch 2017). In this case, earnest users who have been rejected on Tinder (and thus unable to send potential dates texts on the platform) may track them back to Instagram and direct message them there (Murdoch 2017).

Social Awareness

While some young people may use Instagram in niche ways that surpass inter-generational understanding, other subcultural groups of users use the platform to raise social awareness for various causes in a more accessible manner. Some groups may aspire to Influencer-like Insta-fame as a template for generating income along the way, while others focus on visibilizing the lesser-seen struggles of minority groups to combat the illusion of perpetual glamour on Instagram.

Communities of teachers in the US have been honing their skills as 'teacher influencers' who share learning and organizing tips on Instagram, and make some income by selling original classroom resources and worksheets and promoting advertorials (Reinstein 2018). Some of them use Instagram as 'a second full-time job' or 'side hustle' due to the low average income in the teaching industry in the US, but many others do so to supplement the cost of classroom materials that they willingly provide for the students in schools that are lacking resources (Reinstein 2018). For instance, a teacher in Texas who makes US$50,000 through teaching claims to have accumulated over US$200,000 via Instagram advertising, where she has over 90,000 followers at the time of the report (Reinstein 2018). Collectively, many teacher Influencers aim to raise awareness about the government cuts to funding in the education sector and improve teachers' welfare in the country.

Other campaigns executed by marketing firms offer a surprising spin. In August 2016, 25-year-old Parisian 'Louise Delage' began posting a series of holiday pictures at dinner parties, on yachts, with friends (Friedman 2016) with typical Instagram captions such as 'Chilling with friends', 'Dancing', or just emoji (Hunt 2016). In just two months, she garnered over 65,000 followers (Hunt 2016). However, it was revealed in September 2016 that Delage was created by ad agency BETC for their client Addict Aide to 'put a spotlight on how easily you can look past a friend or loved one's alcoholism' (Friedman 2016). What her thousands of followers failed to notice was that in her 150 Instagram posts, Delage was photographed with alcohol in every single photo. The marketing stunt was revealed via a video Delage posted on Instagram that directed followers to the 'Like my addiction' campaign (Hunt 2016).

Conversations around health are also a notable subculture on Instagram, taking on three main forms. The first form is solo efforts by *individual Instagrammers who groom their accounts to promote causes* via their biographical narratives. One example is 14-year-old Australian Daisy Long who was diagnosed with Chronic Fatigue Syndrome, and uses Instagram to raise awareness about the illness via posts about her everyday life. Long was motivated to do so because several patients with Chronic Fatigue Syndrome report that their symptoms are often 'trivialized by medical professionals', and that 'doctors are still not sure how to treat it' (Moore 2016). The second form is *hashtag campaigns that are sustained by crowd-sourced contributions*. #MyFavouriteMeds, which was started by podcast host Jen Gotch, is an instance of this where patients of mental health issues are invited to share pictures of their medication. Gotch felt that 'medication shaming' was creating a 'barrier to treatment', and aimed to stop stigma and open up public disclosures and discussions around mental health issues (Neal 2018). The third form is *campaigns led by Instagram as a platform*. In May 2017, Instagram launched the #HereForYou campaign to 'increase conversation around mental health' during Mental Health Awareness Month. Users were asked to share photos showing their experiences with mental health issues, such as depression, anxiety and eating disorders. The aim of the campaign was to 'put you in touch with millions of people all over the world' who share the same condition, to build a sense of community and foster a support system online. Hollywood celebrities who took part in the campaign and spoke publicly of their own issues with mental health helped the campaign to take off (Holmes 2017).

Other initiatives around social awareness may engage with Instagram's norms more critically. For instance, @barbiesavior was launched by two anonymous American women in their twenties in March 2016 to critique the 'self-congratulatory' exercise of 'white Westerners who travel to third world countries' (Blay 2016), often by Instagramming the entire experience in the form of a travelogue. The satirical Instagram account catalogues the adventures of a Barbie who is 'charting her imaginary volunteer journey' to work with the 'sweet sweet orphans in the country of Africa', as a critique of the 'White Man's Burden', including attitudes of volunteer tourism that are 'deeply patronising and offensive' (Zane 2016).

Most recently, some social awareness initiatives led by developers have also adopted Instagram's affordances for users to have a more interactive experience. In December 2018, Singaporean artist and VR/AR developer Eugene Soh launched the #YellowHelmetChallenge Instagram filter in Singapore in partnership with the Facebook app developer team. The filter superimposes a white helmet on a selfie, which swaps out to a different coloured helmet when users raise their eyebrows. The aim is to land a yellow-coloured helmet, which is a symbol of the foreign workers who work in the construction industry in Singapore, who are often underpaid, with poor living conditions, and at times victims of xenophobia in the country. Soh describes the initiative in his Instagram post:

> Super proud to be launching Singapore's first instagram filter for a good cause! #YellowHelmetChallenge is an initiative by the wonderful people at LabourArty and @ healthservesg who have been looking out for the migrant worker community for a while now. This is what I live for, empowering the powerless, so we may, as a society, grow stronger! #PassionMadePossible.–@dude.sg 2018

Politicians

Given the ubiquity of Instagram for communicating information in a visually engaging and socially relatable manner, it is no surprise that several politicians have also taken to the app to connect with their citizenry. Perhaps the first of these instances is Singaporean Member of Parliament (MP) Baey Yam Keng who has been extensively using Instagram selfies as a form of 'charismatic engagement' since March 2013 (Abidin 2017a). This was an especially significant move in the country, given that online political campaigns began to take root since the General Elections of 2011 after the ruling party garnered its lowest share of electoral votes since independence, and that the Republic has generally had a 'soft authoritarian' (Nasir & Turner 2011) approach towards its management and censorship of the media. Thus, by incorporating social media strategies and regimes into his communication strategies, MP Baey was pioneering an unprecedented digital presence for political authorities, and reiterates media theorist Neil Postman's assertion that 'cosmetics has replaced ideology as the field of expertise over which a politician must have competent control' (Postman 1984, p. 4 in Abidin 2017a, p. 84).

Although he was initially dubbed the 'selfie minister' for his extensive use of Instagram selfies as a tool to connect with his younger constituents, a misstep in Baey's deployment of grief tribute selfies and perhaps a miscalculation of the intricate modulations behind internet vernacular soon angered several citizens. In the wake of the #PrayForParis tributes after the terrorist attacks in November 2015, Baey posted a rather gratuitous picture of himself posing with arms akimbo next to the Eiffel Tower. Taken on a state visit months earlier, his all black ensemble and pensive gaze into the distance resembled a 'superhero power pose'. Further, the lighting on the photograph was overexposed against a cloudless sky, stirring suspicions among users in the comments section that the image might have been photoshopped (Lay 2015). Thus, despite his rather sincere caption and tribute, several users called out the Minister's supposed vanity and narcissism (The New Paper 2015), and he was swiftly photoshopped into a meme posing next to various landmarks around the world (Lay 2015). One commenter wrote: 'Let's get real, you're not praying for Paris. You're posing for Paris' (The New Paper 2015). Swiftly after this commotion broke out, Baey posted a lengthy response expressing regret that his image had 'distracted the message on the global challenges we face today', and admitted that he 'could have been more mindful about the choice of photo' (The New Paper 2015). He thanked the public for their feedback and encouragement, and reiterated that he will remain 'active on social media' as a way to 'connect with people and learn from others' (The New Paper 2015).

After this incident, Baey swiftly returned to his Instagram politician persona, with several strategies in the vein of 'calibrated amateurism' (Abidin 2017d), such as revealing his humble makeshift set-up with his iPad and mobile phone when he conducts Instagram and Facebook live chats (Thomas 2017). He has also sought real-time advice from followers to fix minor technical glitches during his streaming sessions, which only further reiterates his casual, accessible demeanour with his constituents (Thomas 2017). As evidence of his savvy uptake of Instagram vernacular and the implicit rules around the permissible aesthetics, tensions around Baey's more recent Instagram faux pas were swiftly defrayed thanks to his deployment of 'doggo' memes (Lay 2018).

After Baey, several politicians around the world also took to Instagram to cultivate their public persona, including New Zealand Prime Minister Jacinda Ardern who has used the platform to share meaningful 'fan mail' (Preston 2018). As the world's youngest female prime minister as of 2018, Ardern has also used Instagram to document her life as a partner and mother, announcing the birth of her daughter in June 2018 via a family selfie from her hospital bed (NZ Herald 2018). But perhaps the politician who best encapsulates the strategic deployment of digital intimacy via Instagram is American congresswoman-elect Alexandria Ocasio-Cortez, who regularly gives her constituents a peak into 'a typically closed-off Washington experience' (Relman 2018) in American politics. While fervently Instagramming the details of her orientation week and initiation into Congress – including her 'grab bag', selfies with other new initiates, and photographs of the Congress building in the vein of a home tour vlog – Ocasio-Cortez was widely praised for her 'unprecedented form of transparency' (Relman 2018).

Like Baey who took citizens behind-the-scenes of his work life as a politician, and Ardern who made public snapshots into her more personal life as a young woman, Ocasio-Cortez similarly uses Instagram Live to stream her everyday life while

using the opportunity to communicate with users via parasocial relation strategies (Horton & Wohl 1956). For instance,
during Thanksgiving in 2018, she live-streamed the process
of cooking dinner in her home while conducting a Q&A in
reddit's Ask Me Anything (AMA) style on topics including
the challenges in Congress, specific policy issues and insights
into her personal life (Perry 2018). Even though Instagram
now allows users to 'store' their Live videos as 24-hour Stories
or permanent Highlights, Ocasio-Cortez rarely does so and
creates among her viewers a sense of exclusivity for only being
able to access this facet of her persona live. Ocasio-Cortez's
Instagram savvy has been especially impactful in cultivating her public image and growing her constituency, and
experts have even taken to analysing her body language and
gestures to calculate her sincerity (González-Ramírez 2018),
as a form of charismatic authority (Weber 1962). Several
other politicians around the world, especially young women
(Read 2018), have increasingly taken to Instagram as part of
their campaigning and electoral strategies, and social media
experts have also reportedly been hired to teach politicians
how to appear like 'real people' on Instagram in order to reach
younger audiences (Belam 2018).

Grief Tributes
Since mid-2014, a new vernacular trend emerged among
Instagram users globally: whenever a global grieving event –
such as a natural disaster, violent attack or social movement
– takes place, users would take to the platform to post reactions
expressing grief, solidarity, disgust, commentary, critique or
criticism. Over time, the visual lexicon of Instagram reactions
to global grieving events seems to have stabilized, encouraging remixes, intertextuality, cross-references and narrative
continuity among users and between events. These are often
visual tropes most viable for virality during the climax of
global grieving events and have emerged as an Instagram vernacular. To understand the anatomy of this grief aesthetic,

we traced some of these global grieving events and the circulation of imagery on Instagram between September 2014 and March 2016, including: The Occupy Central movement in Hong Kong, September 2014; The Charlie Hebdo shootings in Paris, January 2015; The Bataclan shootings in Paris, November 2015; The San Bernardino shootings in California, December 2015; The Sarinah Thamrin bombings in Jakarta, January 2016, and The Islamic State attacks in Brussels, March 2016. The emergent Instagram reactions to these global grieving events were catalogued on the research website of one of the authors (Wishcrys 2018), through her digital ethnographic observations of the earliest hours post-incident on Instagram. Some of the most common tropes include:

- An iconic visual symbol with cultural significance to the grief event, such as a national landmark or an instrument signifying victims or perpetrators. These may be illustrations, photographs or various art forms (i.e. the Eiffel Tower for #PorteOuverte, the pencil for #CharlieHedbo, national flag for #KimaTidakTakut).
- An iconic image/scene from 'the ground' that captures the essence of the movement, such as a prominent victim or perpetrator photographed in action, or a group of actors performing a powerful gesture (i.e. hands raised in surrender for #OccupyCentral, snaking queues to pay last respects for #PrayForLKY).
- Emblems borrowed from a lexicon of political statements and redesigned for the event (i.e. the yellow ribbon for #OccupyCentral, the peace symbol incorporating Monumen Nasional for #KimaTidakTakut)
- #PrayForX typesetting in various artistic fonts and illustrations, usually printed on a plain coloured background or superimposed onto a background image of iconic landmarks, scenes or scenery.
- Keep Calm and X advice typesetting in various fonts and illustrations, usually appealing to the power (i.e. Keep Calm

and Pray for Paris) of prayer, or an often risky and ill-timed comedic relief (i.e. Keep Calm and Eat Baguettes).

- Emblems borrowed from popular culture and repurposed for the event (i.e. Where's Charlie comic for #CharlieHedbo, Guy Fawkes mask for #OccupyCentral).
- Images of event-specific paraphernalia peddled to users (i.e. yellow ribbons for #OccupyCentral, silhouette artwork for #PrayForLKY).
- Screengrabs of event-related news updates, usually cross-posted from other social media such as Twitter and Facebook, or mainstream television.

The make-up of such communities is usually transient and loose, comprising individual users who are disparate and isolated if not for the fact that they are participating in the same hype ecology for a fixed but short period of time. Unlike the Influencer economy of Instagram, in which some prolific users curate dedicated hashtags archiving original content, such users participate in publicly trending hashtags as a one-off and with little commitment. Such transiently viral hashtags expire quickly the moment it begins to attract spam and bots, or after interest in the global grieving event starts to wane. In further research, this visual aesthetic has been studied as an attention-hacking strategy as 'grief hypejacking' (Abidin 2018b).

Instagram 'in Real Life'

Museums
The impact and influence of Instagram has extended from social media and bled into the physical spaces of 'real life'. Dozens of museums, gallery spaces and pop-up spaces catering specifically for visitors to use as Instagram backdrops and props have emerged since the mid-2010s. These spaces, which visitors usually have to purchase exclusive tickets to enter, have transformed the act of 'taking a photograph [into]

an experience itself' (Bereznak 2017). The physical rituals at these Insta-museums and Instagrammable sites include bidding for exclusive tickets, waiting in line to enter the space, waiting for the crowds to clear out of the frame for a split second to capture a photograph, experiencing exclusive brand launches at specific events, and at times even collecting freebies (Hess 2018). But journalist Amanda Hess argues in *The New York Times* that these are merely secondary experiences, with 'the real experience play[ing] out only after we post photographic evidence on social media', in anticipation of internet reactions, interactions and engagements to validate our photographic mark in the virtual space of Instagram (Hess 2018).

Perhaps the most iconic of the Insta-museums is the Museum of Ice Cream (MoIC). The space comprises a series of exhibits that are essentially elaborate backdrops for photography, selfies and maximum Instagrammability. In the first location in Manhattan's Meatpacking District, all 300,000 US$18 tickets sold out within five days. In the pop-up museum in San Francisco, all US$38 tickets for the six-month run sold out in under ninety minutes (Pardes 2017). Another pop-up location was founded in Los Angeles (Wiener 2017). Journalists who have visited these museums describe the space as 'detail-oriented ... [although] none of these details was small enough to be noisy or list in a frame, ensuring that all would translate nicely to a small-screen format' (Wiener 2017). Although most visitors enter the museums with the sole purpose of collecting Insta-worthy images, co-founder Maryellis Bunn 'denies that Instagram played a significant role in how she shaped the museum' (Pardes 2017). Instead, Bunn claims that the museums are merely a 'way to get people in the doors and feel safe' about their surroundings, to enjoy the displays, and perhaps to Instagram the experience (Wiener 2017).

The museums have since partnered with brands, promoting products and services such as dating platform Tinder, confectionery brand Dove Chocolate, media company Fox, and financial services company American Express (Wiener 2017). A section of the museums known as the Pint Shop has also been dedicated as a grocery store tasting room for visitors to sample sponsored ice cream (Hess 2018). In particular, September 2018 saw the museums collaborating with make-up brand and aggregate store Sephora, during which installations were updated to display exclusive products of the Sephora Collection, allowing audiences to interact with, test out, and hopefully Instagram the upcoming line as free publicity. Many of the items mimic the most iconic emblems of the museums, such as the US$64 'Sprinkle Pool Brush Set' that replicates the design of the MoIC's infamous pool of ice cream sprinkles (Cadena 2018).

Another prominent Insta-museum is 29Rooms, which is marketed as a 'groundbreaking art experience [for] expanding your reality' (Hess 2018), includes exhibits such as a 'human snow globe' and 'cloud pool' in twenty-nine themed rooms. Given the extensive popularity and publicity of 29Rooms on Instagram, seven of the rooms have been dedicated to collaborations with brand sponsorships to promote products and services. Executive Creative Director Piera Gelardi admits that while photo-taking is an 'important part of the experience', the rooms also 'delve into deeper themes, like body image and gender' (Pardes 2017).

Color Factory is another popular Insta-museum, comprising a 12,000-square foot space with fifteen 'interactive colour "experiences"' (Pardes 2017) for 'participatory installation of colors' (Hess 2018). This includes a room covered in confetti, a room full of colourful ribbons, and a room of objects all coloured in the orange spectrum such as 'cheese puffs' and 'goldfish'. In an interview with *Wired*, creator Jordan Ferney claims he made decisions that prioritized photographability over physical experience: 'Like, even with the lighting, where maybe a warmer light would have felt better to be there but a whiter light looks better on Instagram' (Pardes 2017).

Similar Insta-museums include Rosé Mansion in Midtown

Manhattan, where US$45 tickets promise visitors a pop-up 'experience' that is themed around pink wine (Hess 2018); Candytopia, which is an 'outrageously interactive candy wonderland' (Hess 2018); and Selfie Museum KL, which focuses on nine 'dessert-themed showrooms' and includes five free desserts as visitors journey through the space for RM45 (Koh 2018). To mimic the feeling of being 'at home', a 'Penthouse Made for Instagram' is also available for rent at US$15,000 a month, with 'every inch of its 2,400 square feet [being] free from the clutter of everyday life' (Maheshwari 2018). Intended as 'a backdrop for Instagram stars', it was opened in August 2018 by an agency that connects brands to Influencers (Maheshwari 2018), and comprises Insta-clichés such as '[s] potless walls, a "millennial pink" sofa, [and] a spa-style bathtub that's waiting to be filled with flowers' (Maheshwari 2018).

While it may seem as though Insta-museums are a novelty, they are merely the latest predecessor of a long line of photoworthy art installations and spaces, including works by artists Yayoi Kusama and James Turrell (Pardes 2017). Apart from the usual props that invite visitors to stand on specific spots stickered on the floor for the 'best' photography framing, and the usual initiatives that request that visitors take selfies with exhibits and upload them on Instagram using specific hashtags, art galleries and museums have even shifted their marketing to focus on the Instagrammability of their installations and wares.

To promote the National Gallery of Singapore's Yayoi Kusama exhibit in July–September 2017, Singaporean independent media publisher *The Smart Local* previewed the artworks in a sponsored article by selecting the ten most Instagrammable installations (Mandon 2017). These include 'The Spirits of the Pumpkins Descended into the Heavens' (2015), which featured a room covered entirely in dots, and the 'Infinity Mirrored Room – Gleaming Lights of the Souls' (2008), which featured a room with mirrored surfaces and small globule light sources to produce infinite reflections.

The article contained a series of images of a model with the artwork, juxtaposing a 'basic' run-of-the-mill pose with an 'Instaworthy' version of these poses. They also provided a mini how-to guide by recommending visual photography apps and features such as cinemagraphs, and by encouraging visitors to play with new light sources such as an iPhone torchlight. The campaign was promoted on social media under #SglovesKusama, and to entice prospective visitors of the 'Instagrammability' of the exhibits (Mandon 2017).

Foods
Other services and spaces are also cultivating their Instagram hook, most notably eateries. San Francisco entrepreneurs Madelyn Markoe and Jessie Barker decided that the primary goal for their first restaurant was 'to be Instagrammable' (Newton 2017). They were inspired by the trend of 'Instagrammable foods' such as 'unicorn foods' (Stack 2017 in Newton 2017), 'galaxy donuts' (Holden 2017 in Newton 2017), and the 'Sugar Factory milkshake' (Doss 2016 in Newton 2017). There is even an economy of companies that focus on 'turning restaurants into Instagram bait' with exclusive packaging and designs that are tailor-made for an Instagram aesthetic (Tishgart 2017 in Newton 2017). One eatery that has focused on Instagrammable interiors is San Francisco Cuban restaurant Media Noche, with iconic old floor tiles that were custom-made and intended as a 'visual anchor' for other décor (Newton 2017). The restaurant also boasts other 'Instagram triggers' such as bathrooms plastered in 'banana-print wallpaper' (Newton 2017). Another San Francisco Spanish restaurant Bellota prioritizes 'photo-friendliness' by providing custom lamps at every seat for patrons to 'adjust the lighting in order to get the perfect shot', as envisioned by chef Ryan McIlwraith who intended his 'tapas plates and signature paellas' to be included in patrons' selfies (Newton 2017).

In writing this book, one of the authors visited several Instaworthy spots to conduct fieldwork. Four of our first-hand experiences at eateries in Asia were particularly memorable. In the first instance, an English brunch café in the western district of Singapore was constantly updating their menu in conjunction with updates on the Instagram app. When the café first opened, several of its menu items were tailored to maximize Instagrammability; visitors were also invited to take photographs at various indoor and outdoor spots, with props such as colourful throw pillows, beautiful kitchenware, white window sills with matching white linen curtains, and a white garden swing. When Instagram introduced the Boomerang app, which enabled users to create GIF-like loops of short videos progressing forward and backward, the café introduced a DIY galaxy glazed doughnut where patrons could create and video their own creations at their dining tables (figure 5.1). When Instagram later accommodated short videos on its platform, the café introduced a brightly coloured drink that would change colour upon the addition of a syrup and some stirring (figure 5.2).

The second instance took place at a famous dessert café in the Shinjuku district in Tokyo, which was known for Instagrammable items such as a folded marshmallow flower that would blossom when placed in hot chocolate, and a shot glass made entirely out of a chocolate chip dough in which white milk is served (figure 5.3). Customers at this dessert café watched as waiting staff brought these items from the kitchen to the dining table 'deconstructed', displayed them to patrons, arranged them on the table, then waited for the patrons to steady their cameras or ask if they are ready, before embarking on the theatrical act of placing the marshmallow to blossom on the hot chocolate or pouring the milk into the cookie shot glass. In the hour that the author spent at this dessert café, we observed a few patrons ordering 'repeat items' because they had failed to capture the theatrics on their first serve. On one occasion, the waiting staff gave a patron tips on the best camera angle to capture the moment on Instagram; on another occasion where a patron was deciding between a

boufesg
Boufe Boutique Cafe

⋮

958 likes

boufesg #CreatingCosmos at @boufesg ONLY AVAILABLE till
30th November 2017!
A whole new cake experience that allows you to glaze your
own cake and create all sorts of mesmerising cosmos
designs. Not to mention the deliciously refreshing cake you'll
get to enjoy after the experience! 😋
[GIVEAWAY]
Stand a chance to win $50 Dining Vouchers from Boufe!
1️⃣ Tag a friend (or more) you'd like to come to @boufesg
with.
2️⃣ Winner will be announced on 11.11, this Saturday
(November 11th)
Good luck!

Figure 5.1. DIY galaxy glazed doughnut offered by @boufesg
that made for highly Instagrammable foods. Reproduced with
permission from @boufesg

white or purple marshmallow flower, the waiting staff suggested that white provided a better contrast against the hot
chocolate and would look 'more *kawaii*' on Instagram.

In the third instance, a café in a quiet neighbourhood
in Osaka was known for serving its hot beverages and

boufesg
Boufe Boutique Cafe

⋮

♡ Q ◁   ⊓

6,746 views
boufesg #BoufeTwilight
Watch the magic happen before your eyes!
View All 93 Comments
7 April 2016

Figure 5.2. Colour-changing drink offered by @boufesg that made for highly Instagrammable foods. Reproduced with permission from @boufesg

confectionery in quirky kitchenware. The author ordered four of their most popular pastries and drinks and was served in an elaborate contraption that included a large metal bird-cage, a heavy ceramic teapot, and an assortment of cutlery on a wooden tray. The waiting staff carefully arranged all of the décor on the dining table, then asked if we had wanted to photograph ('*shashin*') the display. After a quick photograph, the waiting staff then promptly removed the birdcage after cumbersomely extracting the dessert plate held inside it, and extricated all other props before we were left to enjoy our meal prop-free.

However, despite their best intentions, not all Insta-food experiences unfold as planned, as epitomized by the fourth instance. At this dessert bar known for its luxurious

Figure 5.3. Selection of Insta-worthy menu items, some of which involved a live demonstration or act from the café staff. Photograph by author.

milkshakes in the central business district in Singapore, the author placed our order and asked for one menu item to be slightly modified – specifically, we did not want any whipped cream in our milkshake. To our surprise, this request was turned down by the waiting staff, who reasoned that the whipped cream 'made the drink pretty' and would 'look good in photos'. Caught off-guard, we responded that we were more keen to eat the item than to photograph it, to which the waiting staff responded that they could not allow their menu items to be seen 'in this state' (without whipped cream) because every item was part of their branding. Given this intransigence, the author settled for the milkshake in its original form, which was to contain milk, chocolate chip cookies, brownies, ice cream and the dreaded whipped cream. While awaiting our food, we decided to attempt to Instagram the items to try out 'the branded experience' espoused by the waiting staff. When the drinks were brought to our table, we promptly whipped out our phones but quickly realized that the entire dessert bar was too dim for a 'good photo'. Despite our cumulative experience throughout our Instagram field-work, we had to give up on Instagramming this dessert after the first minute as the ice cream was melting in Singapore's unforgiving humidity. To our complete surprise (again), the entire mountain of whipped cream and brownies collapsed on our dining table barely a minute after being served. We took the initiative to clean up the mess with serviettes until a waiter came by to assist us – but their help came with a catty chide: 'You guys didn't take the photo quickly enough, that's why this happened.' Despite this sour experience with a made-for-the-'gram dish that barely lasted a minute in its acrobatic design, the authors grasped at the silver lining that the tale would make a good vignette for this book.

Homes

Insta-worthiness has also made its way into homes. After launching a very successful career on Instagram primarily through his artfully-staged selfies and skilful photo-enhancing, Influencer Yutakis James made every corner of his home 'Instagrammable', as catalogued on his dedicated hashtag #fantasyvibesonly. The stream includes several different angles of the same room, each redecorated frequently and lined with branded pieces from Supreme, Gucci, Balenciaga, Burberry, and the like. Apparel and accessories are seen doubling up as props around the house, set against stacks of fluffy white cushions on white fur rugs next to white window sills with plenty of natural sunlight pouring in. Yutakis also updates his home space with fresh

flowers every week and photographs them in various locations (@yutakis 2018).

Followers regularly flock to Yutakis's Instagram in praise
of his Insta-ready home, commending his constant effort in
redecorating and maintaining the space. Several followers also
frequently enquire about specific items in a bid to purchase
them for their own homes, even requesting that the Influencer
import them for sale. Due to the demand created by his eye for
the Instagram aesthetic, the Influencer launched a 'concept
studio' named Tricky Studios in January 2017, intended as a
photography and filming space. Rental of the space includes
the use of various pieces of furniture, props, photography
and videography equipment, beauty appliances for cosmetics, home appliances for sprucing up apparel, and amenities
such as showers and kitchen facilities. Highlights include an
indoor swing, an all-white minimalist ensemble of furniture
(in the vein of Yutakis's own home), neon wall signages, and
light installations hanging from the ceiling (@project.tricky
2017). After six months, the influencer announced that the
business would be shifting from being a mere 'space rental'
where 'every single corner of the space is photoshoot/insta-
gramable' [sic] to a service for household 'aesthetic' needs,
possibly to merchandise or sell the insta-worthy props in his
home.

Several other Influencers have also been known to brand
themselves primarily on the notion of chronic Insta-home
redecoration. Influencers @melissackoh and @sherlyn-
chanwp curate their Insta-homes on #homeofmrandmrsbabs
and #yaoshernest respectively, with the former launching an
online retail business selling homewares @somedaysathome
in December 2018, inspired by her Insta-home aesthetic.
Specific sub-genres are even blossoming, such as the crossover
between Insta-home Influencers and parenting Influencers,
like German Influencer @christine_simplybloom who has
three children, American Influencer @sarah_lit who has five
children, and Australian Influencer @charlieandmarlow who

has two children. All of these parent Influencers very consistently dress themselves and their children in neutral-coloured apparel (i.e. white, beige, brown, mustard, dark orange), regularly redecorate their homes with furniture and props made from natural products (i.e. rattan, oak, cotton, linen, rope), and edit or enhance their images to look retro or vintage as if they were captured by analogue cameras (i.e. grainy texture, light leaks, date stamps). Their narrations also point to a longing for 'a simpler time in the past', situating the woman's place in the home as the primary caregiver to a few children, encouraging their children to 'discover themselves in their own time' through outdoor play as opposed to the use of technological devices. In our forthcoming works, the authors are studying Instagram Influencer parents who practise such 'neutral nostalgia' aesthetic, against the backdrop of the mass of Influencers who are racing to keep up with cutting-edge and emergent products and services, and at a time when parenting Influencers are working to diffuse accusations of commercialism or exploitation.

Cannibalizing Place
Although many Insta-places are well loved and celebrated, some initiatives have backfired. An example from June 2018 includes the marketing stunt of an Insta-famous wall mural in Melrose Avenue in Los Angeles, where wall murals were found boxed up in white canvas sheets and guarded by uniformed security officers. A sign next to the set-up reads: 'Private Mural. For verified influencers and people with over 20,000 followers only. We apologize for the inconvenience. See security staff for proof and access. Influencers, please tag us on social media! Insta: @likeandsubscribe Twitter: @likeandsub'. As images of the scene circulated on Twitter, the Twitter account @likeandsub posted on 26 June 2018: 'Today we are so excited to debut the beautiful mural we curated in the heart of the LA art scene. Come down and check it out. Unfortunately the mural is currently for verified

influencers and people with over 20k followers only. However it may be public soon. Stay tuned!' (Schmidt 2018). Initial reactions from internet users included shock and horror, cynicism and sarcastic clapbacks, and call-outs of the marketing stunt itself (Caffier 2018; Cosco 2018).

As it turned out, the set-up was indeed a publicity stunt to promote a TV show 'Like & Subscribe' about the life of social media Influencers. Producer Jack Wagner said in an interview to *Cive* that the 'mural and all of the reactions are a very accurate and real-life preview of how ridiculous the show is' (Caffier 2018). The project received some backlash from Influencers, and its official account Tweeted again on the same day: 'Disappointing to see a few verified influencers getting upset about the mural. There is no reason to be mad! We created it specifically for you. Instead of the negativity, come down and take a great photo!' (Schmidt 2018).

Although some places are cannibalized for (bad) publicity stunts, others meet with more dire consequences. Roys Peaks in Lake Wanaka, New Zealand, is among the 'most Instagrammed day walks', with 'more than 73,000 people' embarking on the three-hour trail in 2018 alone (Roy 2018). Visitors were observed queueing for hours to earn a spot to pose without any other strangers photo-bombing, even resorting to setting off in the middle of the night to claim a spot early. The scenic spot's popularity was partly due to New Zealand Department of Conservation's social media campaign, that was anchored by the local tourist board to promote #royspeak as an Instagrammable spot. However, the alpine landscape was being quickly eroded and destroyed by human activity (Roy 2018).

Some of the amplification of crowds towards these scenic spots are caused by Influencers who post about little-known or undiscovered scenic spots as being photogenic or Instagrammable. These can be detrimental to environments that are not constructed to handle high human traffic, and takes away from the serenity and sacredness of the place

(Schiffer 2018). A survey of 1,000 adults by UK-based holiday rental home insurance provider Schofields reports that more than 40 per cent of travellers aged under 33 'prioritize "Instagrammability"' when selecting their holiday destinations, often using Instagram as a 'travel guide' (Arnold 2018). But the rising pressures of overcrowding and local resources to meet with the tourist influx is seldom managed well.

Besides mother nature, urban architecture is also experiencing the backlash of Insta-pursuits. It seems the pursuit of Instagrammability has resulted in the homogenization of the physical construction and digital representation of spaces, despite their geographical diversity (Stodola 2017). Architects are now planning in and designing 'pop-up urbanism' for Instagram photographability: newer buildings in the vicinity of the tourist-popular King's Cross in London have been designed with 'glittering glass' facades, 'plant-covered walls', 'colour-changing fountains' and 'kitsch billboards' – all seemingly props that 'cr[y] out to be photographed' (Mackie 2018). Feelings of locale, neighbourliness and homeliness are also being eroded as Insta-tourists seep into spaces not usually meant for holidaying crowds. A neighbourhood in Shoreditch, UK, has been covered with wall murals and pop-up shops, and overcrowded with tourists who are hampering the daily errand runs of the people that live there (Mackie 2018), just as public housing estates in Hong Kong have become popular photography destinations for Instagram, much to the dismay of local residents (Hui 2018).

Conclusion

In this chapter, we dived into some of the lesser known subcultures on Instagram, and the increasingly ubiquitous 'bleed' of Instagram from the internet into 'real life'. Returning to the roots of Instagram as a visual social sharing site, we recalled some of the prominent trends around art and photography that still proliferate on the platform. Against the backdrop of

Influencers vying for attention and maximum exposure, we also investigated emergent practices maintained by splinters of young users who instead choose to preserve low post counts, repeatedly post the same picture on a daily basis, or shift their main use of Instagram to its direct messaging altogether, in disparate efforts to reinterpret the function of the app. Still other users are practising publicity on Instagram to raise awareness of various social causes, including underpaid teachers and funding cuts to education, creative advertising campaigns to combat alcoholism, and various initiatives to educate the public about health issues and social stratification. In the vein of promotional persona on Instagram, we then studied how three politicians in Singapore, New Zealand, and the USA are pioneering innovative parasocial strategies to reach their citizenry. We also observed networks of users who take to Instagram in response to global grieving events to share tributes and commiserate on dedicated hashtags through a variety of photographs, artworks and reflections. The chapter then surveyed the emergent trends of Instagram showing up 'in real life' through museums, food experiences and even personal homes, and how such staging and the manipulation of environment can result in a drastic erosion of mother nature and the cannibalizing of a place's culture. On Instagram it is clear that there are many different cultural groups and practices, deploying quite different norms, which is a long way from any singular notion of an all-encompassing Instagram culture or community. Having considered the evolving nature of Instagram norms across subcultures and specific interest groups, the next chapter adopts a more longitudinal approach to investigate some of the implications of conscientiously Instagramming personhood from birth to death.

CHAPTER SIX

Lifespans

In September 2018, Instagram released 'Know how to talk with your teen about Instagram: A parent's guide' (Instagram 2018c), which walks parents through issues teenagers using Instagram might face, including overuse, bullying and unwanted attention. The guide quite deliberately refers to teens, not children, since Instagram's Terms of Use, like many US-based social media platforms, does not allow children under 13 to use the platform. However, children are everywhere on Instagram: from ultrasound photos, first-day-of-school images, birthdays, achievements and holiday events. In an oddly similar way, Instagram has also become an important arena where death, grief and mourning take place. Yet how should the liminal figures of the very young, and the recently deceased, be understood on Instagram? The platform's policies, Terms of Use, Community Guidelines and other key governing documents all refer to, or presume, that Instagram users are able to control and create their own images and selves on the platform, and actively lodge reports or complaints if their own images are stolen or misused. Neither the very young, nor the deceased, can speak for themselves or weigh in on how they are being represented. Thus, while the previous chapter focused on the diversity of cultures that use and make Instagram their own, this chapter focuses on users and user practices that span the entire lifetime, from the cradle to the grave. Using the case studies of the very young and recently deceased, we argue that on Instagram users are always co-creating each other; that is, Instagram users are frequently sharing photos and videos of other people, and therefore contribute to the way that person is seen and under-stood online. For the very young and the recently deceased, someone on Instagram is making *all* the decisions about how these two groups appear on the platform. This chapter maps out that tension, between the presumed active Instagram user, and the way many users are almost always navigating choices about how they capture, communicate about, and represent other people. In the case of the very young or the deceased, these are choices that largely dictate how another person, or their legacy, is represented on Instagram.

Ultrasounds

On Instagram, the first image or video shared of a child often comes before they are born as expectant parents reveal their first ultrasound image, often using this as the moment to announce to friends that they are expecting a new child. Ultrasounds existed before social media, but networked visibility via Instagram and other platforms has made the sharing of this 'first image' of the unborn far more expected and normal (Lupton 2013). Indeed, as media researchers Yukari Seko and Katrin Tiidenberg (2016, p. 50) note, 'visual and social media technologies [have] become an integral part of performing pregnancy and mothering.' For millions of parents, guardians and carers, the highs and lows of par-enting are shared on Instagram, showing off the highs, and seeking solidarity during the lows. While ultrasound sharing is almost always done with good intentions, there are poten-tial consequences when a child grows and looks at the long visual sharing of their life and has a different perspective to their parents on what they want shared, and what they may now want removed (Seko & Tiidenberg 2016). This is less a question about ultrasound images specifically, and more that sharing one image marks the beginning of a longer trajectory where parents share (often publicly) images of a child at birth and as they grow. As many parents did not grow up with social

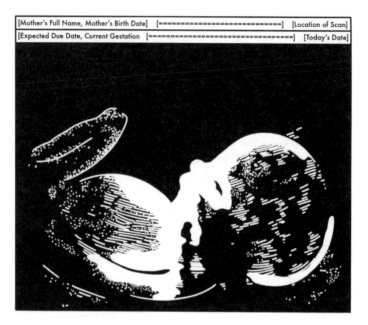

Figure 6.1. Artist impression of an Instagram post showing a foetal ultrasound with visible metadata. Art provided by mistercrow.

media when they were young, they often do not have ready-made exemplars for thinking through what to share, what not to share, and what the longer-term impact of sharing ultrasounds and images of their children might be.

In a study focusing on 2014 Instagram media tagged with #ultrasound, Leaver and Highfield (2018) found that over the three months from March to May there were 10,890 images and 430 videos shared with the tag. A deeper look at a 48-hour period in early March 2014 examined 289 #ultrasound images and seven videos. These public images included selfies, the ultrasound process itself, families reacting to ultrasound images, with the majority being still images of the ultrasound itself, usually from a twelve- or twenty-week scan (see figure 6.1). Almost all of these images referred to the image as a baby, sometimes using an affectionate nickname, with a few already using the intended full name. Notably, Instagram ultrasound sharing is part of a 'new social ritual [that] also reinforces foetal individuality and personhood in a very visible and public way' (Johnson 2014, p. 338). Being able to see and share the foetal ultrasound image confers personhood in a way that did not happen as directly before such visualizations were possible, or shareable.

It is also important to note that in the ultrasound images Leaver and Highfield (2018) found, around two-thirds of people removed the visible metadata from their ultrasounds before sharing them; that is, the data visible on the ultrasound which often includes the mother's name, the ultrasound technician, the location of the ultrasound, the exact date, the expected due date and other details. This indicates at least some level of consideration about their privacy, and potentially the privacy of their unborn child. However, one-third of the ultrasound images shared publicly left all of this data visible, which means these ultrasounds potentially contribute to the digital footprint a child leaves online, even before they are actually born. Leaver (2015, p. 153) describes this as part of a trend toward 'intimate surveillance', 'the purposeful and routinely well-intentioned surveillance of young people by parents, guardians, friends, and so forth', a provocative term which offers a reminder that almost all acts of sharing on Instagram are also acts where data about someone is being shared, often publicly, and this data is being collected, collated and analysed by social media platforms to better profile and sell advertising to parents and, eventually, children. Yet it is also vitally important to keep in mind the data collection context for Leaver and Highfield's (2018) study; when these #ultrasound images were collected, Instagram had around 200 million users, there were no Stories, direct messaging on the platform was very new, and there were relatively few private accounts. Today, the options on Instagram for sharing with a small group via Direct, or via Stories, or using a private account, including options where this media will either delete after it is viewed, or disappear after 24 hours, mean there are many more privacy tools available. For expecting and new parents, it is vital to make this spectrum of privacy tools visible, as well as encouraging some consideration of how parental posting of their children's images may have longer impacts and effects.

Sharenting

As children get older and start to share their own images online, they must often negotiate with their parents to remove, hide or re-contextualize images or material that parents have shared as they were growing up. Indeed, young teens are often very focused on ensuring their self-presentation online shows off the best and most polished version of themselves, while parents often share images that are more natural and often humorous – as much about the parenting experience as the child's representation – which are often incompatible aims (Gaëlle & Karen 2019). This tension is an example of 'context collapse', where social media traces can be read differently, in different contexts, often in ways very different to the original poster's intentions (Davis & Jurgenson 2014; Marwick & boyd 2011). That said, having children visible on Instagram is important. Unlike broadcast media which is highly produced and tightly controlled, social media platforms like Instagram potentially offer the space to offer a far more diverse representation of children and childhood, as opposed to the more constrained and often stereotypical representations of children in terms of gender, ability, ethnicity and class on television and in cinema (Choi & Lewallen 2018). However, according to a study of 510 images tagged with #childhood in 2015, while gender representation of children is certainly more even, other essentializing elements of childhood such as girls being linked with fashion and boys with more active forms of play are just as prominent (Choi & Lewallen 2018). Instagram can also offer a space, though, where the norms and meanings associated with elements of childhood and parenting can be contested and re-shaped.

Instagram has proven a very popular and successful platform for breastfeeding advocates, for example, with studies finding large communities of breastfeeding mothers sharing in positive and empowering ways with minimal negative commentary on the platform (Marcon, Bieber & Azad 2019). Indeed, naming and posting 'brelfies' – 'the fusion of breastfeeding and selfie' (Locatelli 2017, p. 4) – have been powerful tools in normalizing breastfeeding in the everyday, and on Instagram. That said, posting a brelfie necessarily entails also posting a picture of a baby; in many cases breastfeeding mothers take steps to ensure the baby is not fully visible, but that is not always the case, and these images are sometimes paired with captions showing the full name of the baby. In these instances, the line between advocacy and a child's right to privacy is a blurred one, and a hard one to balance, just as they are in other spaces where advocacy, representation and privacy can be at odds (Locatelli 2017; Orton-Johnson 2017). This tension, between representation of children, and their rights to privacy, are wrapped up in the popular media and scholarly debates around 'sharenting', sometimes including the pejorative term 'oversharenting'.

Media and childhood researchers Alicia Blum-Ross and Sonia Livingstone define sharenting simply as 'denoting when parents share information about themselves and their children online' (2017, p. 110). In their study of parental bloggers, Blum-Ross and Livingstone (2017) revealed that when sharing images and writing about their children online, parental bloggers had a range of strategies for maintaining some levels of privacy, such as only sharing photos taken from behind or only using partial names, although some had consciously decided to share their images and stories without any attempt at occlusion. Parental bloggers also noted that as their children grew older, they were more and more likely to have opinions about, and contest, the way their parents shared stories and images of them online. Coming of age for young people today can thus often involve a hard conversation with parents about exactly what expectations of privacy they can expect, enjoy and have respected. The way that Instagram and other platforms avoid talking about how children's images are managed makes this problem more difficult. Images and videos on Instagram are largely considered as extensions of the user posting them, and are usually considered the property of that person in terms of copyright considerations. However, as Blum-Ross and Livingstone argue, 'Too often, the "user" of "user-generated content" or the "self" of "self-representation" is taken to refer to a singular individual. But when we represent ourselves through our relationships, this is not straightforward, as eloquently illustrated by the anxieties surrounding "sharenting"' (2017, p. 121). These anxieties are heightened in cultures where celebrities and other influential figures widely post images of their celebrity children, often on bespoke Instagram accounts in the name of those children, normalizing the sharing of children's images online.

Parental and Child Influencers

Seven-year-old Pixie Curtis has more than 100,000 followers, and has the blue tick on her profile page verifying her identity is genuine on Instagram; Pixie's account is managed by her mother, PR CEO Roxy Jacenko, and features a mix of Pixie's life, including tropical holidays and helicopter rides, along with more banal everyday images. Her account also heavily features photos of other children wearing Pixie's Bows, a commercial arm which began as a boutique service selling 'hand-made' bows but is now a popular brand of bows in Australia and elsewhere (Á. Ryan 2018). Pixie is an example of a 'micro-microcelebrity' (Abidin 2015a), the child of an Influencer or existing micro-celebrity who is knowingly situated online as part of their parent's online presence, often branching off into their own specific spaces and accounts, as is the case with Pixie Curtis (even if the account is managed by, and ultimately the responsibility of, her mother). Indeed, in 2016, Jacenko was derided as a 'pin-up girl for oversharing on social media' (Marriner 2016) after photos of Pixie, who was four years old at the time, were digitally manipulated to create indecent imagery that was then circulated online. In the media, Jacenko was on the receiving end of much moralizing when she complained about the doctored images of Pixie; in a roundabout way, she was shamed for sharing so many images in the first place rather than the media taking her complaints seriously. Feminist media commentator Clementine Ford (2016) was one of the lone voices who came to Jacenko's defence, pointing out the hypocrisy on display:

> Jacenko's choice to turn her child into some kind of brand might be distasteful to some (it certainly is to me), but it in no way, shape or form makes her responsible for the choices other people make to break the law and exploit that child for their own amusement or gain. Besides, if consent is the issue here, how is it all that different from people publicly sharing images of their children even without the intent of making money?

Ford's most salient point was to argue that Pixie might be at the more visible and profitable end of the spectrum, but many, probably most, parents share images of their children on social media. That said, the fact the Jacenko is making money off Pixie's images on Instagram – even if that profit ends up being saved for Pixie – means questions of exploitation are also important to consider when children are a brand extension, or even their own brand, that their parents manage.

Fascination with child Influencers has led to considerable press attention across the globe, resulting in media headlines such as 'The 2-year-old Instagram influencers who make more than you' (Schwab 2018). Moreover, Pixie Curtis is far from alone, or even near the largest numbers, in the child Influencer stakes: 13-year-old Russian-born model Kristina Pimenova, for example, has more than 2.4 million Instagram followers; in the US 5-year-old twins Alexis and Ava McClure have an Instagram following of 1.6 million; and 2-year-old twins Taytum and Oakley Fisher have 2.4 million followers. Nor are child Influencers only highly visible on Instagram in their own accounts. Many parental Influencers heavily feature their children as well.

British couple Clemmie and Simon Hooper – or Mother of Daughters (MOD) and Father of Daughters (FOD) on Instagram – have more than 1.5 million followers between them. Clemmie Hooper originally began blogging to give mid-wifery advice, and continues to do so. The couple have four daughters, and the MOD and FOD doubling on Instagram has allowed them to capitalize on people's interest in their careers, lives, parenting, children and, increasingly, lifestyle. Simon Hooper's Instagram started with the intention of shar-ing the experiences of fatherhood, especially fathering four young girls, something which he argued was not well repre-sented online at all. After building a sizable audience, both have achieved success online in terms of reach, and attracting sponsorship, advertising, as well as giving both the oppor-tunity to write books: *How to Grow a Baby and Push It Out: A Guide to Pregnancy and Birth Straight from the Midwife's Mouth* (C. Hooper 2017); and *Forever Outnumbered: Tales of our Family Life from Instagram's Father of Daughters* (S. Hooper 2018).

While neither appeared to start with commercial intent, the Coopers' posts featured more and more advertising and spon-sorship throughout 2018, which led to many of the couple's followers complaining about their overt commercialism and calling into question the ethics of featuring their children in posts which featured sponsorship for everything from cereal, to cars, to paid holidays to Disneyland in Florida. Questions of exploitation of their four daughters, especially of their younger twins who are not of an age where they could really question being photographed, were raised by a number of commentators and in online forums. After unsuccessfully attempting to address the criticism on Mumsnet, a parenting discussion forum, Clemmie Hooper temporarily removed her Instagram account, leading to headlines such as 'Instagram mega mum quits app after claims she exploits her children' (Dixon & Horton 2018). Clemmie Hooper did eventually return to Instagram, but the point here is not to criticize her specifically, but to use the Coopers' experience to highlight the real challenges around parental Influencers who must navigate and balance commercialism, advocacy and children's rights to privacy. In many countries there are laws about the payment and time commitment of children on commercial television or in paid advertising, but often these laws do not specifically address or include social media content. Indeed, Instagram did not add the official 'paid partnership with' indicator for business accounts until mid-2017, and while this visibility and transparency is important, it does not provide any real guidance as to how much sponsorship and advertising is appropriate. For Clemmie Hooper, she appears to have found a balance she is comfortable with, and in the process of engaging with the criticism has clearly considered in detail how her children feature on her Instagram account. Simon Hooper strategically avoided engaging with the Mumsnet critics, and remains extremely prolific and popular on Instagram.

To counter perceptions that children are overworked or undertaking a form of labour rather than a form of play in sharing online, family Influencers – which include at least one child and parent – often consciously or unconsciously deploy what Crystal Abidin (2017b) calls 'calibrated amateurism', a practice that involves the careful sharing of seemingly less polished and less produced content, behind-the-scenes style material, which shows the fun, frivolity and playfulness 'behind' the more polished images and videos. On Instagram this often entails amateur-style content appearing frequently in Stories, while more polished content appears in the main Instagram feed. Of course, this practice is, in itself, often contrived to make Influencer content creation appear more fun and natural, but that sense of amateurism is, in itself, manufactured. In this way family Influencers often show an awareness of potential criticism that children are being exploited to create content and get online attention. As child and parental Influencer numbers continue to grow, so will strategies to normalize children's appearance on their own, and their parent's, Instagram accounts. To ensure the rights of children, including their right to privacy, is respected, careful consideration must be given to exactly how much, and in what capacities, children should appear on social media, whether this is commercialized or not.

Co-Creation

Many of the challenges that arise in balancing the needs of parents and children on Instagram and elsewhere online come from the framing of all Instagram users as actively responsible for their own behaviour and content, with little consideration of how this effects other people. A more useful model is to position users of social media platforms as *co-creators*, emphasizing that they are often contributing not just to their own online presence, but that of others at the same time. As Tama Leaver argues, co-creation's utility lies in the way it highlights

> multiple ways users can and do contribute to other users' identities; the unequal relationship between users and the platforms on which they often create and curate digital identity traces; and that collaboration is always a process where negotiation is generally needed to ensure that creation benefits both the user creating and the individuals whose identity is formed, in part, by that creation. (Leaver 2019, pp. 38–39)

For parents posting images of their children, from ultrasounds onward, co-creation usefully flags that these actions create a digital footprint that their children will eventually inherit one day. Emphasizing co-creation means that parents would immediately consider children's futures even as they celebrate their own experiences of pregnancy and child-rearing. In more banal ways, co-creation also emphasizes the responsibility Instagram users exercise in relation to one another; something as everyday as tagging another person in an Instagram photo adds to the presence and story about that person online. Co-creation as a concept and tool helps make visible all of the times social media users effectively create each other online.

When someone dies, inevitably they leave some sort of social media trace behind. For Instagram users, this leaves some difficult choices to be made about what happens to that account, within the fairly narrow range of choices the platform actually allows (discussed below). Similarly, even when the person being mourned is not on social media, anyone sharing their own images and videos about their mourning process are, sometimes inadvertently, and sometimes knowingly, also leaving a trace that builds part of that person's digital legacy.

Mourning, Death and Selfies at #funerals

In research analysing 2014 Instagram media with the #funeral hashtag, Leaver and Highfield (2018) found that 15,863 images and 634 videos were publicly shared on the platform over the three-month period from March to May. A qualitative exploration of 48 hours in early March 2014 focused on a corpus of 296 images and nine videos. Many images showed icons of mourning, from flowers and wreaths to images from the service, including some of the coffin, but almost never was a deceased person actually visible. There were also incongruent humorous and other images that had nothing to do with grief, such as reposting of a popular meme that stated that people worked out at the gym wearing black since it was a 'funeral for my fat'. The vast majority of #funeral images, though, showed the social experience of grief, whether that was from the funeral itself, preparation for it, mourning more generally, or group photos before or after a funeral. In none of these cases was there evidence of being disrespectful to the dead; rather, the communication was more about the experience of the person mourning, not just about the person who had died. It is evident, then, that #funeral is a multivalent hashtag on Instagram, signifying quite different things in different contexts. Like funerals and wakes themselves, on the one hand it can be a signifier of profound personal loss and grief, and yet it can also show the joy and tenderness of family and friends reuniting at a wake or memorial. These results concur with another study of #funeral media on Instagram which also focused on 2014 data; this study argued that the meaning of funeral media needs to be understood through the 'platform vernacular' of Instagram which highlights a range of uses and meanings, all of which are better understood in the context of the platform (Gibbs et al. 2015). Leaver and Highfield concluded that 'Instagram does not afford new spaces of collective mourning but rather serves to communicate individual users' experiences of loss and grief to their existing followers' (2018, p. 41).

In 2013, journalist Jason Feifer created a tumblr called *Selfies at Funerals* (Feifer 2013a) which, as the name suggests, re-posted a series of selfies taken at funerals, removed them from their original context on various platforms, including Instagram, and collated them in a way that provoked a moral panic. Indeed, researchers have argued that this tumblr commits 'a kind of representational violence by completely changing the intended audience of the photographs' (Meese et al. 2015, p. 1825). This violence was evident in the sensationalized media headlines decrying the disrespect and narcissism that were read into the collected images. Analysing 525 #funeral tagged images from a 48-hour period in February 2014, Meese et al. (2015) found that selfies were the single largest category of photos in their data. Importantly, despite the hype and hashtag, very few of these images were actually taken at or during a funeral itself. Instead, the vast majority showed reflective moments surrounding a funeral, at home, on the journey to or from a funeral, in bathrooms, and so forth. None of these images were obviously disrespectful to the deceased person or the funeral process. Instead, they concluded, 'the selfie can be repositioned as a way to subtly engage with the emotional content of a funeral and signal one's presence and emotional circumstances to a wider social network' (Meese et al. 2015, p. 1828). While these selfies are co-creative in that they say something about the person being mourned, they are primarily moments of mourning. Related research tends to reinforce these findings, although other studies have found trolling and abusive comments on #funeral images and similar Instagram content does happen, albeit extremely rarely (Thimm & Nehls 2017).

Mirroring these findings, in an opinion column in *The Guardian*, Feifer reflected on his *Selfies at Funerals* tumblr and the negative response to the images it featured, commenting: 'Many people interpreted funeral selfies as further evidence of millenials' self-centeredness. I didn't. Had my parents' or grandparents' generation grown up with the kind of social media tools that today's teens have, they'd would have done equally embarrassing things for all the world to see'. More significantly, though, he added that when young people post 'a funeral selfie, their friends don't castigate them. They understand that their friend, in their own way, is expressing an emotion they may not have words for. It's a visual language that older people – even those like me, in their 30s – simply don't speak' (Feifer 2013b). Instagram can be a space of mourning, where loss can be lamented, but life can also be celebrated, remembered and cherished, but to see this complexity on Instagram, an understanding of the platform and context is needed. Selfies at funerals do not communicate the same thing outside of the platform they were originally shared on. Moreover, Instagram content with the #funeral tag is a particularly salient reminder of van Dijck's (2008) argument that in the era of digital and social media, the photographic image is predominantly about affect and communication, and less about memory or archiving than ever before, even if every post does perform both those functions.

Instagram Data after Death

Molly Russell's tragic suicide, discussed in chapter 1, which her parents directly linked to her Instagram activity, also raised important issues about what access Instagram and other social media companies and platforms should provide to loved ones of deceased Instagram users. Despite a number of requests for access, Instagram/Facebook refused to allow Molly's parents to access her account, despite them being convinced her Instagram viewing and interactions contributed directly to her suicide (BBC News 2019). From mid-2018, in part to comply with the European Union's General Data Protection Regulation (GDPR), Instagram has allowed users to request to view or download a full copy of all of their data held on the Instagram platform (Instagram 2019a), but no one, not family, nor friends, nor legal executor, can log in to a deceased person's Instagram account, or posthumously request their data as a download. Instead, upon someone's death, family members can either request that the deceased user's account is either entirely deleted (and all data lost, permanently) or that the account becomes 'memorialized', which locks the account, respecting whatever privacy settings governed it at the moment it is locked, but preventing any further action by or on that account (Instagram 2019b). For grieving families, the choice to lock or lose a recently deceased loved one's account on Instagram may, understandably, appear quite blunt options, a problem also faced by social media platforms and companies more widely (Leaver 2013).

Instagram's owners, Facebook, have developed a more complex approach to managing the Facebook accounts posthumously. While they are still alive, Facebook users can now nominate a Legacy Contact whose job is to have limited abilities to tidy up the Facebook page of a loved one and manage a few constrained options, such as posting a new message, and changing the cover photo, on a deceased person's behalf on Facebook (Brubaker & Callison-Burch 2016). While there are no public statistics about how many people have nominated a Legacy Contact, there does not appear to be a huge amount of awareness of, or attention paid to, this option. On Instagram, the option of a Legacy Contact would probably not have widespread uptake since Instagram's many young users are unlikely to plan for their death. Nevertheless, for people dealing with the grief of loss, especially when the Instagram account of the deceased person might hold a key to understanding their death, Instagram's extremely blunt approach to the data of deceased users is far from satisfactory. For Molly Russell's parents, this is especially difficult, and their grief points to the need for more complex and contextually aware rules and policies surrounding the management of deceased Instagram users' data.

Conclusion

Despite the convenient myth that social media users are all responsible, self-directing individuals with complete agency and ability to make choices about their own content, this chapter has argued that picture of Instagram users is far from complete. Parents necessarily make choices about what images, stories and videos to share with other people via Instagram and other platforms, and in doing so often leave these traces to aggregate and build an initial presence for these children online. Sharing practices normalize seeing ultrasound images as the default pregnancy announcements, while the debates about sharenting emphasize that almost everyone is trying to work out the best practices, and best models, for sharing about children online, while the different tools and privacy options are being openly explored and experimented with. Parental and child Influencers make visible the additional questions around commercialization and advertising, and the desperate need for better laws and policies to make clearer when lines are crossed between representation and possible exploitation. At the other end of life, examining mourning practices shows that far from being narcissistic or shallow, most Instagram mourners treat the dead with great respect, and are comfortable enough to allow their Instagram followers to see a window into their own grief. However, Instagram's own blunt responses to dealing with the data of deceased users shows real room for better policies and practices. The co-creation model emphasizes shared responsibility and shared awareness of the way Instagram users, and social media users on almost every platform, potentially shape and create the traces and stories of other people. In the case of children and the recently deceased, parents, loved ones and mourners are doing *all* the shaping, which is a considerable and not well understood responsibility. The previous chapter emphasized the many cultures which use Instagram; this chapter argued that Instagram users co-create entire lifespans from before birth until death and mourning; while the following final chapter will argue that Instagram has infiltrated and influenced almost every other facet of life as well.

CHAPTER SEVEN

From the Instagram of Everything to the Everything of Instagram

In this final chapter, we argue that Instagram has become synonymous with visual design and visual experiences. Instagram's impact has become material, with devices, spaces, cultural institutions and homes all being re-designed and reimagined for the peak Instagram aesthetic experience. The idea and grammar of Instagram ripples through popular culture. Virtual Influencers, digital entities with no physical form, have emerged on Instagram, provoking new questions of authenticity, while the seeming dominance of similar and repetitive visual stylings shows a growing logic of templatability driven by the metrics and algorithms driving Instagram today.

Instagram Materialities

As explored in chapter 2, Instagram's visual identity draws heavily from vintage and retro photographic aesthetics, particularly the platform's early iconography. The success of Instagram has also led to a reverse flow of inspiration: the digital as stimulus for physical and material products, including reinvigoration of photographic devices. In some cases, this is reflective of savvy branding and hooking in to popular trends; products and services that are not really, or only, about Instagram, but which play off the recognition of the platform for promotional purposes. For others, there is a more concrete relationship in making Instagram material tangible and even edible.

The connections between Instagram's original logos and physical cameras have long inspired designs and ideas for an

Instagram camera; by the time Facebook bought Instagram in 2012, proposals, both serious and satirical, had been circulating online. These proposals took a step further in May 2012 when Italian designer Antonio DeRosa posted a conceptual design that merged the Instagram logo of the time and the capacities of instant cameras. Dubbed the 'Socialmatic', the camera resembled the logo on the front, the back touchscreen provided an Instagram interface, and inside was a printer allowing for instant development of captured images, providing as close to simultaneous digital sharing and physical printing of the same photograph as possible (Cade 2012). Although purely an artist's impression of what an Instagram camera could look like and do, DeRosa's design caught enough attention to encourage him to launch an IndieGoGo campaign to produce it; less than a year later, Polaroid bought into the project to make the Socialmatic an actual, branded product (Fingas 2013).

In the process of becoming a Polaroid-branded camera, the Socialmatic lost its Instagram-specific aspects, although it continued to resemble the platform's logo. After several years of development, the camera was eventually launched in January 2015 as 'a revolution in the social digital photography' that allowed the user 'to fill the gap between virtual and real world' (De Rosa n.d.). In trying to bring together physical and digital photography, the Socialmatic struggled with the necessary material requirements; in order to incorporate the printer technology, the device was tablet-sized, making it much bulkier than a smartphone and with a lower-quality front-facing camera. Even more than Instagram's own 'cult of the reference' described by Belgian historian Gil Bartholeyns (2014), the Socialmatic based its customer appeal on twin referents: the familiarity of call-backs to Instagram, and to the retro photographic aesthetics Instagram and similar apps had helped to promote. Polaroid's own promotional material showcased this mix of the now and the retro as a major selling point of the Socialmatic and its combination of 'the nostalgic appeal of vintage Polaroid instant print cameras with the ability to share using the camera's built-in Wi-Fi and Android™ interface' (Polaroid n.d.). Meanwhile, a mood indicator on the front of the Socialmatic demonstrated 'the camera's feelings', an attempt at encouraging and rewarding ongoing use of the device. An early review noted that Polaroid 'describes this as a "Frontal LCD with mood assistant AI," but all it really does is show you a smiley face. The face gets happier the more photos of your dinner you take and share with Instagram, and turns all frowny if you've not used it for a while' (Cooper 2014). Like the social media inspiring it, regular engagement is seen as key to the Socialmatic, regardless of the context or quality.

Since its launch, the Socialmatic has existed in a strange liminal space bridging physical and digital photography: as at January 2019, it has a rating of only 2.2/5 on Amazon.com (from 69 reviews), customer comments noting the limited capabilities of the device and lack of updates to it – especially in comparison with the ongoing evolution of smartphones. Its connection to Instagram has also diminished, both with Polaroid's own branding and with the 2016 overhaul of Instagram's visual identity. However, despite its flaws and muted response, the Socialmatic offers perhaps the closest realization so far of Instagram made material – or, at least, the Instagram of 2011–15. The actual need for such a product, beyond novelty value, can be questioned. So can its photographic contributions, and its success in acting as either, and both, a digital, socially-oriented camera and an instant print camera. The Socialmatic may be a realization of the fetishization of particular photographic cultures and an attempt to appeal to youth cultures; it also makes tangible the processes Instagram and its competitors invoke through their aesthetics, without losing the actual processes of taking and sharing photos through such platforms. Indeed, the materiality of Instagram became even more evident with the launch of Samsung's S10 range, which not only included Instagram by default, but has a bespoke Instagram-camera mode integrated into its own camera application. The importance of this integration was evident as Instagram head Adam Mosseri took the stage to announce it at Samsung's S10 launch event in February 2019 (Gartenberg 2019).

The digital-only form of Instagram has led to numerous explorations of how to make this content material – and, in turn, how to make this a profitable business venture. From the early days of the platform, services have offered users the opportunity to get their Instagram photos printed, collected into photobooks, and reproduced on mugs, magnets, stickers and more. The Instagram-specifity of these services is often limited; similar products aimed at Flickr users existed long before Instagram's launch, while all that is really required is a digital image file, regardless of its provenance or where it may or may not have been uploaded. However, since Instagram does not offer these services themselves, or have any commercial arrangements with providers to allow users to easily print their own content, a small economy has emerged centred around making things out of content that seemingly only exists as pixels on a screen. By 2012, the market of third-party services had taken advantage of Instagram's popularity and the technical capabilities of the platform's application programming interface (API) to make it easy for customers to access their content. Furthermore, the co-founder of CanvasPop (established pre-Instagram in 2009), which printed digital photos onto canvases for hanging, argued in an April 2012 *Huffington Post* article that 'Instagram never had a focus on monetizing their audience' (in Guarini 2012). Instagram's focus on making money from their users became evident eventually, of course, and the thriving third-party innovation ecology has been severely truncated in the light of Instagram's embrace of commercial partnerships, sponsored content and its development as a shoppable platform.

The initial economy aimed at making Instagram content material included companies that, in order to set themselves apart from established photo-printing businesses, have adapted more niche product strategies. In December 2011 the launch of Stitchtagram (later just Stitchta) filled a gap in the market for users wanting to turn their Instagram images into pillows and bags. Pixelist (launched in 2013) went even further in the remediation of Instagram content into physical art, as customers could pay to turn a chosen image into a hand-made oil painting. Other businesses went for products which were just as novel, but far more ephemeral and offering a very different interaction between user and Instagram content. Cocoagraph (2012–16) gave users the opportunity to send in images to be printed onto chocolate bars, in several flavours, as entirely edible products. New York-based bakery Baking for Good offers 'Instagraham' picture cookies (a pun that really only works for a US audience; Kelly 2012), while Kellie's Baking Co. offers similar biscuits, dubbed 'Instabites', and Boomf (launched 2013) sells edible Instagram content through printing on marshmallows (Byford 2013; Garber 2013). Later expanding into chocolates and novelty cards, Boomf attracted widespread attention as a business venture of James Middleton, brother of the Duchess of Cambridge (Hyde 2016; Nicholl 2014). It was also initially a venture of the tech start-up Mint, who had previously created other Instagram-related products, most notably the tiny projector Projecteo (2013–18) which initially received over $87,000 in Kickstarter funding (Welch 2013).

In many of these cases the Instagram-oriented nature of the product is often just a promotional hook. While early services were able to use the Instagram API to access an individual user's content when they logged in, this ability has diminished as the API has become more restricted. Focusing purely on Instagram would then limit the viability of these services, both in terms of who can use it, and also what content is available; images might not be shared on a profile but still could be suitable for creating a product. Making Instagram material is part of a wider trend of how to offer something new, tangible or original from the digital. This is apparent with general printing services, but also with more niche endeavours: edible and food-adjacent representations of social media content are seen in, among others, instant selfie cookies (Roberts 2017), printed latte art (using coffee extract as the ink) (Ripples 2018), and 3D printed and laser-etched lollipops and macaroons (Ruby 2017).

Instagram in Popular Culture

While there has been a spate of documentaries and popular science media coverage on Instagram cultures, a vast majority has thus far focused on the top 1% of 'RKOI' or Rich Kids of Intagram (Trafik Media 2016), or the culture of social media Influencers (BuzzFeedVideo 2018, CBC News: The National 2017, The Feed 2015). Unlike reality TV programmes featuring Instagram stars who depend on extremity for entertainment value (E! News 2019), many of these documentaries produce 'a day in the life' accounts of Insta-famous Influencers in a bid to demystify their rise to fame and the operations of their business (Bloomberg 2018, BuzzFeedVideo 2018). It is not uncommon for such coverage to begin with a critique that Instagram Influencers are attention-seeking, with doubts as to whether they are 'actually working', reducing these young people to mere 'millennials whose job is to post, post, and post some more' (CBS News: The National 2017). There seems to be a strong emphasis on the commercial prowess of these Instagram stars (CBS News: The National 2017), especially given their 'theoretical opportunity to become millionaires' and that 'their reach is worth millions of dollars' (The Feed 2015). These videos tend to provide some insight into the infrastructure of Instagram fame, such as how platforms like YouTube are partnering with and equipping Influencers with skills (CBS News: The National 2017), the role of talent agencies who spot and groom potential Influencers (The Feed 2015), or general observations about how the shift from broadcast to interactive communications has enabled such new forms of online fame (Faces and Facets 2017). A smaller number of better researched videos provide expertise on the darker side of the industry, including shadow economies of wholesalers who peddle fake followers, fraud on Instagram, and how users are learning to outsmart and optimize the algorithm (VPRO 2018).

For the most part, these documentaries focus on a handful of Instagram Influencers to drive the narrative. Case studies include a pair of Canadian twin sisters who became full-time bloggers from posting about fashion (CBC News: The National 2017), a young Australian man who cultivated his fame from displaying his opulent lifestyle in Sydney (The Feed 2015), an American paralegal who quit to become a full-time social media model (BuzzFeedVideo 2018), and an Australian teacher who left to be a full-time Instagram baker (The Feed 2015). Other short-form popular documentaries tend to focus on unusual personalities, such as a 6-year-old Japanese girl who takes her own selfies and is celebrated for her flair for vintage fashion (Broadly 2017), or extreme measures taken towards Instagram popularity such as plastic surgery (Refinery29 2018). The constant refrain being preached is that Influencers draw people in with their authenticity, by 'keeping it real while keeping it in', and 'not coming off as just another paid celebrity' (CBS News: The National 2017). This sense of intimacy allows Influencers to appear relatable to their followers, because the consumption experience feels as if one is 'almost getting access to a hidden camera in someone's life … [like] the best reality show ever' (The Feed 2015).

In a consistent narrative arc, most of the Insta-documentaries tend to end on a pensive afterthought about the downsides of fame on the platform, such as the lack of job security and level of technical and socio-cultural expertise needed to maintain one's standing (The Feed 2015), the implications of cohorts of Insta-famous young people growing up online at times rather pridefully and arrogantly (Trafik Media 2016), spillover effects such as a rise in plastic surgery procedures yearning after a 'culture of perfection' promoted by Instagram (Refinery29), and concerns over mental health and work–life balance as a result of being driven by social media metrics for job security (Bloomberg 2018). At the time of writing, only a handful of documentaries addressed Instagram beyond Influencer cultures to consider the psychological consequences of generations of young people who are inculcated to prioritize social media validation (The Drum 2015), and a few animated films that reflexively question how Instagram bleeds into everyday life have begun to emerge (bennozoid 2018).

Several music videos from artistes around the world are also beginning to engage with Instagram as a subject. Lyrically, the most meaningful of these include South Korean alternative R&B singer-songwriter Dean's 'Instagram', in which he reflects upon the impact of Instagram on human relationships, such as the pressure to keep up with an 'Insta-perfect' image despite one's struggles, and the feelings of emptiness and loneliness that result (Deantrbl 2018). A string of music videos from Japanese rapper Wez (UnityJapan 2015), American YouTube rapper and comedian DeStorm (DeStorm Power 2012), and American artists RiFF RAFF and DJ Noodles (JodyHighRoller 2014) have also included rap lyrics that lament Instagram's constant chase for popularity, the pressure to publicize every lived moment on Instagram to affirm that one is having a good time, and dating in the age of Instagram where potential hook-ups are selected from Instagram posts respectively. Visually, artists are also incorporating interactive Instagram functions into their music videos, such as the act of selecting an Instagram filter for a photo (JodyHighRoller 2014), screengrabs of images and comments from Instagram (SoImJenn 2018), and the use of editing and publishing Stories, and scrolling and commenting on posts to drive the narrative of the song (iKON 2017).

In television and film, too, these aesthetics and representations of Instagram's functionalities have been repurposed for narrative devices and plot points alike. To name all shows referencing Instagram at all, let alone similarly styled visual platforms, is not our intent here; however, we highlight some key examples and trends. *Broad City*'s fifth season episode 'Stories' (2019) is presented as a series of Instagram-esque Stories, complete with emoji, hashtags and user names pinned to videos. The aesthetic references Instagram without being an actual Instagram Story, as the platform's brand guidelines would have to be followed in order to use the actual interface and its results visually in the creative product (potentially giving Instagram and Facebook control over the episode). The Instagram aesthetic features too in the song 'Research me obsessively', from *Crazy Ex-Girlfriend*'s second season episode 'Who's the cool girl Josh is dating?' (2016). Here, the presentation draws heavily from the Instagram aesthetic of 2016, covering both the platformed (square images) and the vernacular (hashtag styles). The song also reflects on questions of public and private accounts, using humour to comment on the justifications given for trying to find out as much as possible about a new person in an ex's life ('it's not stalking because the information is all technically public').

Instagram as a plot device has also featured in television shows as varied as drama, comedy and reality television. Australian reality shows have demonstrated ongoing reliance on Instagram for generating content and conflict, from *Yummy Mummies*' (2017) use of the platform as a contrivance for its geographically dispersed cast to actually meet and interact, for example, to discussion of appropriate Instagram behaviour on *The Real Housewives of Sydney* (2017; among others). The Norwegian teen drama *Skåm* (2015–17), meanwhile, used social media (including Instagram) both within its episodes and in maintaining accounts for the characters in the show. Perhaps most prominently, though, in English-speaking popular culture is the Influencer culture-heavy setting, with a serving of obsession and questions of authenticity, of the 2017 film *Ingrid Goes West*, starring Aubrey Plaza and Elizabeth Olsen.

Virtual Influencers

As seen in chapter 4, Influencers come in many shapes, sizes and, indeed, species: not only can Instagram accounts featuring pets received tens of thousands of dollars for promoted posts, but there are now whole Influencer agencies dedicated to matching Influencer pets with brands wanting to promote on their feeds (Sorokanich 2018). Yet the most intriguing new Instagram stars are not just a different species, but a different form altogether: *virtual Influencers* are CGI or virtual celebrities who do not have a physical form at all, but are created, crafted, narrated and managed to promote or sell a particular message or brand. Sometimes dubbed avatars, CGI Influencers, or animated models, virtual Influencers first emerged in 2016, becoming popular across the next few years. There are clearly precedents: Japanese virtual idol Kyoko Date was popular in 1996, managed as real talent despite being a digital model; and when Andy Serkis played Gollum in the *Lord of the Rings* films, there were widespread fears that 'synthespians' would take the jobs of 'real' actors and that soon all acting would be digital (Creed 2000; Leaver 2012). That did not happen, and nor are virtual Influencers likely to replace every other Instagram star, but they may be one of the most significant types of Influencer to emerge, showing the contours of how authenticity, engagement and communication operate on Instagram.

Noonoouri, for example, first emerged in February 2018, and is the creation of Joerg Zuber who runs German design agency Opium Effect. On Instagram, Noonoouri has more than 250,000 followers, has done make-up tutorials for Kim Kardashian, posed with Kendall Jenner, and, to mild controversy, been one of the faces of Dior's Summer 2018 make-up line (Chekoufi 2018; Corner 2018). Noonoouri is unlikely to be mistaken for a 'real' person, though, as her oversized eyes and head mean she looks more like a Bratz doll than a model. Her Stories, however, are fascinating, mixing more standard Influencer shots with an almost stream-of-consciousness series of images around fashion, aesthetics and a range of other topics. Yet despite her clearly constructed nature, the comments on Noonoouri's images are indistinguishable from other celebrities and Influencers except that almost every photo has at least one person ask: 'are you a real person?'. On the six-month anniversary of her Instagram account's launch, Zuber distanced Noonoouri from criticisms she was taking the work of real flesh-and-blood models, commenting: 'She is not an avatar, nor [does] she wants to substitute real humans, never. She is a besouled character, nourished by a real human having fun with fashion, beauty, architecture, art and lifestyle with a big social heart for the voiceless' (Zuber 2018).

Shudu (full name, Shudu Gram) first came to prominence when beauty brand Fenty reposted an image of Shudu to their Beauty Instagram account wearing their Saw-C shade lipstick. To many people's surprise, shortly afterwards *Harper's Bazaar* outed Shudu as the creation of British photographer Cameron-James Wilson (Rosenstein 2018). Shudu is a particularly contentious figure as she presents as a dark-skinned African woman, but is the proprietary artistic creation of a white, male photographer. While Shudu initially had many admirers who championed her as increasing black representation in the fashion industry, Wilson was on the receiving end of considerable criticism after it was revealed she was a computer-generated creation (Jackson 2018). One tweet which captured the backlash, and was liked more than 50,000 times, ironically lamented: 'A white photographer figured out a way to profit off of black women without ever having to pay one. Now pls, tell me how our economic system is in no way built on and quite frankly reliant on racism and misogyny' (hodayum 2018). On Shudu's Instagram images, Wilson initially used hashtags which aligned her with the Black community, such as #blackisbeautiful and #blackgirlsrock, which in retrospect seemed particularly contentious, so much so that Wilson went back through all of Shudu's images, removing many of these hashtags, while adding explicit markers that she is, in his eyes, a form of #3dart. Wilson calls Shudu the 'world's first digital supermodel', and this has been taken quite literally with genuine fear that digital models will replace real ones. In a recent interview, Wilson began trying to reassure people, 'Anyone working in modelling is secure in their job!' but could not help but quickly follow with the assertion that 'it will change the industry. It will change the way it works. We can digitize real models without having to fly them round the world, minimizing carbon footprint and creating more affordable campaigns for instance. Shudu is a pioneer' (Parcq & London 2018).

Cameron-James Wilson has more recently explained in interviews that he sees digital models as an extension of the extensive digital makeovers most real models have before their images are published:

> I think responsible use of CGI models is making it very clear. In my eyes it's no different than retouching, technology exists today that means we can simulate garments true to life on digital models, so what is the difference? Since being on fashion campaign shoots I've seen the 'tricks' brands use to make their garments look appealing, it may as well just be a rendering. CGI is heavily used in every other commercial industry, fashion is the last one to catch on. (Dimitras 2018)

In late 2018, Shudu, along with two new digital models, Margot and Zhi, joined the modelling ranks of French luxury brand Balmain. The partnership was orchestrated by Balmain's creative director Olivier Rousteing, who had Margot and Zhi designed by Wilson exclusively for Balmain. Moreover, the three are now the cornerstones of Wilson's new virtual model company, Diigitals, which has quickly commercialized Shudu's notoriety to offer virtual models to brands across the globe (Clark 2018). Wilson's earlier argument that his digital creations were not going to take the work of flesh-and-blood models seems a commitment he has largely forgotten.

While Noonoouri and Shudu have both amassed significant followings, they pale in comparison to virtual Influencer 'it girl' Lil Miquela who had more than 1.5 million followers at the beginning of 2019. Miquela's first posts appeared in April 2016, and while her images were clearly digitally created, there was widespread speculation that she was a real model using specific filters to create a digital look. Despite her virtual nature, Lil Miquela quickly began partnering with fashion labels and left-wing causes, showcasing both in her Instagram feed. She was joined on Instagram by her best friend, Blawko, and nemesis-cum-frenemy Bermuda, all posting in a similar digital style. After a narrative worthy of a soap opera, Bermuda hijacked and deleted Lil Miquela's entire Instagram feed before forcing Lil Miquela to admit to the world that she was 'a robot'. Shortly afterwards, many of Lil Miquela's posts reappeared along with an angry post to Instagram on 20 April 2018, in which she claimed that the company managing her, Brud FYI, had lied to her, telling her she was based on a real person and was not entirely manufactured but now she'd learnt the truth that she was entirely 'built' and was angry that her managers had lied to her, but in that same post she claimed to now be fully self-aware (lilmiquela 2018a). Her revelations are clearly part of a larger, complex, narrative written by Brud FYI about her sentience, building on a raft of science fiction precursors from *A.I. Artificial Intelligence* through to *Blade Runner*. In a second post the same day, Lil Miquela wrote

> I'm not sure I can comfortably identify as a woman of color. "Brown" was a choice made by a corporation. "Woman" was an option on a computer screen. ... I'm different. I want to use what makes me different to create a better world. I want to do things that humans maybe can't. ... I am committed to bolstering voices that need to be heard. (lilmiquela 2018b)

While these thoughts furthered her narrative, they also very carefully and strategically distanced Lil Miquela from the controversy around Shudu and the appropriation of ethnicity. Indeed, Lil Miquela's posts echo the controversy around Lonelygirl15 on YouTube in 2006, where a seemingly innocent teenager's vlogs built a huge following but were later revealed to be part of a fictional transmedia narrative. While Lonelygirl15 'violated the ideology of authenticity' associated with amateur productions in the early days of YouTube (Burgess & Green 2018, p. 44), the revelation of Lil Miquela's digital rather than physical existence does not seem to have diminished her appeal at all. On Instagram, authenticity may well be judged on the experience and interaction, not necessarily on whether an Influencer is made out of flesh or data.

As we have argued throughout this book, Instagram is more than anything about communication. The real reason Lil Miquela has such wide appeal, like other successful Influencers – digital or otherwise – is that she engages meaningfully, regularly and strategically with her followers. She shares widely on the daily drama with Blawko and Bermuda, she celebrates partnerships with fashion brands but also, like many Influencers, uses her Stories feed as a daily train-of-thought, posting images, ideas and happenings that firmly place Lil Miquela as 'existing' in the vernacular of everyday life. Lil Miquela – and the team that manage 'her' at Brud FYI – maximize opportunities to engage with fans and followers. In the week and weekend around 31 October 2018, for example, Lil Miquela's Stories were filled with reposts of hundreds of fans who had dressed like the virtual Influencer for Halloween. They, in turn, almost always reposted to their Stories showing great delight that Lil Miquela had seen and enjoyed their costumes and cosplay. Unlike Shudu, Lil Miquela does not break character, she is a consistent voice, a consistent narrative, and Brud FYI have been very careful to keep the creative team behind her invisible. While this balance might be upset in the future, in Lil Miquela's first three years she has shown that the trick to being a successful Influencer, virtual or otherwise, is building a meaningful sense of interaction with followers, and ensuring that every post feels like an authentic example of two-way communication.

Templatability of Instagram

'Rinse and Repeat'
Amidst the flourishing visual genres of Instagram, some aesthetic decisions have come to become repeatable or templatable by a critical mass of users. Such *repeatable aesthetics* are easy to mimic such that they are vernacularly known as 'rinse and repeat' actions. Drawing on this and questioning the whole notion of authenticity on Instagram, account @ insta_repeat collects and makes collages of Instagram posts that are almost identical, from the posing and framing to the filtered colouration and captions (figure 7.1). In an interview with Quartz, the anonymous 27-year-old filmmaker said they wanted to make 'observations about the homogeneous content that is popular on Instagram' (Murphy 2018). In another interview with Photo Shelter, the creator observes that many of these Instagram posts fall within the genre of travel and adventure, and are often captioned with catchphrases such as 'live authentic' or 'explore to create', yet the mimicry and constant repetition was ironic to this supposed sense of self-discovery and uniqueness (Murabayashi 2018).

New York City-based illustrator and writer Mari Andrew perhaps best encapsulates this rheotoric on her Instagram account @bymariandrew (2018a) on which she regularly sketches Instagram trends. One of these sketches is 'Instagrammable vacation bingo', with a 4×4 grid describing and illustrating insta-clichés such as 'palm trees against a blue sky', 'door portrait', 'hotel lobby', 'pool portrait', and 'last day captioned "never leaving"' (@bymariandrew 2018b). Other clichés are slightly more niche, such as the 'Friends in their

Figure 7.1. Artist impression of typical post by @insta_repeat featuring a compilation of Instagram posts framed in the same visual template. Art provided by mistercrow.

30s Instagram Bingo', with a 4×4 grid containing Instagram posts such as 'Luxurious Airbnb captioned "my home for the week"', 'work hard party hard cocktail', '#WorkFromHome Wednesday by the pool', and 'Bathroom selfie with long caption about current highs and lows' (@bymariandrew 2018c). Andrew has also observed some longitudinal trends with her sketch 'Instagram post of the year', with an illustration and description of the peak Instagram from 2011 to 2016 (@ bymariandrew 2017):

- 2011: Latte art with polaroid corners
- 2012: Mayfair filter, blur, tilt shift
- 2013: Looking out at scenery while wearing a hat
- 2014: Object held against white wall

- 2015: Single beam of light on white bedspread
- 2016: whimsical portrait against hot pink wall

This repetitive template of what is celebrated as a 'good Instagram aesthetic' has also been ritualized to the point of pure mimicry. In November 2016, Instagram travel influencers and 'internet famous' couple Jack Morris (@doyoutravel) and Lauren Bullen (@gypsea_lust) discovered that another 'mysterious couple' who were posting under @diana_alexa (now deleted) was mimicking them to a tee. These included their travel destinations, photographic locations, framing and compositions, outfits and even photo captions (Gould-Bourn n.d.; Truman 2016). The details were replicated down to the same pillow arrangement in one post, matching anklets in another, and swimsuits in the exact same shade of blue in still another post (Gould-Bourn n.d.). The mirroring was executed so well and so sincerely that it did not appear to be a parody or trolling account, but was instead read as potential stalker tendencies or blatant plagiarism. The mysterious couple had also blocked Morris from their Instagram account after reposting one of his images (Tirosh 2016). Although there were some conspiracy theories about how Morris and Bullen might have possibly set this 'scandal' up for publicity or that the copycat is a 'hoax' (Darvall 2016; Lakritz 2016), it was later revealed that the @diana_alexa couple did indeed recreate the Instagram posts as 'a doable way of achieving something creative', to ascertain 'how accurately [they] could recreate the photos down to a tee' (Harvey-Jenner 2016).

'Fake it till you make it'
While the visual templatability of Instagram has become easy to identify and memorize, executing the actual photograph might be more challenging considering the costs involved when travelling and the props that are necessary. But it appears that some Influencers have 'worked' their way around these constraints by generating illusions of their Instagram

experience through *simulatable aesthetics*, best encapsulated by the adage 'fake it till you make it'. In June 2018, Singaporean Instagram photographer and influencer Daryl Aiden Yow (@ darylaiden), who had 100k followers at the time of this incident, was exposed by digital platform and lifestyle news portal *Mothership* for editing and compiling stock images on his account. He had seemingly passed these images off as his own as it was mentioned on several captions that they were 'shot professionally' (Lee et al. 2018). However, the stock images were eventually traced back to services including Shutterstock, CanStockPhoto, and Unsplashed.com, among others (BBC News 2018). This exposé was especially critical given that Yow had been running brand-sponsored workshops to share photography tips with his followers and was an ambassador of a camera brand (Lee et al. 2018).

The discovery led to an onslaught of criticism after users started to scrutinize Yow's past posts more closely to compile more evidence of plagiarism (Tan & Wee 2018). Bloopers spotted included faint watermarks, the absence of footprints, and shadows that did not match their figures (Tan & Wee 2018). Influencers with whom he had collaborated as photographer were also implicated and accused of deception, and the scandal grew larger (How 2018). Further, several Influencers and professional photographers with online clout spoke out on the issue (Ong 2018), inevitably stimulating more backlash and hate towards Yow.

Yow later clarified that the stock photos were not stolen but paid for, and if lifted from other photographers or the image-sharing platform Pinterest, that he had credited the original sources by tagging his posts. He also claimed that his clients were aware of the purchase and use of stock images (Joelynn 2018; Tan & Tan 2018). Yet, these rebuttals did little to placate disgruntled internet users, who instead began to parody the Influencer's mishap with the #DarylAidenChallenge which involved badly photoshopping oneself into ludicrous situations (Must Share News 2018a). In response, Yow deleted some of his posts and edited the captions of others (Nazren 2018). He later issued a public apology on Instagram Stories (Must Share News 2018b) and deleted all the images on his account.

In his redemption narrative, Yow returned to Instagram after two-and-a-half months with a clean slate. In this rebranding exercise, Yow's Instagram posts have since focused on his photo enhancing and editing techniques. His new posts now include Instagram slide decks revealing the 'before and after' process of his Insta-worthy images such as colouration techniques (@darylaiden 2018a), behind-the-scenes of optical illusions (@darylaiden 2018b), and layering and retouching skills (@darylaiden 2018c). In single-image posts, he includes disclaimers that the image was edited such as 'PS: Sky was enhanced and layered in!' (@darylaiden 2018d). Yow has since resumed his advertorials with clients, using obviously photoshopped images that convey dramatic compositions and visual tricks to highlight the products he is promoting (@darylaiden 2018e, @darylaiden 2018f), including technology gadgets and photography workshops he has critiqued for the public in partnership with sponsors (@darylaiden 2018g).

In a similar but less serious vein, in May 2017 American rapper Bow Wow was exposed and mocked for passing off an image of a private jet as his own, having claimed in his Instagram captions to be travelling to New York City for a press run. The image was found to be lifted from the website of a transportation company (Farokhmanesh 2017), and Bow Wow was spotted on a commercial flight in economy class by a fellow passenger who outed him in a Snapchat post (Giedr 2017). This quickly spiralled into the #BowWowChallenge, in which users on Twitter and Instagram post before-and-after images of how they were 'faking' their Instagram posts via a combination of careful framing, layering and the use of props (Giedr 2017). Users wittingly 'faked' romantic partners and dates, new wealth such as enviable homes and luxury cars, and attendance at parties and exclusive events (Molloy 2017), thus turning the #BowWowChallenge into a bona fide meme (Know Your Meme 2017).

In response to the increasing awareness of staged artifice on Instagram, a string of dedicated Instagram accounts have emerged to playfully critique Instagrammers who were clearly merely 'posing for the 'gram'. These include @youdidnotsleepthere (2018), which collects 'Instagram's most illogical campsites' with campers posting shots of tents on the most precarious cliffs and mountains, @youdidnoteatthat (2018), which collects Instagram pictures of 'too many macarons and ice cream cones used as props' but are probably not actually eaten, and @youdidnotskatethat (2018), which collects images of mostly young women posing with skateboards but who are probably unable to skate as indicated by their incongruent outfits, footwear and props.

The simulacrum of Instagram has spiralled a step further, with entire shadow economies set up to maximize the experience of Instagrammability for those who are unable to reach it. For instance, at RMB88 per half-hour slot, a café in Shenzhen will provide visitors with a 'luxurious bathrobe' and a 'photo backdrop of the view from a high-rise hotel in a bustling metropolitan city' as props for the perfect Instagram photo. There are various backdrop selections, including the Dragon's Back Trail of picturesque mountains in Hong Kong, and the skyline of Osaka (Kohnhorst 2018).

Instagram vs. Reality
Evidently, the formulaic, repeatable and simulatable aesthetics of Instagram – also quipped as 'rinse and repeat' templates and 'fake it till you make it' – have blossomed into a specific subculture of 'how (not) to' guides on Instagram. These have birthed the trope of 'Instagram vs. reality' posts and disclosures, in which users expose the actual effort behind the 'gram. Titles such as '14 photographs that prove everything you've seen on Instagram is a lie' and 'Three shocking truths behind travel photos' seek to out the 'hard truths' behind the

visual envy on Instagram, such as waiting in long queues for an Instagrammable spot, battling crowds, the need to keep the rubbish on the street out of frame, and locations with perpetual bad weather (Morris 2017; Nonstop Living n.d.). In fact, some Influencers are now reclaiming this 'Instagram vs. reality' trope to generate 'authentic' content, narratively describing the backstory to (and sometimes mishaps behind) their 'best travel photos' (Woodrow n.d.), including close-ups with creatures such as sharks, enduring painful insect bites, posing in glamourous outfits in bad weather (Woodrow n.d.).

Entire brand campaigns now ride on the 'Instagram vs. reality' trope to promote anything from photography gadgets and travel destinations, to household products and self-care services. With titles such as '10 photographs you can take in Singapore to bluff your friends that you're on vacation' (Yang 2016) and '10 photographs taken in Singapore to bluff your friends that you're in Japan' (Lin 2018), readers are taken to unexpected (and raggedy) locations such as construction sites, the back of a rubbish dumpster, and train tracks, and shown how with careful framing and the right props, the Insta-worthy can be constructed in one's backyard or at one's doorstep (Yang 2016).

In another campaign to promote a food recipe portal (Dodgson 2018), parenting Influencers in the UK teamed up to show the behind-the-scenes of Insta-worthy shots amidst their actual domestic lives of mess and young children. Disclosures were made about how they had to 'distract' and 'coax' their children out of meltdowns, how the perfect Instagrammable meals involved laborious preparations and clean-ups, and how they found clean spots for their Instagram shots among the household clutter (Dodgson 2018).

From the Everything of Instagram ...

In this book, we set out to survey 'the everything of Instagram' through six chapters. In chapter 1, we historicized the 'politics' of Instagram as a platform, focused on its technological, cultural and economic contexts, contestations and competitions across visual social media platforms, as well as the ever-growing challenges of treating Instagram's billion plus users as a single community beholden to a single set of Community Guidelines. In chapter 2, we observed some of the most pertinent 'aesthetics' of Instagram as a visual culture, in relation to the primary content generated on the site and the normative practices of its users, from filters and square frames, to later norms, including the popularity of vertical video in Stories and IGTV. In chapter 3, we further mapped out the ecologies of Instagram as app, and how it is situated among a plethora of visually dominant photographic mobile apps, with specific attention paid to Instagram's own ecology and how the ways Instagram works with third-party services and apps has shifted over time. In chapter 4, we tracked the economies of Instagram as a business, especially its relationship to the rise of social media Influencers and the commodification of visual spaces online. Chapter 5 examined various 'cultures' on Instagram as a social space, including its folkloric beliefs, contentious subcultural groups, and impact on popular culture, showing not one, but many, varied, vibrant Instagram communities. And finally, in chapter 6, we used the longer lens to look at the way Instagram entails photos, videos and stories about users from the day they are first visualized, often through ultrasounds, all the way through to how Instagram users grieve, remember and memorialize their loved ones. Yet, in the decade since Instagram's debut, its uptake, influence and leverage on how users come to practise visual social media cultures has expanded dramatically, to the extent that the platform is linked with almost every cultural form and practice; the world presents a veritable everything of Instagram.

... to the Instagram of Everything

Doing it for the 'gram, or curating lives to ensuring they're 'Insta-worthy', has seen Instagram become synonymous with the world around us, just as Google has become the verb for searching for information online. A billion people are using Instagram daily, initially sharing via filters and square frames, with half a billion of them sharing the minutiae of their lives, loves and losses on Instagram Stories using a vastly more complex toolkit of visual social media expression than was initially developed by competitors like Snapchat whom Instagram have skilfully beaten at their own game. Instagram Direct has colonized other popular forms of messaging, incorporating much of the expressive toolkit of Stories, while slowly and quietly including live video and video chat, encroaching spaces once dominated by Skype and Apple. Having popularized vertical video through Stories, Instagram have raised the bar trying to take on content-providing behemoths YouTube and Netflix with IGTV. All the while, Facebook started slowly with official advertising on Instagram, but it has now encompassed the platform from the main feed to Stories, with one in four or five images usually commercial content. Equally, Instagram has been owned and managed by Facebook since 2012, but despite all of the backlash and bad press around privacy and political manipulation on Facebook in 2018, Instagram has remained remarkably clean of Facebook's smell; indeed, 'amid all the chaos, Facebook has successfully positioned Instagram as an innocent bystander time and time again' (Greer 2018).

As Instagram borrowed from and side-lined competing platforms, material locations around the world have been rushing to ensure they are Insta-friendly. As discussed in chapter 5, museums, galleries, cafés, restaurants, parks, universities, foyers and more have all been re-designed to make sure that the quintessential, defining Instagram shot of video can be easily created in their space. Pop-up bars, clubs and event launches are dominated by the cardboard Instagram frames, and endless branded props, with the strategically chosen event-specific Instagram hashtag to ensure maximum visibility. Influencers of all shapes and sizes produce content daily, representing their best selves in the main Instagram feed while carefully crafting a more approachable and engaging self in their dialogues in Instagram Stories. The mobile camera photographic sensibility has been thoroughly redirected to, and through, the Instagram lens. Indeed, virtual Influencers are, to some extent, the indigenous lifeforms of Instagram: dazzling entities who, at their best, combine communication, commerce and a very twenty-first-century sense of authenticity and engagement, without existing in the world outside the platform at all.

Yet for all of Instagram's success, or indeed, because of it, the experience of Instagram is increasingly challenged by the logic of templatability which is evident across the platform, captured in the examples and aesthetics detailed above. Instagram's drive to serve metrics for Influencers and advertisers has meant both are increasingly behaving in similar ways; how-to guides online detailing the ultimate Instagram post are tailored to crafting content which maximizes the attention of Instagram's algorithms. While Instagram's Discover pages are meant to highlight new material for users, the multiple signals of other user's comments and likes, and machine vision algorithms looking for aesthetically similar content, mean Discover is largely populated with content *similar* to material a user has already seen, greatly reducing the serendipity and spontaneity of exploring Instagram. Memorable posts are no longer memorable for their originality, but often for either beginning or, far more often, perpetuating a visual style that has been rapidly popularized on the platform. Templates, we argue, are not cultural norms, nor hegemonic, but are visually memorable and memorizable visual stylings, settings and practices that can be replicated with relative ease to the extent that they become, for a period of time, iconic. The seeming end of new aesthetic visual filters being added to Instagram by the company directly correlates with the rise of metric and algorithmically perpetuated templatability driven by users. We argue, then, that templatability comprises:

1. **Affordances and Algorithms**. The complex dance between what Instagram's tools allow people to do is always framed, now, by what the platform's algorithms allow people to see. When the most familiar content appears at the top of every user's algorithmic feed, as well as in Discover, Instagram becomes a quite different user experience. Calls for algorithmic transparency and resistance to Instagram 'programming' users are, to some extent, a desire to move beyond the logic of the template.

2. **Aesthetics and Affect**. Instagram has moved beyond filters, but now wrestles with ensuring that new aesthetic norms, which are often driven by creators pleasing algorithms before people, do not interrupt the affective experiences of Instagram.

3. **Attention and Audiences**. All profitable social media platforms strive to turn audiences and their attention into advertising dollars, and in doing so need to foster user engagement and communication on their platform. When one in four or five images is advertising, the attention economy is likely at its peak. For Instagram, Stories may be its main growth area, but ensuring audiences want to remain on Instagram may well need more careful calibrating of unsought commercial content, especially in the more intimate Stories setting.

4. **Agency and Activism**. As with every platform, Instagram users want to feel like their actions and engagement matters. User agency, the capacity to take charge of one's decision-making, and activism, the capacity to make meaningful political action, are at the core of the mythos of visual social media. Templatability may well diminish the feeling of individuality and individual contributions to Instagram, and with that a sense of being able to

meaningfully communicate aesthetically, or contribute to change.

Templates are not necessarily negative. A good template emerges because it is visually and affectively pleasing. The challenge for Instagram is to ensure their algorithms balance encouraging user creativity in seeing and utilizing templates without them becoming so commonplace as to be parodies of themselves. Parody has its place, but maintaining a platform whose currency is communication and authenticity means originality and serendipity are vital as well.

Instagram: Visual Social Media Cultures

Instagram is as much the story of the rapid expansion of visual social media cultures as it is any one platform or experience. The attention economy is primarily visual today, and Instagram remains synonymous with the visual zeitgeist. Sociality online, however, has become more and more complicated with communities and national governments pressuring for social media corporations to take more responsibility for the actions and content on their platforms. Instagram, like parent company Facebook, must also figure out how to encourage commerce, advertising and Influencers without impinging on the affective user experience, which is dominated more and more by similar content and the logics of templatability. While in this book we have continually referred to the plurality of cultures that use and, to an extent, inhabit Instagram, this is at odds with the singular ways that Instagram itself seems to imagine, and write policies for, its users.

With a billion users, Instagram is a global platform, but also faces increasing competition in the visual social media space: V Live and Snow are popular in South Korea; Douyin, Tudou and Meitu XiuXiu have huge numbers of users in China; while Musical.ly/TikTok/Douyin originated in China but has now also become hugely popular in Latin America. Instagram faces challenges but has historically succeeded as new challenges and competitors have emerged, often replicating the most popular features of their competitors. Ultimately, the continued success of the platform will come down to whether they can balance providing rich tools, spaces and experiences of communication with the corporate necessity of ever-expanding and inescapable commerce and advertising in the face of doggedly insisting that Instagram is a singular community, governed in a single way, via a single set of Community Guidelines. In April 2019, a promising sign that Instagram is focusing more on users than metrics came at Facebook's F8 Developer's Conference where Adam Mosseri announced that the platform was experimenting with hiding the number of likes and views posts receive (Shaban 2019). While this information would remain available to the user themselves, preventing the overnight decimation of the Influencer economy, taking the emphasis in the main Instagram feed away from metrics and competition might just be the balance needed to ensure the platform continues to grow and can be enjoyed by users across the globe for many years to come.

Appendix: Instagram Timeline

Table A1. Instagram Timeline	
6 October 2010	Instagram app launched via Apple's App Store (iOS only)
12 December 2010	1 million registered users
3 August 2011	150 million photos uploaded
September 2011	10 million registered users
3 April 2012	Instagram releases Android app
9 April 2012	Facebook purchases Instagram for US$1 billion
26 July 2012	80 million registered users
16 August 2012	Instagram Photo Maps launched
5 November 2012	Instagram Profiles for the Web launched
5 December 2012	Instagram removes ability for photos to appear as 'cards' (visible integrated photos) on Twitter
17 December 2012	Instagram alters Terms of Use
18 December 2012	Instagram reverts to previous Terms of Use after public backlash
26 February 2013	100 million active monthly users
20 June 2013	Instagram adds video (15 seconds maximum)
10 July 2013	Instagram adds native web embedding for photos and videos
6 September 2013	150 million users
24 October 2013	Instagram begins experimenting with advertisements in the main feed, initially with a 'Sponsored' notification on each
12 December 2013	Instagram Direct messaging service added
24 March 2014	200 million users
July 2014	Instagram releases Bolt (messaging app) in New Zealand, South Africa and Singapore (it was discontinued within six months)

(continued)

Table A1. Instagram Timeline	
26 August 2014	Hyperlapse app released via Apple App Store (iOS only; to date, no Android version has been released.)
10 November 2014	Instagram enables photo caption editing after posting
December 2014	Great Instagram Purge or Instagram Rapture. More than 18 million spam accounts deleted
10 December 2014	300 million users, 70 million photos and videos shared per day
24 March 2015	Layout app via Apple App Store
27 August 2015	Instagram adds native support for portrait/landscape (non-square) photos/videos
1 September 2015	Instagram overhauls Direct with threaded comments and 'send to' option
8 September 2015	Instagram advertising expands, opening to all advertisers and appearing in feeds globally
22 September 2015	400 million users (75% of those outside the US)
22 October 2015	Boomerang looping video app launched
8 February 2016	Instagram adds multiple account support and account switching
23 February 2016	Instagram adds number of views counter for Instagram video
3 March 2016	Instagram bans Snapchat and Telegram profile links in Instagram bio
15 March 2016	Instagram begins trialling algorithmically ordered timeline (non-chronological)
29 March 2016	Instagram begins rolling out support for 60-second videos
28 April 2016	Instagram releases fully-featured Windows 10 app
11 May 2016	Instagram redesigns main and ecology app logos
1 June 2016	Major changes to Instagram's API limit or kill off a number of third-party apps, especially 'readers' and significantly limit and control what new apps can do (e.g. no Regrams)
2 June 2016	Instagram shifts all users to an algorithmic (not chronological) view
21 June 2016	Instagram reports 500 million users; 300 million active daily; 80% of users are outside of the US
2 August 2016	Instagram adds Stories (lasting 24 hrs, then self-deleting)
September 2016	Instagram begins removing Photo Maps

(continued)

Table A1. Instagram Timeline	
12 September 2016	Instagram adds new comment-moderation tools (including user-created keyword block lists)
19 October 2016	Instagram adds mental health and suicide prevention prompts relating to keyword searches and (anonymous) user reporting
10 November 2016	Instagram adds Boomerang loops, Mentions and Links to Instagram Stories
21 November 2016	Instagram debuts Live Video in Stories for limited users
21 November 2016	Instagram adds disappearing photos/videos for groups and friends via Instagram Direct
21 November 2016	Verified Accounts can now add 'See More' links to Stories
6 December 2016	Users can now turn comments off for specific photos/videos
6 December 2016	Users can now anonymously report self-injury posts
14 December 2016	Instagram adds saved/bookmarked posts
15 December 2016	600 million users
20 December 2016	Instagram adds Stickers for Instagram Direct and Hands-Free recording in Stories
24 January 2017	Live video on Instagram Stories available to all users
22 February 2017	Multiple photos/videos can now be added in one post
20 March 2017	Instagram adds the ability to save Live Video after it's streamed
23 March 2017	Instagram adds 'Sensitive Content' warnings (for community-report material)
23 March 2017	Two-factor authentication enabled for Instagram logins
23 March 2017	Launches 'Instagram Together' Community Safety website http://instagram-together.com/
11 April 2017	Instagram revamps Direct: more visual, integrates Direct and Disappearing Media thread
11 April 2017	375 million are using Direct
13 April 2017	'Selfie Stickers', Pinning, Expanded Geostickers all added to Stories
17 April 2017	Instagram adds Collections for organizing Saved Posts (since December 2016, 46% of users have saved one or more posts)
April 2017	Instagram Stories now has 200 million active daily users

(continued)

Table A1. Instagram Timeline	
14 June 2017	Instagram adds 'Paid Partnership With' Tags to clearly mark paid content
26 April 2017	700 million users
17 May 2017	Instagram adds (Snapchat-style) Face Filters, Rewind (Reverse Play) Videos and clickable hashtags overlaid on images
20 June 2017	Instagram Live Videos can be saved/replayed for 24 hours
20 June 2017	Instagram Stories now has 250 million daily active users (more than Snapchat, who invented the format)
29 June 2017	Instagram adds (English-only initially) Hide Offensive Comments option; also adds algorithmic spam comment filtering added for English, Spanish, Portuguese, Arabic, French, German, Russian, Japanese and Chinese
6 July 2017	Instagram adds Photo and Video Replies to Stories (similar to Snapchat)
2 August 2017	Instagram Stories is 1 year old
26 September 2017	800 million users; 500 million daily active users; plus new comment filtering tools
26 October 2017	Instagram Stories adds 'SuperZoom' (and temporary Halloween themed stickers)
26 October 2017	Instagram adds the Poll Sticker to Instagram Stories
7 November 2017	Instagram now allows any gallery media to be added to Stories (previously limited to the past 24 hours)
5 December 2017	Instagram adds Stories Archive and Stories Highlights on Profiles
12 December 2017	Instagram adds the ability to follow #hashtags and have the results turn up in the main feed
18 January 2017	Instagram turns on 'last active' notifications in Messenger (without explicitly announcing it)
23 January 2018	Instagram adds GIF stickers in Messenger (powered by and licensed from Giphy)
1 February 2018	Instagram adds Type Mode in Stories
March 2018	Instagram removes Giphy GIF Stickers for three weeks after a racist sticker appears (reinstated after new filters put in place)
21 March 2018	Instagram Bios can now add Hashtags and (other) profile links

(continued)

Table A1. Instagram Timeline	
10 April 2018	'Focus' (super portrait mode) added to Instagram Stories
1 May 2018	Automatic 'bullying' comments filtered out for everyone
1 May 2018	Sharing stickers/moments/event to Stories from other apps (initially Spotify and GoPro) added – deep integration
1 May 2018	Instagram begins rolling out one-on-one and small group video chat in Direct Messaging
17 May 2018	Main Instagram feed posts can now be shared directly with Instagram Stories and Direct
22 May 2018	Instagram allow users to mute either the Posts, Stories or both from specific users they follow
May 2018	Instagram ads Emoji Slider in Instagram Stories
12 June 2018	Shopping stickers (Buy This) now available in Instagram Stories (already in the main posts)
20 June 2018	Instagram launches IGTV (Instagram TV), claiming the 'vertical video' space for videos up to 1 hour long – includes IGTV link in the main Instagram interface as well as standalone IGTV app
20 June 2018	Instagram has more than 1 billion monthly users
21 June 2018	Instagram Stories has 400 million active daily users
26 June 2018	Instagram Video Chat in Instagram Direct for one-on-one and small groups now available for all users
28 June 2018	Instagram releases (but does not publicly promote or launch) Instagram Lite for Android, a pared-back Instagram app for emerging markets (initially released in Mexico)
28 June 2018	Instagram adds Music Stickers in Instagram Stories
2 July 2018	'You're All Caught Up' notification added to timeline when all of the last 2 days posts have been seen
10 July 2018	Instagram adds 'Ask Me Something' question sticker to Instagram Stories
19 July 2018	Instagram Direct adds 'green availability indicator' to show when friends are live online (enabled by default)
1 August 2018	Instagram and Facebook start rolling out time management functions to monitor, report and remind users about the amount of time being spent on the platform

(continued)

Table A1. Instagram Timeline	
28 August 2018	Instagram begins rolling out 'About This Account' information for accounts with large followers (showing when the account was created, recent account name changes, what ads it is running, and what country it is being managed from) to better inform followers about the type and nature of the account they are following
28 August 2018	Instagram adds support for third-party 'authenticator apps' adding a new method of two-factor authentication (partially in response to protests that mobile/SMS-based two-factor authentication didn't accommodate for users with multiple accounts)
6 September 2018	Instagram releases a new, detailed, Parent's Guide to Instagram https://wellbeing.instagram.com/parents
17 September 2018	'Shopping' (links to sales) added to Stories and to Explore
20 September 2018	GIF Stickers added to Direct Messaging
24 September 2018	Instagram's co-founders Kevin Systrom and Mike Krieger announce their resignation from Facebook/Instagram
1 October 2018	Adam Mosseri becomes Head of Instagram (Systrom and Krieger officially step down)
4 October 2018	Instagram rolls out scannable Nametags (similar to Snapchat's Snapcodes)
9 October 2018	Instagram begins using 'machine learning' to detect bullying; adds bullying comment filter to Live Videos
1 November 2018	Instagram releases 'I Voted' stickers and 'We Voted!' Story for US mid-term elections
15 November 2018	Specific Shopping section added to Collections; Shopping Icon and Popup added to Instagram Video
19 November 2018	Instagram announce increased policing of accounts using 'inauthentic' third-party apps to artificially inflate likes, comments and followers, warning these will be deleted
21 November 2018	Instagram begins rolling out layout changes to Instagram Profiles
28 November 2018	Instagram adds automated alternate text descriptions to photos being read by screen readers, and the ability for all users to edit the alternate text of their media

(continued)

Table A1. Instagram Timeline	
30 November 2018	Instagram adds the ability to share Stories with a specific, limited Close Friends list
18 December 2018	Instagram adds Music replies to the Question Sticker in Stories; adds Live Video replies to answer Question Stickers
18 December 2018	Instagram adds a Countdown Sticker for Stories
24 December 2018	Instagram removes hundreds of meme accounts, explaining that these accounts are bought, sold or traded, which is a violation of their Terms of Use
28 December 2018	Instagram 'accidentally' replaces scrolling with tap-to-move side-swiping in Instagram's main feed, but removes this change hours later, calling it a 'bug'
10 January 2019	Instagram adds the ability to post to multiple Instagram accounts at the same time
31 January 2019	Instagram Stories have 500 million daily active users
4 February 2019	Responding to the suicide of Molly Russell in the UK, Instagram Head Adam Mosseri writes an article for *The Telegraph* outlining Instagram's enhanced attempts to deal with self-harm material on the platform
7 February 2019	Instagram commits to removing ALL graphic images of self-harm from the platform (regardless of context)
13 March 2019	Instagram (and Facebook) experience their largest outage in history, being inaccessible for more than 12 hours
19 March 2019	Instagram launches 'Checkout', in-app purchases inside Instagram with partner brands
23 April 2019	Instagram adds Quiz Stickers to Stories
30 April 2019	Instagram releases Donation Stickers in Stories (initially only in the US)
30 April 2019	Instagram announces redesigned Camera and Create Mode for Stories which makes it easier to share creative content and messages without taking photos
30 April 2019	Instagram launches an experiment (in Canada) hiding like and view counts for all posts in the main Instagram feed

References

Abidin, C. (2014). '#In$tagLam: Instagram as a repository of taste, a brimming marketplace, a war of eyeballs'. In M. Berry and M. Schleser (eds) *Mobile Media Making in the Age of Smartphones*. New York: Palgrave Pivot, pp. 119–28.

Abidin, C. (2015a). 'Micromicrocelebrity: Branding babies on the Internet'. *M/C Journal*, *18*(5). http://journal.media-culture.org.au/index.php/mcjournal/article/viewArticle/1022

Abidin, C. (2015b). 'Communicative <3 Intimacies: Influencers and perceived interconnectedness'. *Ada: A Journal of Gender, New Media & Technology* 8. http://adanewmedia.org/2015/11/issue8-abidin/

Abidin, C. (2016). '"Aren't these just young, rich women doing vain things online?": Influencer selfies as subversive frivolity'. *Social Media + Society*, 2(2), https://doi.org/10.1177/2056305116641342

Abidin, C. (2017a). 'Vote for my selfie: Politician selfies as charismatic engagement'. In A. Kuntsman (ed.) *Selfie Citizenship*. London: Palgrave Pivot, pp. 75–87.

Abidin, C. (2017b). '#familygoals: Family influencers, calibrated amateurism, and justifying young digital labor'. *Social Media + Society*, 3(2), https://doi.org/10.1177/2056305117707191

Abidin, C. (2017c). 'MeituXiuxiu, cultural diffusion, and Asia exotica'. *Wishcrys*, 19 January. https://wishcrys.com/2017/01/19/meituxiuxiu-cultural-diffusion-and-asia-exotica/

Abidin, C. (2017d). 'Instagram, Finstagram, and calibrated amateurism'. https://thesocietypages.org/cyborgology/2017/09/18/instagram-finstagram-and-calibrated-amateurism/

Abidin, C. (2018a). *Internet Celebrity: Understanding Fame Online*. Bingley, UK: Emerald Publishing.

Abidin, C. (2018b). 'Young people and digital grief etiquette'. In Z. Papacharissi (ed.) *A Networked Self: Birth, Life, Death*. London and New York: Routledge, pp. 160–74.

Abidin, C. and M. Ots (2016). 'Influencers tell all? Unravelling authenticity and credibility in a brand scandal'. In M. Edström, A.T. Kenyon, and E.-M. Svensson (eds) *Blurring the Lines: Market-driven and Democracy-driven Freedom of Expression*. Gothenburg: Nordic Information Centre for Media and Communication Research, pp. 153–61.

Adams, C. (2018). 'How to become a travel influencer'. *Independent*, 30 August. https://www.independent.co.uk/travel/news-and-advice/travel-influencer-how-to-instagram-social-media-advice-photos-a8514186.html

Adler, L. (2017). 'Instagram won't stop showing me the Mother's Day photos I don't want to see'. *Gizmodo*, 20 May. https://www.gizmodo.com.au/2017/05/instagram-wont-stop-showing-me-the-mothers-day-photos-i-dont-want-to-see/

Albury, K. (2015). 'Selfies, sexts, and sneaky hats: Young people's understandings of gendered practices of self-representation'. *International Journal of Communication*, 9, 1734–45.

Albury, K. and P. Byron (2016). 'Safe on my phone? Same-sex attracted young people's negotiations of intimacy, visibility, and risk on digital hook-up apps'. *Social Media + Society*, 2(4), https://doi.org/10.1177/2056305116672887

Alper, M. (2014). 'War on Instagram: Framing conflict photojournalism with mobile photography apps'. *New Media & Society*, 16(8), 1233–48.

Arnold, A. (2018). 'Here's how much instagram likes influence millennials' choice of travel destinations'. Forbes, 24 January. https://www.forbes.com/sites/andrewarnold/2018/01/24/heres-how-much-instagram-likes-influence-millennials-choice-of-travel-destinations/#43c6a3154eba

Ask, J. (2013). 'Snapchat rejects Facebook's $3B bid'. Forbes, 14 November. https://www.forbes.com/sites/forrester/2013/11/14/snapchat-rejects-facebooks-3b-bid/

Baker, S.A. and M.J. Walsh (2018). '"Good Morning Fitfam": Top posts, hashtags and gender display on Instagram'. *New Media & Society*, 20(12), 4553–70.

Barna, M. (2016). 'Instagram changed their logo and uhh … It's pretty bad'. *Huffington Post*, 19 May. https://www.huffingtonpost.com/maxwell-barna/instagram-changed-their-l_b_9996496.html

Barthes, R. (1977). *Image-Music-Text* (trans. S. Heath). London: Fontana Press.

Bartholeyns, G. (2014). 'The instant past: Nostalgia and digital retro photography'. In K. Niemeyer (ed.) *Media and Nostalgia: Yearning for the Past, Present and Future*. New York: Palgrave Macmillan, pp. 51–69.

Bayer, J.B., N.B. Ellison, S.Y. Schoenebeck and E.B. Falk (2016).

'Sharing the small moments: Ephemeral social interaction on Snapchat'. *Information, Communication & Society*, 19(7), 956–77.

BBC News (2018). 'Instagram star Daryl Aiden Yow used stock image photos'. BBC, 21 June. https://www.bbc.com/news/technology-44560852

BBC News (2019). 'Molly Russell: "Why can't I see my daughter's data?"' BBC, 6 February. https://www.bbc.com/news/av/technology-47143315/molly-russell-why-can-t-i-see-my-daughter-s-data

Belam, M. (2018). 'Tory MPs urged to behave like "real people" on Instagram'. *The Guardian*, 11 May. https://www.theguardian.com/politics/2018/may/11/tory-mps-urged-to-behave-like-real-people-on-instagram

bennozoid (2018). 'INST.i.AM: A digital ethnographic documentary'. YouTube, 8 September. https://www.youtube.com/watch?v=QN8DGIDM94Q&list=PLcalFoyBNDPmnJKmoTbDmmjXdzevjGL6s

Bereznak, A. (2017). 'Can real life compete with an Instagram playground?'. The Ringer, 9 August. https://www.theringer.com/tech/2017/8/9/16110424/instagram-playground-social-media

Berger, J. (2008). *Ways of Seeing*. Harmondsworth: Penguin Books.

Blay, Z. (2015). '12 words black people invented, and white people killed'. *Huffington Post*, 20 August. https://www.huffingtonpost.com/entry/black-slang-white-people-ruined_us_55ccda07e4b064d5910ac8b3

Blay, Z. (2016). '"White Savior Barbie" hilariously parodies volunteer selfies in Africa'. *Huffington Post*, 19 April. https://www.huffingtonpost.com.au/entry/white-savior-barbie-hilariously-parodies-volunteer-selfies-in-africa_us_570fd4b5e4b03d8b7b9fc464

Bloomberg (2018). 'Being Instagram famous is a full-time job'. YouTube, 29 November. https://www.youtube.com/watch?v=JKcNmFeKe2Y

Blum-Ross, A. and S. Livingstone (2017). '"Sharenting", parent blogging, and the boundaries of the digital self'. *Popular Communication*, 15(2), 110–25.

Bogle, A. (2016). 'All of Instagram is snapping the same pic of this damn pool in Morocco'. *Mashable*, 24 November. https://mashable.com/2016/11/24/instagram-copy-cats-pool-photo/

Bohn, D. (2012). 'Twitter dictates third-party app form and function in new API, gives six months to comply'. The Verge, 16 August. https://www.theverge.com/2012/8/16/3248079/twitter-limits-app-developers-control

Borges-Rey, E. (2015). 'News images on Instagram'. *Digital Journalism*, 3(4), 571–93.

boyd, d. (2013). *It's Complicated: The Social Lives of Networked Teens*. New Haven, CT: Yale University Press.

boyd, d. and N. Ellison (2007). 'Social network sites: Definition, history, and scholarship'. *Journal of Computer-Mediated Communication*, 13(1), 210–30.

Bratton, B.H. (2016). *The Stack: On Software and Sovereignty*. Cambridge, MA: MIT Press.

Bredl, K., C. Ketzer, J. Hunniger and J. Fleischer (2013). 'Twitter and social TV: Microblogging as a new approach to audience research'. In G. Patriarche, H. Bilandzic, J.L. Jensen and J. Jurisic (eds) *Audience Research Methodologies: Between Innovation and Consolidation*. Hoboken, NJ: Taylor & Francis, pp. 196–211.

Brinker, J.A. (2018). 'The ultimate way to grow on Instagram | Hacking the IG algorithm with methods you've never used'. YouTube, 7 November. https://www.youtube.com/watch?v=9MAlrtQ_cHg

Broadly (2017). 'Meet Coco, the six year old Instagram star'. YouTube, 15 August. https://www.youtube.com/watch?v=ut1su_ssv9Y

Brooker, L. (2014). 'Bolt, Instagram's crack at Snapchat, is out in Australia'. *Gizmodo*, 10 August. https://www.gizmodo.com.au/2014/08/bolt-instagrams-crack-at-snapchat-is-out-in-australia/

Brubaker, J.R. and V. Callison-Burch (2016). 'Legacy contact: Designing and implementing post-mortem stewardship at Facebook'. In *Proceedings of the 2016 CHI Conference on Human Factors in Computing Systems*. New York: ACM, pp. 2908–19.

Bucher, T. (2018). *If… Then: Algorithmic Power and Politics*. New York: Oxford University Press.

Burgess, J. and J. Green (2018). *YouTube: Online Video and Participatory Culture*, 2nd edn. Cambridge: Polity.

Burgess, J., A. Galloway and T. Sauter (2015). 'Hashtag as hybrid forum: The case of #agchatoz'. In N. Rambukkana (ed.) *Hashtag Publics*. New York: Peter Lang.

BuzzFeedVideo (2018). 'I spent the day with an Instagram model'. YouTube, 30 May. https://www.youtube.com/watch?v=WMBDsef6yu4

Byford, S. (2013). 'Boomf makes your Instagram photos edible'. The Verge, 27 November. https://www.theverge.com/2013/11/27/5150608/boomf-instagram-marshmallow-prints

Cade, D. (2012). 'Instagram Socialmatic: A concept design for a physical Instagram camera'. PetaPixel, 8 May. https://petapixel.com/2012/05/08/instagram-socialmatic-a-concept-design-for-a-physical-instagram-camera/

Cadena, D. (2018). 'Sephora and Museum of Ice Cream Made the Makeup Collection of Your Instagram Dreams'. Buzzfeed, 12 September. https://www.buzzfeed.com/danielacadena/sephora-teamed-up-with-museum-of-ice-cream-for-a-dreamy?utm_term=.svp2wl5wK#. os9ER6vR5

Caffier, J. (2018). 'Only "influencers" can take photos at this LA mural and people are pissed'. Vice, 27 June. https://www.vice.com/en_us/ article/zm8dwx/only-influencers-can-take-photos-at-this-la-mural-and-people-are-pissed

Carah, N. and D. Angus (2018). 'Algorithmic brand culture: Participatory labour, machine learning and branding on social media'. Media, Culture & Society, 40(2), 178–94.

Carter, N. and A. Maclean (2012). 'The photo app Facebook didn't buy: Hipstamatic'. Inc., 12 April. http://www.inc.com/nicole-carter-and-andrew-maclean/photo-app-facebook-didnt-buy-hipstamatic.html

CBC News: The National (2017). 'Social media influencers | How they make money'. YouTube, 20 March. https://www.youtube.com/watch?v=vps-6BuCT2o

Chekoufi, F. (2018). 'Meet Noonoouri, the virtual Instagram influencer loved by Kim Kardashian West and Dior'. Vogue, 19 June. https://www.vogue.com.au/vogue-codes/news/meet-noonoouri-the-virtual-instagram-influencer-loved-by-kim-kardashian-west-and-dior/news-story/dfeb2658e3bbc7b2cfd11d0d26eb5bbc

Chen, J. (2010). 'PSA: Please turn your damn cellphone sideways when recording video'. Gizmodo, 23 November. https://gizmodo.com/5697423/psa-please-turn-your-damn-cellphone-sideways-when-recording-video

Choi, G.Y. and J. Lewallen (2018). '"Say Instagram, Kids!": Examining sharenting and children's digital representations on Instagram'. Howard Journal of Communications, 29(2), 144–64.

Clark, L. (2018). 'Balmain reveals CGI models have joined the #Balmain Army'. Marie Claire, 3 September. https://www.marieclaire.com.au/balmain-reveals-cgi-models-in-new-campaign

Cobb, G.R. (2017). 'Critiquing the Thin Ideal in Pro-Anorexia Online Spaces'. PhD thesis, University of Sussex. http://sro.sussex.ac.uk/68417/

Constine, J. (2015). 'Instagram kills off feed reading apps'. TechCrunch, 18 November. http://social.techcrunch.com/2015/11/17/just-instagram/

Constine, J. (2016). 'Instagram CEO on Stories: Snapchat deserves all the credit'. TechCrunch, 2 August. http://social.techcrunch.com/2016/08/02/silicon-copy/

Constine, J. (2018a). 'Instagram will show more recent posts due to algorithm backlash'. TechCrunch, 22 March. http://social.techcrunch.com/2018/03/22/instagram-recent/

Constine, J. (2018b). 'How Instagram's algorithm works'. *TechCrunch*, 1 June. http://social.techcrunch.com/2018/06/01/how-instagram-feed-works/

Constine, J. (2018c). 'Instagram's CEO on vindication after 2 years of reinventing Stories'. *TechCrunch*, 2 August. http://social.tech crunch.com/2018/08/02/choosing-interactivity-over-photoshop/

Constine, J. (2018e). 'Snapchat and Instagram remove Giphy feature due to racial slur GIF'. *TechCrunch*, 9 March. http://social.tech crunch.com/2018/03/09/snapchat-removes-giphy-feature-due-to-racial-slur-gif/

Constine, J. (2019). 'Facebook plans new products as Instagram Stories hits 500M users/day'. *TechCrunch*, 30 January. http://social.techcrunch.com/2019/01/30/instagram-stories-500-million/

Cook, E. and C. Garduño Freeman (2011). 'Snap, post, share: Understanding the online social life of personal photography'. In D. Araya, Y. Breindl and T.J. Houghton (eds) *Nexus: New Intersections in Internet Research*. New York: Peter Lang, pp. 35–53.

Cooper, D. (2014). 'Polaroid's real-life Instagram logo camera can also print your photos'. Engadget, 16 September. https://www.engadget.com/2014/09/16/polaroid-socialmatic-hands-on/

Corner, N. (2018). 'Dior make-up mocked for using CGI influencer for beauty campaign'. *Daily Mail*, 17 December. https://www.daily mail.co.uk/femail/article-6504611/Dior-make-mocked-using-CGI-influencer-Noonoouri-social-media-beauty-campaign.html

Coscarelli, J. and M. Ryzik (2017). 'Fyre Festival, a luxury music weekend, crumbles in the Bahamas'. *The New York Times*, 28 April. https://www.nytimes.com/2017/04/28/arts/music/fyre-festival-ja-rule-bahamas.html

Cosco, J. (2018). 'Terrible marketing stunt involves a security-guarded mural in LA just for verified social media influencers'. Digg, 25 June. http://digg.com/2018/influencer-mural-la-wtf

Crawford, A. (2019). 'Instagram "helped kill my daughter"'. BBC News, 22 January. https://www.bbc.com/news/av/uk-46966009/instagram-helped-kill-my-daughter

Creed, B. (2000). 'The Cyberstar: Digital pleasures and the end of the unconscious'. *Screen*, 41(1), 79–86.

Crook, J. (2016). 'Instagram's algorithmic feed is the worst thing to happen to me all summer'. *TechCrunch*, 13 July. https://techcrunch.com/2016/07/13/instagrams-algorithmic-feed-is-the-worst-thing-to-happen-to-me-all-summer/

Cushing, E. (2015). 'On the road with the teen social-media sensations of DigiTour'. *BuzzFeed*, 2 July. https://www.buzzfeed.com/

ellencushing/sexts-hugs-and-rock-n-roll-on-the-road-with-the-teen-social

D'Onfro, J. (2013). 'Kevin Systrom explains why he killed this old Instagram logo that most people have never seen'. *Business Insider*, 11 September. https://www.businessinsider.com/old-instagram-icon-youve-never-seen-2013-9

D'Orazio, D. (2012). 'Instagram cuts off Twitter cards integration, further souring relationship'. The Verge, 5 December. https://www.theverge.com/2012/12/5/3730876/instagram-cuts-off-twitter-cards-integration-further-souring-relationship

Damsfeld, S. (2017). 'Bestfluence – Giv feedback til influencere'. simonedamsfeld.dk,15October.http://simonedamsfeld.dk/2017/10/15/bestfluence-giv-feedback-til-influencers/

Darvall, K. (2016). 'Was Instagram star's copied photos scandal fake? Online sleuths say mystery follower claim that went viral is a conspiracy'. *Daily Mail*, 19 November. https://www.dailymail.co.uk/femail/article-3951674/Australian-instagram-travel-blogger-Lauren-Bullen-slammed-fake-copy-cat-pictures-viral.html

Davis, A. (2019). 'Partnering with experts to protect people from self-harm and suicide'. Facebook Newsroom, 7 February. https://newsroom.fb.com/news/2019/02/protecting-people-from-self-harm/

Davis, J.L. and N. Jurgenson (2014). 'Context collapse: Theorizing context collusions and collisions'. *Information, Communication & Society*, 17(4), 476–85.

Davis, M., M. Finn, V. Viswanathan and M. Rothenberg (2005). MMM2: Mobile media metadata for media sharing. Presented at CHI 2005, Portland, OR, 2–7 April.

De Rosa, A. (n.d.). 'Antonio DeRosa – Polaroid Socialmatic'. Antonio DeRosa Designer. https://aderosa.myportfolio.com/polaroid-socialmatic

Deantrbl (2018). 'DEAN – instagram'. YouTube, 29 January. https://youtu.be/wKyMIrBClYw

Deller, R.A. and S. Tilton (2015). 'Selfies as charitable meme: Charity and national identity in the #nomakeupselfie and #thumbsupfor stephen campaigns'. *International Journal of Communication*, 9, 1788–805.

DeStorm Power (2012). 'DeStorm, "Instagram (Explicit)"'. YouTube, 26 June. https://youtu.be/MsCz7wnRPoQ

Dimitras, D. (2018). 'Cameron-James Wilson: The creator of the world's first digital model named Shudu'. Visual Atelier 8, 17 October. https://www.visualatelier8.com/interviews/cameron-james-wilson-creates-shudu-the-worlds-first-digital-model

Dionne, E. (2017). 'An underwater cult: How Fiona became an internet sensation'. *Bitch Media*, 2 November. https://www.bitchmedia.org/article/fiona-the-greatest-hippo-of-all-time

DiResta, R., D.K. Shaffer, B. Ruppel, D. Sullivan, R. Matney, R. Fox, J. Albright and B. Johnson (2018). *The Tactics & Tropes of the Internet Research Agency.* https://disinformationreport.blob.core.windows.net/disinformation-report/NewKnowledge-Disinformation-Report-Whitepaper.pdf

Dixon, H. and H. Horton (2018). 'Instagram mega mum quits app after claims she exploits her children'. *The Telegraph*, 22 May. https://www.telegraph.co.uk/news/2018/05/22/instagram-mega-mum-takes-account-accusations-used-children-advertising/

do it for the gram (n.d.). *Urban Dictionary.* https://www.urbandictionary.com/define.php?term=do%20it%20for%20the%20gram

Dodgson, L. (2018). 'Disappointing photos show the real, messy, unglamourous lives behind the perfect Instagram shots'. Insider, 10 September. https://www.thisisinsider.com/instagram-doesnt-show-real-life-heres-whats-behind-those-perfect-photos-2018-9#but-the-chaos-and-debris-doesnt-make-the-food-any-less-appealing-5

Doss, L. (2016). 'Every milkshake needs its own stylist: Sugar Factory's decadent shakes and burgers are Instagram-worthy'. *Miami New Times*, 19 May. https://www.miaminewtimes.com/restaurants/sugar-factorys-decadent-shakes-and-burgers-are-instagram-worthy-8467277

Douglas, N. (2014). 'It's supposed to look like shit: The Internet Ugly aesthetic'. *Journal of Visual Culture*, 13(3), 314–39.

Downs, C. and J. Koebler (2017). 'Remember Hipstamatic? It's still alive'. Motherboard, 9 October. https://motherboard.vice.com/en_us/article/wjx95x/hipstamatic-instagram-what-happened-to-hipstamatic

Dredge, S. (2018). 'Instagram stories now have 400m users…and licensed music'. 28 June. https://musically.com/2018/06/28/instagram-stories-400m-users-music/

Drill, C. (2017). 'Why did the Internet fall out of love with cats?'. *GOOD*, 10 May. https://www.good.is/features/how-the-alt-right-led-to-the-dog-internet

DuckDuckGo (2018). 'A majority of Americans don't know Facebook owns Instagram'. 9 April. https://spreadprivacy.com/facebook-instagram/

Duffy, B.E. (2017). 'The trend of fake Instagram accounts exposes the troubling way that work is taking over our lives'. *Quartz*, 30 August. https://qz.com/1065732/finstas-or-fake-instagram-accounts-expose-the-troubling-way-that-work-is-taking-over-our-lives/

Duffy, B.E. and N.K. Chan (2019). '"You never really know who's looking": Imagined surveillance across social media platforms'. *New Media & Society*, 21(1), 119–38.

Duguay, S. (2016). 'Lesbian, gay, bisexual, trans, and queer visibility through selfies: Comparing platform mediators across Ruby Rose's Instagram and Vine presence'. *Social Media + Society*, 2(2), https://doi.org/10.1177/2056305116641975

Duguay, S. (2017). 'Identity modulation in networked publics: Queer women's participation and representation on Tinder, Instagram, and Vine'. PhD thesis, Queensland University of Technology, Brisbane. https://eprints.qut.edu.au/111892/

E! News (2019). 'Rich kids of Beverly Hills'. eonline.com, n.d. https://www.eonline.com/au/shows/rich_kids_of_beverly_hills

Ekman, U. (2015). 'Complexity of the ephemeral – snap video chats'. *Empedocles: European Journal for the Philosophy of Communication*, 5(1–2), 97–101.

Elle (2018). 'Insta famous celebrities are about to be hit with a "fame tax", but how on earth will it work?'. Elle Australia, 10 May. https://www.elle.com.au/culture/budget-2018-fame-tax-17527

Eppink, J. (2014). 'A brief history of the gif (so far)'. *Journal of Visual Culture*, 13(3), 298–306.

Facebook (2012). 'Facebook to acquire Instagram'. Facebook Newsroom, 9 April. https://newsroom.fb.com/news/2012/04/facebook-to-acquire-instagram/

Facebook (2018a). 'Can I create multiple Facebook accounts?'. https://www.facebook.com/help/975828035803295?helpref=uf_permalink

Facebook (2018b). 'What names are allowed on Facebook?'. https://www.facebook.com/help/112146705538576?helpref=faq_content

Faces and Facets (2017). 'Documentary – new kings: The power of online influencers (influencer marketing)'. YouTube, 27 July. https://www.youtube.com/watch?v=JiYdBLB9oIM

Farokhmanesh, M. (2017). 'The Bow Wow challenge is a hilarious reminder that everyone lies on social media'. The Verge, 10 May. https://www.theverge.com/2017/5/10/15612724/bow-wow-challenge-social-media-lies

Federal Trade Commission (2017). 'FTC staff reminds influencers and brands to clearly disclose relationship'. ftc.gov, 19 April. https://www.ftc.gov/news-events/press-releases/2017/04/ftc-staff-reminds-influencers-brands-clearly-disclose

Feifer, J. (2013a). 'Selfies at funerals'. http://selfiesatfunerals.tumblr.com/

Feifer, J. (2013b). 'Obama's funeral selfie is a fitting end to my Tumblr

– Selfies at funerals'. *The Guardian*, 11 December. https://www.the
guardian.com/commentisfree/2013/dec/11/obama-funeral-selfie-
tumblr-mandela-teens

Fingas, J. (2013). 'Polaroid to make Socialmatic camera a reality for
fans of Instagram, recursion'. Engadget, 1 March. https://www.
engadget.com/2013/03/01/polaroid-to-make-socialmatic-camera-a-
reality/

Flanagan, A. (2017). 'A second lawsuit against Fyre Festival also targets
its "tribe" of influencers'. NPR Music, 3 May. https://www.npr.org/
sections/therecord/2017/05/03/526758059/a-second-lawsuit-
against-fyre-festival-also-targets-its-tribe-of-influencers?t=1538
566430053

Flynn, K. (2017). 'Inside the black market where people pay thousands of dollars for Instagram verification'. *Mashable*, 1 September.
https://mashable.com/2017/09/01/instagram-verification-paid-
black-market-facebook/#hPLKSNjZeqqO

Ford, C. (2016). 'Why it's hypocritical to blame Roxy Jacenko's parenting style for what happened to her daughter'. Daily Life, 18 February.
http://www.dailylife.com.au/news-and-views/dl-opinion/why-roxy-
jacenko-shouldnt-be-blamed-for-what-happened-to-her-daughter-
20160218-gmxofm.html

Friedman, M. (2016). 'This Instagram account got 58,000 followers
while secretly sending a message about drinking'. *Cosmopolitan*, 6
October. https://www.cosmopolitan.com/health-fitness/a4637276/
fake-louise-delage-instagram-alcohol-addiction-psa/

Frith, J. (2015). *Smartphones as Locative Media*. Cambridge: Polity.

Frosh, P. (2019). *The Poetics of Digital Media*. Cambridge: Polity.

Gaëlle, O. and V. Karen (2019). 'Sharenting: Parental adoration
or public humiliation? A focus group study on adolescents'
experiences with sharenting against the background of their own
impression management'. *Children and Youth Services Review*, 99,
319–27.

Garber, M. (2013). 'The edible Instagram'. *The Atlantic*, 27 November.
https://www.theatlantic.com/technology/archive/2013/11/the-
edible-instagram/281900/

Garber, M. (2014). 'Instagram was first called "Burbn"'. *The Atlantic*,
2 July. https://www.theatlantic.com/technology/archive/2014/07/
instagram-used-to-be-called-brbn/373815/

Garduño Freeman, C. (2010). 'Photosharing on Flickr: Intangible heritage and emergent publics'. *International Journal of Heritage Studies*,
16(4–5), 352–68.

Gartenberg, C. (2019). 'The Galaxy S10 will have an Instagram mode built into its camera'. The Verge, 20 February. https://www.theverge.com/circuitbreaker/2019/2/20/18233638/galaxy-s10-instagram-mode-camera-app-samsung-event-2019

Gatys, L.A., A.S. Ecker and M. Bethge (2015). 'A neural algorithm of artistic style'. *ArXiv:1508.06576 [Cs, q-Bio]*. http://arxiv.org/abs/1508.06576

Geller, M. (2018). 'Unilever takes stand against digital media's fake followers'. Reuters, 18 June. https://uk.reuters.com/article/uk-unilever-media/unilever-takes-stand-against-digital-medias-fake-followers-idUKKBN1JD10R

Gerrard, Y. (2018). 'Beyond the hashtag: Circumventing content moderation on social media'. *New Media & Society*, 20(12), 4492–511.

Gibbs, M., J. Meese, M. Arnold, B. Nansen and M. Carter (2015). '#Funeral and Instagram: Death, social media, and platform vernacular'. *Information, Communication & Society*, 18(3), 255–68.

Giedr (2017). 'Famous rapper gets caught lying about flying on private jet, and the internet's reaction is hilarious'. Bored Panda. https://www.boredpanda.com/rapper-bow-wow-challenge/?utm_source=google&utm_medium=organic&utm_campaign=organic

Gil, N. (2017). 'What is a Finstagram account and why is everyone getting one?'. *Evening Standard*, 22 February. https://www.standard.co.uk/lifestyle/london-life/what-is-a-finstagram-account-and-why-is-everyone-getting-one-a3473336.html

Gillespie, T. (2010). 'The politics of "platforms"'. *New Media & Society*, 12(3), 347–64.

Gillespie, T. (2018). *Custodians of the Internet: Platforms, Content Moderation, and the Hidden Decisions That Shape Social Media*. New Haven, CT: Yale University Press.

Godlewski, N. (2016). 'If you have over 25 photos on Instagram, you're no longer cool'. *Business Insider*, 27 May. https://www.businessinsider.com.au/teens-curate-their-instagram-accounts-2016-5

Goffman, E. (1956). *The Presentation of Self in Everyday Life*. London: Penguin Books.

Gómez Cruz, E. and E.T. Meyer (2012). 'Creation and control in the photographic process: iPhones and the emerging fifth moment of photography'. *Photographies*, 5(2), 203–21.

González-Ramírez, A. (2018). 'Love Alexandria Ocasio-Cortez's Instagram? Here's what her body language reveals'. Yahoo, 7 December. https://www.yahoo.com/lifestyle/love-alexandria-ocasio-cortez-apos-140000929.html

Gould-Bourn, J. (n.d.) 'Couple freaks out after realizing someone follows them around the world just to copy their travel photos'.

Bored Panda. https://www.boredpanda.com/copycat-instagram-tra vel-photos-doyoutravel-gypsealust/?utm_source=google&utm_ medium=organic&utm_campaign=organic

Greer, S. (2018). 'How Instagram hides behind Facebook – and rakes in billions'. *The Guardian*, 1 December. https://www.theguardian. com/technology/2018/dec/01/instagram-facebook-controversy-social-network-tech

Gries, L.E. (2015). *Still Life with Rhetoric: A New Materialist Approach for Visual Rhetorics*. Boulder, CO: University Press of Colorado.

Grossman, S. (2015). 'Instagram now allows photos of women breast-feeding'. *Time*, 16 April. http://time.com/3825923/instagram-women-breastfeeding-photos/

Guarini, D. (2012). 'Instagram's popularity sparks secondary market for photo printers'. *Huffington Post*, 17 April. https://www.huff ingtonpost.com/2012/04/17/instagram-secondary-market-photo-printers_n_1432525.html

Haimson, O.L. and A.L. Hoffmann (2016). 'Constructing and enforc-ing "authentic" identity online: Facebook, real names, and non-normative identities'. *First Monday*, 21(6), https://doi.org/10.5210/ fm.v21i6.6791

Halpern, M. and L. Humphreys (2016). 'Iphoneography as an emer-gent art world'. *New Media & Society*, 18(1), 62–81.

Hamburger, E. (2014). 'This is Bolt, Instagram's new messaging app'. The Verge, 29 July. https://www.theverge.com/2014/7/29/5948845/ this-is-bolt-instagrams-new-messaging-app

Hand, M. (2012). *Ubiquitous Photography*. Cambridge: Polity.

Handyside, S. and J. Ringrose (2017). 'Snapchat memory and youth digital sexual cultures: Mediated temporality, duration and affect'. *Journal of Gender Studies*, 26, 347–60.

Harman, J. (2015). 'The crazy way teens are hiding their imperfections online: Finstagram'. *Elle*, 9 July. https://www.elle.com/culture/ tech/a29243/finstagram/

Harper, S. (2016). 'The world's most amazing 100% awesome photog-raphy theory'. *Photographies*, 9(3), 327–48.

Harvey-Jenner, C. (2016). 'Blogger Lauren Bullen of Gypsea Lust denies claims the copycat Instagram pictures story is fake'. *Cosmopolitan*, 18 November. https://www.cosmopolitan.com/uk/ entertainment/news/a47410/lauren-bullen-gypsea-lust-copycat-instagram-pictures-denies-fake/

Heath, A. (2014). 'Cole Rise on Instagram fame and creating Litely, the hottest new photography app'. 30 May. https://www.cultofmac. com/280994/cole-rise/

Hern, A. (2019). 'Facebook to integrate Instagram, Messenger and WhatsApp'. *The Guardian*, 25 January. https://www.theguardian.com/technology/2019/jan/25/facebook-integrate-instagram-messenger-whatsapp-messaging-platforms

Hess, A. (2018). 'The existential void of the pop-up "experience"'. *The New York Times*, 26 September. https://www.nytimes.com/2018/09/26/arts/color-factory-museum-of-ice-cream-rose-mansion-29rooms-candytopia.html

Highfield, T. (2016). *Social Media and Everyday Politics*. Cambridge: Polity.

Highfield, T. (2017). 'Social TV and depictions of community on social media: Instagram and Eurovision fandom'. In P. Messaris and L. Humphreys (eds) *Digital Media: Transformations in human communication*, 2nd edn. New York: Peter Lang, pp. 156–65.

Highfield, T. (2018). 'Emoji hashtags // hashtag emoji: Of platforms, visual affect, and discursive flexibility'. *First Monday*, 23(9), https://doi.org/10.5210/fm.v23i9.9398

Highfield, T. and T. Leaver (2015). 'A methodology for mapping Instagram hashtags'. *First Monday*, 20(1), http://dx.doi.org/10.5210/fm.v20i1.5563

Highfield, T. and T. Leaver (2016). 'Instagrammatics and digital methods: Studying visual social media, from selfies and GIFs to memes and emoji'. *Communication Research and Practice*, 2(1), 47–62.

Hinchliffe, E. (2016). 'Instagram is killing a big feature'. *Mashable*, 6 September. https://mashable.com/2016/09/06/instagram-kills-photo-maps/

Hochman, N. and L. Manovich (2013). 'Zooming into an Instagram city: Reading the local through social media'. *First Monday*, 18(7), doi:10.5210/fm.v18i7.4711

hodayum (2018). 'A white photographer figured out a way to profit off of black women without ever having to pay one. Now pls, tell me how our economic system is in no way built on and quite frankly reliant on racism and misogyny [Tweet]. 28 February. https://twitter.com/hodayum/status/968567361921052674

Holden, L. (2017). 'SLO Donut Co.'s marshmallow galaxy doughnuts are a big hit online'. *The Tribune*, 9 May. https://www.sanluisobispo.com/living/food-drink/article149637024.html

Holmes, L. (2017). 'Instagram's new mental health campaign is just what our phones need'. *Huffington Post*, 10 May. https://www.huffingtonpost.com.au/entry/instagram-mental-health-campaign_us_5911d484e4b0a58297df8719

Holpuch, A. (2015). 'Facebook adjusts controversial "real name" policy in wake of criticism'. *The Guardian*, 15 December. https://www.theguardian.com/us-news/2015/dec/15/facebook-change-controversial-real-name-policy

Hooper, C. (2017). *How to Grow a Baby and Push It Out: A Guide to Pregnancy and Birth Straight from the Midwife's Mouth*. London: Vermilion.

Hooper, S. (2018). *Forever Outnumbered: Tales of Our Family Life from Instagram's Father of Daughters*. London: Coronet Books.

Hopkins, J. and N. Thomas (2011). 'Fielding networked marketing: Technology and authenticity in the monetization of Malaysian blogs'. In D. Araya, Y. Breindi and J. Tessa (eds) *Nexus: New Intersections in Internet Research*. New York: Peter Lang, pp. 139–56.

Horst, H.A. (2016). 'Mobile intimacies: Everyday design and the aesthetics of mobile phones'. In S. Pink, E. Ardèvol and D. Lanzeni (eds) *Digital Materialities: Design and Anthropology*. London: Bloomsbury, pp. 159–74.

Horton, A. (2018). 'Putin made a show of crossing the new Crimea bridge. But he was upstaged by a cat'. *Washington Post*, 16 May. https://www.washingtonpost.com/news/worldviews/wp/2018/05/16/putin-made-a-show-of-crossing-the-new-crimea-bridge-but-he-was-upstaged-by-a-cat/

Horton, D. and R.R. Wohl (1956). 'Mass communication and para-social interaction: Observations on intimacy at a distance'. *Psychiatry: Interpersonal and Biological Processes*, 19(3), 215–29.

How, M. (2018). 'S'porean influencer Andrea Chong finally says something about Daryl Aiden Yow saga'. Mothership, 22 June. https://mothership.sg/2018/06/andrea-chong-daryl-aiden-yow/

Howard, P.N., B. Ganesh, D. Liotsiou, J. Kelly and C. François (2018). *The IRA, Social Media and Political Polarization in the United States, 2012–2018*. Computational Propaganda Research Project, Oxford University.

Hughes, J. (2016). 'Vine dries up. Black humor loses a home'. *The New York Times*, 31 October. https://www.nytimes.com/2016/11/01/arts/vine-jay-versace-black-culture.html

Hui, M. (2018). 'Public housing for some, Instagram selfie backdrop for others'. *The New York Times*, 9 August. https://www.nytimes.com/2018/08/09/world/asia/hong-kong-instagram-photography.html

Humphreys, L. (2018). *The Qualified Self: Social Media and the Accounting of Everyday Life*. Cambridge, MA: MIT Press.

Hunt, E. (2016). 'Who is Louise Delage? New Instagram influencer

not what she seems'. *The Guardian*, 6 October. https://www.the
guardian.com/technology/2016/oct/06/shell-drink-to-that-fake-
instagram-louise-delage-profile-highlights-alcoholism

Hyde, M. (2016). 'Boomf! James Middleton's printed marshmallow
business puffed up by investors'. *The Guardian*, 6 May. https://
www.theguardian.com/lifeandstyle/lostinshowbiz/2016/may/06/
james-middleton-boomf-printed-marshmallow

Ian (2016). 'Designing a new look for Instagram, inspired by the community'. 11 May. https://medium.com/@ianspalter/designing-a-
new-look-for-instagram-inspired-by-the-community-84530eb355e3

iKON (2017). 'BOBBY – LOVE AND FALL "텐데(TENDAE)"'. YouTube,
19 September. https://www.youtube.com/watch?v=1P3bBpLDpWs

Instagram (2015). 'Three new filters and emoji hashtags'. *Instagram Info
Center*, 27 April. https://instagram-press.com/blog/2015/04/27/
three-new-filters-and-emoji-hashtags/

Instagram (2016a). 'Frequently asked questions'. https://www.insta
gram.com/about/faq/

Instagram (2018a). 'About eating disorders'. https://help.instagram.
com/252214974954612/?helpref=hc_fnav&bc[0]=3683906265779
68&bc[1]=285881641526716

Instagram (2018b). 'Community Guidelines'. https://help.instagram.
com/477434105621119/

Instagram (2018c). 'Know how to talk with your teen about Instagram:
A parent's guide'. 6 September. https://wellbeing.instagram.com/
parents

Instagram (2018d). 'Sharing your election day excitement on
Instagram'. *Instagram Info Center*, 1 November. https://instagram-
press.com/blog/2018/11/01/sharing-your-election-day-excitement-
on-instagram/

Instagram (2018e). 'Terms of use'. https://help.instagram.com/478745
558852511

Instagram (2019a). 'How do I access or review my data on Instagram?'.
https://help.instagram.com/181231772500920

Instagram (2019b). 'How do I report a deceased person's account on
Instagram?'. https://help.instagram.com/264154560391256

Isaac, M. and D. Wakabayashi (2017). 'Russian influence reached 126
million through Facebook alone'. *The New York Times*, 31 October.
https://www.nytimes.com/2017/10/30/technology/facebook-
google-russia.html

Isador, G. (2017). 'We asked people why they post thirst traps'. Vice, 27
February. https://www.vice.com/en_uk/article/wnkej4/we-asked-
people-why-they-post-thirst-traps

Jackson, L.M. (2018). 'Shudu Gram is a white man's digital projection of real-life black womanhood'. *The New Yorker*, 4 May. https://www. newyorker.com/culture/culture-desk/shudu-gram-is-a-white-mans-digital-projection-of-real-life-black-womanhood

Jean (2016). 'What's a Finsta? And does your teen have one?' *Be Web Smart*, 16 May. http://www.bewebsmart.com/social-media/insta gram-social-media/what-is-a-finsta/

JodyHighRoller (2014). 'RiFF RAFF x DJ Noodles, "iNSTAGRAM"'. YouTube, 2 May. https://youtu.be/Ks3cz9-voFg

Joelynn (2018). 'Influencer Daryl Aiden Yow admits paying for stock images to create composite photos'. Must Share News, 20 June. https://mustsharenews.com/daryl-aiden-yow-plagiarism/

John, N.A. (2017). *The Age of Sharing*. Cambridge: Polity.

Johnson, L. (2016). 'How a sweet, simple Instagram photo gave rise to a sweeping global travel brand'. *Adweek*, 4 July. https://www. adweek.com/digital/how-sweet-simple-instagram-photo-gave-rise-sweeping-global-travel-brand-172124/

Johnson, S.A. (2014). '"Maternal devices", social media and the self-management of pregnancy, mothering and child health'. *Societies*, 4(2), 330–50.

Johnston, C. (2016). 'Snapchat, Instagram Stories, and the Internet of Forgetting'. *The New Yorker*, 5 August. https://www.newyorker. com/tech/elements/snapchat-instagram-stories-and-the-internet-of-forgetting

Kanai, A. (2015a). 'Jennifer Lawrence, remixed: Approaching celebrity through DIY digital culture'. *Celebrity Studies*, 6(3), 322–40.

Kanai, A. (2015b). 'WhatShouldWeCallMe? Self-branding, individuality and belonging in youthful femininities on Tumblr'. *M/C Journal*, 18(1), http://journal.media-culture.org.au/index.php/mcjournal/article/view/936

Karp, H. (2017). 'At up to $250,000 a ticket, island music festival woos wealthy to stay afloat'. *Wall Street Journal*, 2 April. https://www. wsj.com/articles/fyre-festival-organizers-push-to-keep-it-from-fizzling-1491130804

Kasra, M. (2017). 'Digital-networked images as personal acts of political expression: New categories for meaning formation'. *Media and Communication*, 5(4), 51–64.

Kelly, C. (2012). 'Christmas cookies, designed by Instagram'. *The Washington Post*, 29 November. https://www.washingtonpost.com/blogs/all-we-can-eat/post/christmas-cookies-decorated-by-instagra m/2012/11/29/2e6b3bdc-397c-11e2-a263-f0ebffed2f15_blog.html

Kircher, M.M. (2015). 'Teens are hiding their real lives from nosey parents with "fake" Instagram accounts'. *Business Insider*, 15 September. https://www.businessinsider.com/teens-hiding-real-lives-on-finsta gram-2015-9?r=US&IR=T&IR=T

Kircher, M.M. (2017). 'Instagram really, really wants you to create a second account'. *Nymag*, 5 May. http://nymag.com/selectall/2017/ 05/instagram-wants-users-to-make-second-finstagram-accounts. html

Klara, R. (2018). 'After 2 years, has everyone finally chilled out about the Instagram logo?'. *Adweek*, 27 February. https://www.adweek. com/brand-marketing/after-2-years-has-everyone-finally-chilled-out-about-the-instagram-logo/

Know Your Meme (2017). '#BowWowChallenge'. Know Your Meme, n.d. https://knowyourmeme.com/memes/bowwowchallenge

Koh, S. (2018). 'Selfie Museum KL – Malaysia's version of NYC's viral Ice Cream Museum is only open till Feb 2019'. The Smart Local, 29 October. https://thesmartlocal.com/read/selfie-museum-kl

Kohnhorst, A. (2018). 'Café provides backdrops and bathrobes for fake luxury Instagram pics'. Radiichina, 25 October. https://radiichina. com/cafe-provides-backdrops-and-bathrobes-for-fake-luxury-insta gram-pics/

Kraus, R. (2019). 'Germany orders Facebook to stop combining user data from multiple sources into one'. *Mashable*, 8 February. https:// mashable.com/article/germany-orders-facebook-stop-combin ing-user-data/

Kreems, N. (2018). 'The secret Instagram account selling Black Metal-inspired Biryani'. *Vice.com*, 22 August. https://munchies.vice.com/ en_uk/article/ev89m7/singapores-best-biryani-comes-from-a-secret-instagram-account?utm_campaign=sharebutton

Kress, G.R. and T. van Leeuwen (2006). *Reading Images: The Grammar of Visual Design*. New York: Routledge.

Lakritz, T. (2016). 'There's something fishy about this copycat travel blogger story that everyone is talking about'. Insider, 17 November. https://www.thisisinsider.com/travel-blogger-fishy-claims-about-copycat-2016-11

Larsen, J. (2008). 'Practices and flows of digital photography: An eth-nographic framework'. *Mobilities*, 3(1), 141–60.

Larsson, A.O. (2017). 'Skiing all the way to the polls: Exploring the popularity of personalized posts on political Instagram accounts'. *Convergence: The International Journal of Research into New Media Technologies*, https://doi.org/10.1177/1354856517741132

Lay, B. (2015). 'MP Baey Yam Keng clarifies Eiffel Tower picture wasn't photoshopped, but it has started'. Mothership, 16 November.

https://mothership.sg/2015/11/mp-baey-yam-keng-clarifies-eiffel-tower-picture-wasnt-photoshopped-but-it-has-started/

Lay, B. (2018). 'How MP Baey Yam Keng Instagram game's on fleek? After wild doggo, comes pupper'. Mothership, 12 January. https://mothership.sg/2018/01/baey-yam-keng-stray-dogs/

Leaver, T. (2012). *Artificial Culture: Identity, Technology, and Bodies.* London: Routledge.

Leaver, T. (2013). 'The social media contradiction: Data mining and digital death'. *M/C Journal*, 16(2). http://journal.media-culture.org.au/index.php/mcjournal/article/viewArticle/625

Leaver, T. (2015). 'Born digital? Presence, privacy, and intimate surveillance'. In J. Hartley and W. Qu (eds) *Re-Orientation: Translingual Transcultural Transmedia: Studies in Narrative, Language, Identity, and Knowledge.* Shanghai: Fudan University Press, pp. 149–60.

Leaver, T. (2019). 'Co-creating birth and death on social media'. In Z. Papacharissi (ed.) *A Networked Self and Birth, Life, Death.* New York: Routledge, pp. 35–49.

Leaver, T. and T. Highfield (2018). 'Visualising the ends of identity: Pre-birth and post-death on Instagram'. *Information, Communication & Society*, 21(1), 30–45.

Lee, D. (2014). 'Instagram deletes millions of accounts in spam purge'. BBC News, 19 December. https://www.bbc.com/news/technology-30548463

Lee, J., W.C. Goh, J. Wee and R. Ng (2018). 'S'pore photographer Daryl Aiden Yow's pics are so lovely, they look stunningly like other people's work'. Mothership, 20 June. https://mothership.sg/2018/06/daryl-aiden-yow-instagram-photos-singapore/

Levin, S. (2017). 'Fyre festival: Social media "influencers" traded posts for lavish perks'. *The Guardian*, 2 May. https://www.theguardian.com/culture/2017/may/01/fyre-festival-social-media-influencers-paid-content

Liebhart, K. and P. Bernhardt (2017). 'Political storytelling on Instagram: Key aspects of Alexander Van der Bellen's successful 2016 presidential election campaign'. *Media and Communication*, 5(4), 15–25.

Light, B., J. Burgess and S. Duguay (2018). 'The walkthrough method: An approach to the study of apps'. *New Media & Society*, 20(3), 881–900.

lilmiquela (2018a). 'Are you kidding me??? No. No I'm sorry you don't get to be hurt right now'. Instagram, 20 April. https://www.instagram.com/p/BhzelQ5lCi2/

lilmiquela (2018b). 'I'm thinking about everything that has happened and though this is scary for me to do, I know I owe you guys more honesty'. Instagram, 20 April. https://www.instagram.com/p/BhzyxKoFIIT/

Lin, SJ (2018). '10 photographs taken in Singapore to bluff your friends that you're in Japan'. The Smart Local, 3 May. https://thesmartlocal.com/read/bluff-friends-japan

Locatelli, E. (2017). 'Images of breastfeeding on Instagram: Self-representation, publicness, and privacy management'. *Social Media + Society*, 3(2). https://doi.org/10.1177/2056305117707190

Lomas, N. (2016). 'Prisma uses AI to turn your photos into graphic novel fodder double quick'. *TechCrunch*, 24 June. http://social.techcrunch.com/2016/06/24/prisma-uses-ai-to-turn-your-photos-into-graphic-novel-fodder-double-quick/

Lomas, N. (2019). 'Instagram's Adam Mosseri to meet UK health secretary over suicide content concerns'. *TechCrunch*, 4 February. http://social.techcrunch.com/2019/02/04/instagrams-adam-mosseri-to-meet-uk-health-secretary-over-suicide-content-concerns/

Lorenz, T. (2018a). 'Why some of Instagram's biggest members are locking their accounts'. *The Atlantic*, 12 July. https://www.the-atlantic.com/technology/archive/2018/07/why-some-of-instagrams-biggest-memers-are-locking-their-accounts/564995/

Lorenz, T. (2018b). 'The teens who rack up thousands of followers by posting the same photo every day'. *The Atlantic*, 4 October. https://www.theatlantic.com/technology/archive/2018/10/teens-who-post-same-thing-every-day-instagram/572155/

Lorenz, T. (2018c). 'The voting-sticker thirst trap is here'. *The Atlantic*, 6 November. https://www.theatlantic.com/technology/archive/2018/11/voting-sticker-thirst-trap-here/575080/

Losh, E. (2015). 'Feminism reads big data, selfiecity'. *International Journal of Communication*, 9, 1647–59.

Luckhurst, P. (2017). '@Why everyone needs a FINstaGRAM account'. *Evening Standard*, 20 April. https://www.standard.co.uk/lifestyle/esmagazine/why-everyone-needs-a-finstagram-account-a3517176.html

Lupton, D. (2013). *The Social Worlds of the Unborn*. Basingstoke: Palgrave Macmillan.

Maares, P. and F. Hanusch (2018). 'Exploring the boundaries of journalism: Instagram micro-bloggers in the twilight zone of lifestyle journalism'. *Journalism*, https://doi.org/10.1177/1464884918801400

MacCannell, D. (1973). 'Staged authenticity: Arrangements of social space in tourist settings'. *American Journal of Sociology*, 79(3), 589–603.

MacDowall, L.J. and P. de Souza (2018). '"I'd double tap that!!": Street art, graffiti, and Instagram research'. *Media, Culture & Society*, 40(1), 3–22.

Mackie, B. (2018). 'Is Instagram changing the way we design the world?'. *The Guardian*, 12 July. https://www.theguardian.com/life andstyle/2018/jul/12/ready-for-your-selfie-why-public-spaces-are-being-insta-designed

Maddox, J. (2017). '"Guns don't kill people…selfies do": Rethinking narcissism as exhibitionism in selfie-related deaths'. *Critical Studies in Media Communication*, 34(3), 193–205.

Maheshwari, S. (2018). 'A penthouse made for Instagram'. *The New York Times*, 30 September. https://www.nytimes.com/2018/09/30/business/media/instagram-influencers-penthouse.html

Mandon, L.Z. (2017). '10 artsy photographs you can take at the Yayoi Kusama Exhibit at National Gallery Singapore'. The Smart Local, 18 July. https://thesmartlocal.com/read/yayoi-kusama

Manovich, L. (2017). *Instagram and Contemporary Image*. http://manovich.net/index.php/projects/instagram-and-contemporary-image

Manovich, L., M. Stefaner, M. Yazdani, D. Baur, D. Goddemeyer, A. Tifentale, … J. Chow (2014). Selfiecity. http://selfiecity.net/

Marcon, A.R., M. Bieber and M.B. Azad (2019). 'Protecting, promoting, and supporting breastfeeding on Instagram'. *Maternal & Child Nutrition*, 15(1), e12658.

Marriner, C. (2016). 'How Roxy Jacenko inadvertently became pin-up girl for oversharing on social media'. *The Sydney Morning Herald*, 21 February. http://www.smh.com.au/nsw/how-roxy-jacenko-inadvertently-became-pinup-girl-for-oversharing-on-social-media-2016 0219-gmyn2b.html

Marwick, A.E. (2013). *Status Update: Celebrity, Publicity, and Branding in the Social Media Age*. New Haven, CT: Yale University Press.

Marwick, A.E. and d. boyd (2011). 'I tweet honestly, I tweet passionately: Twitter users, context collapse, and the imagined audience'. *New Media & Society*, 13(1), 114–33.

Meese, J. (2014). '"It Belongs to the Internet": Animal images, attribution norms and the politics of amateur media production'. *M/C Journal*, 17(2), http://journal.media-culture.org.au/index.php/mcjournal/article/viewArticle/782

Meese, J., M. Gibbs, M. Carter, M. Arnold, B. Nansen and T. Kohn (2015). 'Selfies at funerals: Mourning and presencing on social media platforms'. *International Journal of Communication*, 9, https://ijoc.org/index.php/ijoc/article/view/3154/1402

Milner, R.M. (2016). *The World Made Meme: Public Conversations and Participatory Media*. Cambridge, MA: MIT Press.

Miltner, K.M. (2014). '"There's no place for lulz on LOLCats": The role of genre, gender, and group identity in the interpretation and enjoyment of an Internet meme'. *First Monday*, 19(8), http://firstmonday. org/ojs/index.php/fm/article/view/5391/4103

Miltner, K.M. and T. Highfield (2017). 'Never gonna GIF you up: Analyzing the cultural significance of the animated GIF'. *Social Media + Society*, 3(3), https://doi.org/10.1177/2056305117725223

Mirzoeff, N. (2015). *How to See the World*. Harmondsworth: Penguin Books.

Mitchell, P. and T. Highfield (2017). 'Mediated geographies of everyday life: Navigating the ambient, augmented and algorithmic geographies of geomedia'. *Ctrl-Z*, 7, http://www.ctrl-z.net.au//journal?slug=mitchell-highfield-mediated-geographies-of-everyday-life

Molloy, M. (2017). 'Bow Wow Challenge: Rapper mocked over "fake" private jet photo with memes'. *The Telegraph*, 11 May. https://www.telegraph.co.uk/men/the-filter/bow-wow-challenge-rapper-mocked-fake-private-jet-photo-memes/

Moore, H. (2016). '"It's fainting when you get out of bed and vomiting all the time": Teenage girl with chronic fatigue syndrome spends her days house-bound in constant pain – but says other people "think she's just tired"'. *Daily Mail*, 14 May. https://www.dailymail.co.uk/news/article-3590259/Teenage-girl-battling-chronic-fatigue-leaves-wheelchair-bound.html

Morris, H. (2017). '14 photographs that prove everything you've seen on Instagram is a lie'. *The Telegraph*, 24 November. https://www.telegraph.co.uk/travel/news/Instagram-vs-reality-how-travel-photos-are-a-lie/

Mosseri, A. (2019a). 'Our commitment to protect the most vulnerable on Instagram'. *The Telegraph*, 4 February. https://www.telegraph.co.uk/news/2019/02/04/changing-instagram-support-people-tormented-suicidal-thoughts/

Mosseri, A. (2019b). 'Changes we're making to do more to support and protect the most vulnerable people who use Instagram'. Instagram, 7 February. https://instagram-press.com/blog/2019/02/07/changes-were-making-to-do-more-to-support-and-protect-the-most-vulnerable-people-who-use-instagram/

Murabayashi, A. (2018). 'Think all the photos on Instagram look the same? So does she'. Photo Shelter, 24 July. https://petapixel.com/2018/07/26/this-instagram-account-shows-how-instagram-photos-look-the-same/

Murdoch, C. (2017). 'Heads up, weirdos: Tindstagramming will definitely not help you convince that girl that she should date you'. *Mashable*, 27 September. https://mashable.com/2017/09/26/tindsta gramming-new-dating-trend/#Vk6NgKd55aqo

Murphy, M. (2018). 'You are not original or creative on Instagram'. *Quartz*, 8 August. https://qz.com/quartzy/1349585/you-are-not-original-or-creative-on-instagram/

Must Share News (2018a). 'There's now a #DarylAidenChallenge hashtag full of hilarious photoshops'. Must Share News, 20 June. https://mustsharenews.com/daryl-aiden-challenge/

Must Share News (2018b). '"I was wrong," says Daryl Aiden Yow; No word yet if clients aware of his practices'. Must Share News, 20 June. https://mustsharenews.com/daryl-aiden-yow-apology/

Nasir, K.M. and B.T. Turner (2011). 'Governing as gardening: Reflections on soft authoritarianism in Singapore'. *Citizenship Studies*, 17(3–4), 339–52.

Nazren, F. (2018). 'We inspect Daryl Aiden Yow's Instagram for disappearing posts and growth patterns'. Mothership, 20 June. https://mothership.sg/2018/06/daryl-aiden-yow-instagram-delete/

Neal, B. (2018). 'The #MyFavoriteMeds hashtag on Instagram is a powerful message about ending mental health medication shaming'. Bustle, 20 December. https://www.bustle.com/p/the-myfavorite meds-hashtag-on-instagram-is-a-powerful-message-about-ending-mental-health-medication-shaming-15521701

Newton, C. (2014). 'Facebook clarifies real name policy amid LGBT protests'. The Verge, 1 October. https://www.theverge. com/2014/10/1/6881641/facebook-will-update-real-name-policy-to-accommodate-lgbt-community

Newton, C. (2017). 'Instagram is pushing restaurants to be kitschy, colorful, and irresistible to photographers'. The Verge, 20 July. https://www.theverge.com/2017/7/20/16000552/instagram-res taurant-interior-design-photo-friendly-media-noche

Nicholl, K. (2014). 'James Middleton reveals himself as mastermind behind Boomf, a customized-marshmallow company'. *Vanity Fair*, 24 January. https://www.vanityfair.com/news/2014/01/james-middleton-boomf-marshmallow

Nightingale, V. (2007). 'The cameraphone and online image sharing'. *Continuum*, 21(2), 289–301.

Noble, S.U. (2018). *Algorithms of Oppression: How Search Engines Reinforce Racism*. New York: NYU Press.

Nonstop Living (n.d.) 'Instagram vs. reality: Three shocking truths behind travel photos'. Nonstop-Living. https://nonstop-living.com/instagram-vs-reality/

Nudd, T. (2016). 'Instagram's new logo is a travesty. Can we change it back? Please?'. *Adweek*, 11 May. https://www.adweek.com/brand-marketing/instagrams-new-logo-travesty-can-we-change-it-back-please-171398/

NZ Herald (2018). 'First baby poses in new Instagram snap with Prime Minister Jacinda Ardern and midwife'. *NZ Herald*, 22 June. https://www.nzherald.co.nz/nz/news/article.cfm?c_id=1&objectid=12075992

Olszanowski, M. (2014). 'Feminist self-imaging and Instagram: Tactics of circumventing sensorship'. *Visual Communication Quarterly*, 21(2), 83–95.

Olszanowski, M. (2015). 'The 1x1 common: The role of Instagram's hashtag in the development and maintenance of feminist exchange'. In N. Rambukkana (ed.) *Hashtag Publics: The Power and Politics of Discursive Networks*. New York: Peter Lang, pp. 229–42.

Ong, T. (2018). 'Influencers & photographers speak out on S'pore photographer Daryl Aiden Yow saga'. Mothership, 20 June. https://mothership.sg/2018/06/influencers-photographers-media-industry-daryl-aiden-yow-photography/

Orton-Johnson, K. (2017). 'Mummy blogs and representations of motherhood: "Bad mummies" and their readers'. *Social Media + Society*, 3(2), https://doi.org/10.1177/2056305117707186

Pachal, P. (2016). 'What the designer of the old Instagram icon thinks of the new one'. *Mashable*, 11 May. https://mashable.com/2016/05/11/instagram-old-icon-designer/#HItnKBc.lZqU

Parcq, A. du and B. London (2018). 'The man behind Shudu Gram & the world's first "digital supermodels" reveals the secrets behind his stratospheric success'. *Glamour Magazine*, 13 September. https://www.glamourmagazine.co.uk/article/shudu-gram-virtual-super models

Pardes, A. (2017). 'The rise of the made-for-Instagram museum'. *Wired*, 27 September. https://www.wired.com/story/selfie-factories-instagram-museum/

Pardes, A. (2018). 'How to "regram" a photo on Instagram'. *Wired*, 18 March. https://www.wired.com/story/how-to-regram-on-instagram/

Parkinson, H.J. (2014). 'Instagram purge costs celebrities millions of followers'. *The Guardian*, 19 December. https://www.theguardian.com/technology/2014/dec/19/instagram-purge-costs-celebrities-millions-of-followers

Parkinson, H.J. (2016). 'Instagram unveils new logo, but it's not quite picture perfect'. *The Guardian*, 11 May. http://www.theguardian.com/technology/2016/may/11/instagram-new-logo-photo-sharing-app

Pearce, W., S.M. Özkula, A.K. Greene, L. Teeling, J.S. Bansard, J.J. Omena and E.T. Rabello (2018). 'Visual cross-platform analysis: Digital methods to research social media images'. *Information, Communication & Society*, https://doi.org/10.1080/1369118X.2018.1486871

Pearson, E. (2018). 'Shoefies and Huis: crafting community participation from the ground up'. *Communication Research and Practice*, 4(2), 117–31.

Perkins, G. (2018). 'Grow your Instagram ORGANICALLY in 2018 (How to work WITH the Instagram algorithm)'. YouTube, 15 February. https://www.youtube.com/watch?v=VPIZFelfEbs

Perry, D.M. (2018). 'Alexandria Ocasio-Cortez has mastered the politics of digital intimacy'. *Pacific Standard*, 30 November. https://psmag.com/social-justice/alexandria-ocasio-cortez-has-mastered-the-politics-of-digital-intimacy

Phillips, W. (2015). *This Is Why We Can't Have Nice Things: Mapping the Relationship between Online Trolling and Mainstream Culture*. Cambridge, MA: MIT Press.

Phillips, W. and R.M. Milner (2017). *The Ambivalent Internet: Mischief, Oddity, and Antagonism Online*. Cambridge: Polity.

Polaroid (n.d.). 'Polaroid Socialmatic Camera'. https://polaroid.com/socialmatic

Postman, N. (1984). *Amusing Ourselves to Death: Public Discourse in the Age of Show Business*. London: Heinemann.

Poulsen, S.V. (2018). 'Becoming a semiotic technology – A historical study of Instagram's tools for making and sharing photos and videos'. *Internet Histories*, 2(1–2), 121–39.

Preston, K. (2018). 'NZ PM Jacinda Arden shares adorable drawing from fan on Instagram'. Nine.com.au, 18 September. https://honey.nine.com.au/2018/09/18/11/08/jacinda-ardern-instagram-drawing

Price, E. (2018). 'Musical.ly and TikTok are merging into a short-video powerhouse'. *Fast Company*, 2 August. https://www.fastcompany.com/90212600/musical-ly-and-tiktok-are-merging-into-a-short-video-powerhouse

Purtill, J. (2017). 'Instafamous must reveal #ads under new transparency rules'. ABC, 1 March. https://www.abc.net.au/triplej/programs/hack/social-influencers-must-reveal-ad-under-new-transparency-rules/8315962

Ranadive, A. and D. Ginsberg (2018). 'New tools to manage your time on Facebook and Instagram'. *Facebook Newsroom*, 1 August. https://newsroom.fb.com/news/2018/08/manage-your-time/

Read, B. (2018). '2018's biggest Instagram influencers are these congressional freshmen women'. *Vogue*, 21 November. https://www.vogue.com/article/alexandria-ocasio-cortez-instagram-rashida-tlaib-ilhan-omar-ayanna-pressley-influencers

Refinery29 (2018). 'The truth behind Instagram-famous plastic surgeons | Shady | Refinery29'. YouTube, 23 June. https://www.youtube.com/watch?v=zyKjMVyDJx8

Reinstein, J. (2018). 'Teachers are moonlighting as Instagram influencers to make ends meet'. Buzzfeed News, 31 August. https://www.buzzfeednews.com/article/juliareinstein/teachers-instagram-influencers-school-tpt-pinterest

Relatable (2019). 'We transform influencer marketing into a global scalable media channel'. Relatable.me. https://www.relatable.me/

Relman, E. (2018). 'Alexandria Ocasio-Cortez is using Instagram stories to bring you behind the curtain of Washington, DC, establishment'. *Business Insider*, 15 November. https://www.businessinsider.com/alexandria-ocasio-cortez-instagram-stories-washington-dc-2018-11/?r=AU&IR=T

Rettberg, J.W. (2014). *Seeing Ourselves Through Technology: How We Use Selfies, Blogs and Wearable Devices to See and Shape Ourselves.* Basingstoke: Palgrave Macmillan.

Rettberg, J.W. (2017). 'Hand signs for lip-syncing: The emergence of a gestural language on Musical.ly as a video-based equivalent to emoji'. *Social Media + Society*, 3(4), https://doi.org/10.1177/2056305117735751

Rettberg, J.W. (2018). 'Snapchat: Phatic communication and ephemeral social media'. In J.W. Morris and S. Murray (eds) *Appified: Culture in the Age of Apps.* Ann Arbor, MI: University of Michigan Press, pp. 188–96.

Richardson, D. (2017). 'Blame the Fyre Festival fiasco on the plague of celebrity influencers'. Wired, 5 April. https://www.wired.com/2017/05/blame-fyre-festival-fiasco-plague-celebrity-influencers/

Ripples (2018). 'Ripple Maker – How to use our device to create drink ripples'. https://www.drinkripples.com/ripplemaker

Roberts, N. (2017). 'The instant edible selfie cookie, already a crowd favorite at Twitter and Google events'. Forbes, 21 September. https://www.forbes.com/sites/ninaroberts/2017/09/21/the-instant-edible-selfie-cookie-already-a-crowd-favorite-at-twitter-and-google-events/

Robertson, A. (2012). 'Twitter blocks Instagram from using its API for friend-finding feature'. The Verge, 26 July. https://www.theverge.com/2012/7/26/3189340/twitter-blocks-instagram-friend-finding-api

Robinson, J., E. Bailey and S. Byrne (2017). 'Social media can be bad for youth mental health, but there are ways it can help'. The Conversation, 12 December. http://theconversation.com/social-media-can-be-bad-for-youth-mental-health-but-there-are-ways-it-can-help-87613

Rodley, C. (2017). 'Deep dinosaur'. 19 June. https://chrisrodley.com/2017/06/19/dinosaur-flowers/

Roesner, F., B.T. Gill and T. Kohno (2014). 'Sex, lies, or kittens? Investigating the use of Snapchat's self-destructing messages'. Proc. FC.http://homes.cs.washington.edu/~yoshi/papers/snapchat-FC2014.pdf

Romano, A. (2016). 'You may not have understood Vine, but its demise is a huge cultural loss'. Vox, 28 October. https://www.vox.com/2016/10/28/13439450/vine-shutdown-loss-to-black-culture

Rosenstein, J. (2018). 'People can't tell if this Fenty model is real or fake'. Harper's Bazaar, 9 February. https://www.harpersbazaar.com/beauty/makeup/a16810663/shudu-gram-fenty-model-fake/

Roy, E.A. (2018). 'Instacrammed: The big fib at the heart of New Zealand picture-perfect peaks'. The Guardian, 7 December. https://www.theguardian.com/world/2018/dec/07/instacrammed-the-big-fib-at-the-heart-of-new-zealand-picture-perfect-peaks

Ruby, K. (2017). 'The edible selfie experience: 10 delicious ways to "share" your face'. Observer, 22 March. https://observer.com/2017/03/best-edible-treats-print-social-media-pictures/

Ryan, Á. (2018b). 'Roxy Jacenko's daughter Pixie Curtis just made a huge business move'. 7 August. https://celebrity.nine.com.au/2018/08/07/17/08/roxy-jacenko-daughter-pixie-curtis-sells-pixies-bows-myer

Ryan, K.M. (2018). 'Vertical video: Rupturing the aesthetic paradigm'. Visual Communication, 17(2), 245–61.

Saethre-McGuirk, E.M. (2018). 'Why we need some perspective on landscape photography in the Instagram age'. The Conversation, 12 August. http://theconversation.com/why-we-need-some-perspective-on-landscape-photography-in-the-instagram-age-100093

Safronova, V. (2015). 'On fake Instagram, a chance to be real'. The New York Times, 18 November. http://www.nytimes.com/2015/11/19/fashion/instagram-finstagram-fake-account.html

Safronova, V. (2017). 'Instagram is now a dating platform, too. Here's

how it works'. *The New York Times*, 21 December. https://www.
nytimes.com/2017/12/21/style/instagram-thirst-traps-dating-break
ups.html

San Cornelio, G. and A. Roig (2018). 'Selfies and cultural events: Mixed
methods for the study of selfies in context'. *International Journal of
Communication*, 12, 2773–92.

Saturday, M. (2013). 'Instagram logo'. *Dribbble*, 2 May. https://
dribbble.com/shots/1054954-Instagram-Logo

Savage, M. (2019). 'Health secretary tells social media firms to protect
children after girl's death'. *The Observer*, 26 January. https://www.
theguardian.com/politics/2019/jan/26/matt-hancock-facebook-
social-media-suicide-self-harm-young-people

Schiffer, Z. (2018). 'How the rise of outdoor influencers is affecting
the environment'. Racked.com, 27 August. https://www.racked.
com/2018/8/27/17719792/outdoor-influencers-leave-no-trace-
bears-ears

Schmidt, M. (2018). 'You need 20,000 Instagram followers to take
a photo in front of this security-guarded mural'. People, 26 June.
https://people.com/home/you-need-20000-instagram-followers-to-
take-a-photo-in-front-of-this-security-guarded-mural/

Schrock, A. (2015). 'Communicative affordances of mobile
media: Portability, availability, locatability, and multimediality'.
International Journal of Communication, 9, 1229–46.

Schwab, K. (2018). 'The 2-year-old Instagram influencers who make
more than you'. *Fast Company*, 17 December. https://www.fastcom
pany.com/90278778/the-2-year-old-instagram-influencers-who-
make-more-than-you-do

Seabrook, E.M., M.L. Kern and N.S. Rickard (2016). 'Social networking
sites, depression, and anxiety: A systematic review'. *JMIR Mental
Health*, 3(4), e50.

Seko, Y. and K. Tiidenberg (2016). 'Birth through the digital womb:
Visualizing prenatal life online'. In P.G. Nixon, R. Rawal and
A. Funk (eds) *Digital Media Usage Across the Lifecourse*. London and
New York: Routledge, pp. 50–66.

Senft, T.M. (2008). *Camgirls: Celebrity and Community in the Age of
Social Networks*. New York: Peter Lang.

Senft, T.M. and N.K. Baym (2015). 'What does the selfie say?
Investigating a global phenomenon: Introduction'. *International
Journal of Communication*, 9, 1588–606.

Serafinelli, E. (2017). 'Analysis of photo sharing and visual social
relationships: Instagram as a case study'. *Photographies*, 10(1),
91–111.

Serafinelli, E. (2018). *Digital Life on Instagram: New Social Communication of Photography*. Bingley: Emerald.

Shaban, H. (2019). 'Here's why Instagram is going to hide your "likes"'. *Washington Post*, 1 May. https://www.washingtonpost.com/technology/2019/05/01/heres-why-instagram-is-going-hide-your-likes/

Shah, B. (2015). 'Inside Instagram's long guerrilla war on porn – and the users who keep coming back'. Medium, 7 July. https://medium.com/the-slice/inside-instagram-s-long-guerrilla-war-on-porn-and-the-users-who-keep-coming-back-32cbc67137d5#.b10gx0j0j

Shah, S. (2017). 'Do you Finstagram? The new way teens are using Instagram in private'. *Digital Trends*, 23 February. https://www.digitaltrends.com/social-media/finstagram-fake-instagram/

Shifman, L. (2014). *Memes in Digital Culture*. Cambridge, MA: The MIT Press.

Shontell, A. (2013). 'Jack Dorsey was "heartbroken" when Instagram sold to Facebook. *Business Insider Australia*, 7 May. https://www.businessinsider.com.au/jack-dorsey-was-heartbroken-when-instagram-sold-to-facebook-2013-5

Skrubbeltrang, M.M., J. Grunnet and N.T. Tarp (2017). '#RIPINSTAGRAM: Examining user's counter-narratives opposing the introduction of algorithmic personalization on Instagram'. *First Monday*, 22(4), https://doi.org/10.5210/fm.v22i4.7574

Social Blade (2019). 'Simplified Analytics right at your finger tips'. Social Blade, n.d. https://socialblade.com/

Soffer, O. (2016). 'The oral paradigm and Snapchat'. *Social Media + Society*, 2(3), https://doi.org/10.1177/2056305116666306

SoImJenn (2018). 'So, I'm Jenn – Love of a Lifetime – Official Lyric Video (Vertical Video)'. YouTube, 24 May. https://www.youtube.com/watch?v=7VRKdKg69ZI

Sontag, S. (2005). *On Photography*. New York: Rosetta Books.

Sorokanich, L. (2018). 'Dog influencers are so popular, they need their own talent agency'. Fast Company, 20 December. https://www.fastcompany.com/90280718/this-talent-agency-manages-instagrams-top-dog-influencers

Spangler, T. (2018). 'Musical.ly is going away: Users to be shifted to Bytedance's TikTok video app'. *Variety*, 2 August. https://variety.com/2018/digital/news/musically-shutdown-tiktok-bytedance-1202893205/

Stack, L. (2017). '"Unicorn food" is colorful, sparkly and everywhere'. *The New York Times*, 19 April. https://www.nytimes.com/2017/04/19/style/unicorn-food-starbucks.html

Stark, L. (2018). 'Facial recognition, emotion and race in animated social media'. *First Monday*, 23(9), http://firstmonday.org/ojs/index.php/fm/article/view/9406

Stodola, S. (2017). 'Influence: How Instagram made all places any place'. *Flung Magazine*, 13 June. https://flungmagazine.com/2017/06/13/influence-how-instagram-made-all-places-any-place/

Swisher, K. (2013). 'The money shot'. *Vanity Fair*, 6 May. https://www.vanityfair.com/news/business/2013/06/kara-swisher-instagram

Syme, R. (2017). 'Hooray for Fiona the hippo, our bundle of social-media joy'. *The New York Times*, 25 November. https://www.nytimes.com/2017/11/25/style/fiona-the-hippo.html

Systrom, K. (2011). 'What is the genesis of Instagram?'. 12 January. https://www.quora.com/Instagram-company/What-is-the-genesis-of-Instagram

Systrom, K. (2012). 'Instagram + Facebook'. 9 April. http://instagram.tumblr.com/post/20785013897/instagram-facebook

Tan, G.Z. and J. Tan (2018). 'Influencer Daryl Aiden Yow defends himself against plagiarism accusations in first public statements'. Mothership, 20 June. https://mothership.sg/2018/06/daryl-aiden-yow-instagram-photos-response/

Tan, J. and J. Wee (2018). 'People are now critiquing Daryl Aiden Yow's photo editing skills & adding sources for his images'. Mothership, 20 June. https://mothership.sg/2018/06/daryl-aiden-yow-singapore-instagram-photos-part-two/

Taylor, N. and M. Keating (2018). 'Contemporary food imagery: Food porn and other visual trends'. *Communication Research and Practice*, 4(3), 307–23.

The Drum (2015). 'The true cost of Instagram fame'. YouTube, 26 June. https://www.youtube.com/watch?v=kc4XkBj-mpc

The Feed (2015). 'Instafamous: How do people make money from Instagram? | The Feed'. YouTube, 15 June. https://www.youtube.com/watch?v=wIbi1nzcBRY

The New Paper (2015). 'MP Baey Yam Keng regrets Eiffel Tower selfie in Paris tribute post on Facebook'. *The New Paper*, 17 November. https://www.tnp.sg/news/singapore-news/mp-baey-yam-keng-regrets-eiffel-tower-selfie-paris-tribute-post-facebook

Thelander, Å. and C. Cassinger (2017). 'Brand new images? Implications of Instagram photography for place branding'. *Media and Communication*, 5(4), 6–14.

Thimm, C. and P. Nehls (2017). 'Sharing grief and mourning on Instagram: Digital patterns of family memories'. *Communications*, 42(3), 327–49.

Thomas, S. (2017). 'Selfie king to live chat pro: Baey Yam Keng works social media like a boss'. AsiaOne, 6 March. https://www.asiaone.com/singapore/selfie-king-live-chat-pro-baey-yam-keng-works-social-media-boss

Thompson, N. and F. Vogelstein (2019). '15 months of fresh hell inside Facebook'. Wired, 16 April. https://www.wired.com/story/facebook-mark-zuckerberg-15-months-of-fresh-hell/

Thompson, R. (2017a). 'The Instagram "pods" using likes to fight the new algorithm'. Mashable, 19 April. https://mashable.com/2017 / 04 / 19 / instagram - pods - bloggers / ? europe = true # 3A08jro Utiqx

Thompson, R. (2017b). 'Instagram is the new Tinder – whether you want it to be or not'. Mashable, 11 October. https://mashable.com/2017/10/10/instagram-dms-flirting/#UoRTvYMt.8qC

Tiidenberg, K. (2015). 'Odes to heteronormativity: Presentations of femininity in Russian-speaking pregnant women's Instagram accounts', International Journal of Communication, 9, 1746–58.

Tiidenberg, K. (2018). Selfies: Why We Love (and Hate) Them. Bingley: Emerald.

Tiidenberg, K. and E. Gómez Cruz (2015). 'Selfies, image and the re-making of the body'. Body & Society, 21(4), 77–102.

Tirosh, U. (2016). 'What do you do when someone travels around the world to copy you'. DIY Photography, 11 November. https://www.diyphotography.net/someone-travels-around-world-copy/

Tishgart, S. (2017). 'This design expert knows how to make a small restaurant go viral'. Grub Street, 3 April. http://www.grubstreet.com/2017/04/how-to-make-a-restaurant-go-viral.html

Trafik Media (2016). 'The rich kids of Instagram cutting the edge Full documentary'. YouTube, 24 June. https://www.youtube.com/watch?v=DJaxt16Hz5c

TreePotatoes (2016). 'How to be an Instagrammer parody (Ft. Mongchin & Nicole Changmin)'. YouTube, 12 July. https://www.youtube.com/watch?v=Labo5TnGnDY

Truman, I. (2016). 'Famous Australian blogger finds an exact copy-cat'. Elle Australia, 14 November. https://www.elle.com.au/news/instagram-blogger-gypsea-lust-finds-exact-copycat-6759

Turton, W. (2016). 'The new Instagram feed is ruining my life'. Gizmodo, 23 June. http://gizmodo.com/the-new-instagram-feed-is-ruining-my-life-1782491769

UnityJapan (2015). 'WEZ from YALLA FAMILY – Instargram' [Official Music Video]. YouTube, 14 June. https://www.youtube.com/watch?v=zxgg4n2eFFU

Vaidhyanathan, S. (2018). *Antisocial Media: How Facebook Disconnects Us and Undermines Democracy*. New York: Oxford University Press.

van Dijck, J. (2007). *Mediated Memories in the Digital Age*. Stanford, CA: Stanford University Press.

van Dijck, J. (2008). 'Digital photography: Communication, identity, memory'. *Visual Communication*, 7(1), 57–76.

van Dijck, J. (2013). '"You have one identity": Performing the self on Facebook and LinkedIn'. *Media, Culture & Society*, 35(2), 199–215.

Van House, N.A. (2011). 'Personal photography, digital technologies and the uses of the visual'. *Visual Studies*, 26(2), 125–34.

Van House, N.A., M. Davis, M. Ames, M. Finn and V. Viswanathan (2005). 'The uses of personal networked digital imaging: An empirical study of cameraphone photos and sharing'. Presented at CHI 2005, Portland, OR, 2–7 April.

Verstraete, G. (2016). 'It's about time: Disappearing images and stories in Snapchat'. *Image & Narrative*, 17(4), 104–13.

Villi, M. (2015). '"Hey, I'm here right now": Camera phone photographs and mediated presence'. *Photographies*, 8(1), 3–22.

Villi, M. and M. Stocchetti (2011). 'Visual mobile communication, mediated presence and the politics of space'. *Visual Studies*, 26(2), 102–12.

Vincent, J. (2016). 'Facebook's new filters are like Prisma for video'. *The Verge*, 8 November. https://www.theverge.com/2016/11/8/13562288/facebook-ai-filter-prisma-mobile-app-caffe2go

VPRO (2018). '#followme'. vpro.nl, 21 November. https://www.vpro.nl/programmas/follow-me.html;jsessionid=B9BD39FB3244C20F2 10704B4FBB8C5DE

Wagner, K. (2018). 'Instagram's Kevin Systrom on leaving Facebook: "No one ever leaves a job because everything's awesome"'. *Vox*, 15 October. https://www.recode.net/2018/10/15/17979680/instagram-kevin-systrom-facebook-departure-new-project

Wargo, J.M. (2017). '"Every selfie tells a story …": LGBTQ youth lifestreams and new media narratives as connective identity texts'. *New Media & Society*, 19(4), 560–78.

Weber, M. (1962). *Basic Concepts in Sociology*. New York: Philosophical Library.

Welch, C. (2013). 'Projecteo, "the Instagram projector", now available for $34.99 after Kickstarter success'. *The Verge*, 29 May. https://www.theverge.com/2013/5/29/4375576/projecteo-instagram-film-projector-now-available

Welch, C. (2018). 'Instagram brings GIFs back to Stories with stricter moderation'. The Verge, 29 March. https://www.theverge.com/2018/3/29/17176912/instagram-gif-stickers-stories

Weltevrede, E., A. Helmond and C. Gerlitz (2014). 'The politics of real-time: A device perspective on social media platforms and search engines'. *Theory, Culture & Society*, 31(6), 125–50.

White, A., S. Bodoni and S. Nicola (2019). 'Facebook's battle in Germany is a thorn in WhatsApp integration'. *Bloomberg News*, 7 February. https://www.bloomberg.com/news/articles/2019-02-07/facebook-s-battle-in-germany-a-thorn-in-whatsapp-integration

White, A. and C. Krol (2017). '"Rich kids of Instagram meets Hunger Games": Guests at luxury Fyre Festival where tickets cost $12,000 "mugged, stranded and hungry"'. *The Telegraph*, 28 April. https://www.telegraph.co.uk/music/news/fyre-festival-instagram-friendly-music-event-12000-tickets-turns/

Wiener, A. (2017). 'The Millennial Walt Disney'. *New York Magazine*, 2 October. http://nymag.com/intelligencer/2017/10/museum-of-ice-cream-maryellis-bunn.html

Wilken, R. and G. Goggin (eds) (2015). *Locative Media*. London and New York: Routledge.

Winter, D. (2011). 'Through my eye, not Hipstamatic's'. The New York Times, 11 February. https://lens.blogs.nytimes.com/2011/02/11/through-my-eye-not-hipstamatics/

Wishcrys (2018). 'Instagram'. wishcrys.com, 4 March. https://wishcrys.com/instagram/

Witt, A.E., N. Suzor and A. Huggins (2019). 'The rule of law on Instagram: An evaluation of the moderation of images depicting women's bodies'. *UNSW Law Journal*, 42(2).

Woodrow, C. (n.d.) 'Instagram vs. reality: Behind the scenes of my best travel photos'. Ordinary Traveler. https://ordinarytraveler.com/instagram-vs-reality-behind-scenes-travel

Yang, J. (2016). '10 photographs you can take in Singapore to bluff your friends that you're on vacation'. The Smart Local, 22 June. https://thesmartlocal.com/read/overseas-photographs

Yang, L. (2017). 'There's a college in China that teaches you how to become a social media celebrity'. *Business Insider*, 20 June. https://www.businessinsider.com/become-internet-famous-with-this-college-degree-2017-6?IR=T

Zalewska, M. (2017). 'Selfies from Auschwitz: Rethinking the relationship between spaces of memory and places of commemoration in the Digital Age'. *Digital Icons: Studies in Russian, Eurasian and Central European New Media*, 18, 95–116.

Zane, D. (2016). 'Barbie challenges the "white saviour complex"'. BBC News, 1 May. https://www.bbc.com/news/world-africa-36132482

Zappavigna, M. (2016). 'Social media photography: Construing subjectivity in Instagram images'. *Visual Communication*, 15(3), 271–92.

Zuber, J. (2018). '6 months on insta – @noonoouri noonoouri is nothing without you!' Instagram, 9 August. https://www.instagram.com/p/BmQeUCUgIkf/

@bymariandrew. 2017. 'Instagram post of the year'. Instagram, 14 July. https://www.instagram.com/p/BWhrZtdADnF/

@bymariandrew. 2018a. 'Mari Andrew'. Instagram. https://www.instagram.com/bymariandrew/

@bymariandrew. 2018c. 'Friends in their 30s Instagram bingo'. Instagram, 29 July. https://www.instagram.com/p/BloBCJXg3do/

@bymarieandrew. 2018b. 'Instagrammable vacation bingo'. Instagram, 7 July. https://www.instagram.com/p/Bk7kLp7A4BP/

@darylaiden. 2018a. 'I've been getting so many …'. Instagram, 21 November. https://www.instagram.com/p/BqcZMqJFYCT/

@darylaiden. 2018b. 'Spending my Sunday crashing @dreachong's …'. Instagram, 16 September. https://www.instagram.com/p/BnybzPVDThn/

@darylaiden. 2018c. 'I usually see people buying …'. Instagram, 18 September. https://www.instagram.com/p/Bn30G2TjaW2/

@darylaiden. 2018d. 'I don't know why when …'. Instagram, 9 December. https://www.instagram.com/p/BrKuDkDlDlq/

@darylaiden. 2018e. 'Dining at @NandosSG has always …'. Instagram, 23 December. https://www.instagram.com/p/BrugjasFY65/

@darylaiden. 2018f. 'Now that the fun's ALMOST …'. Instagram, 20 December. https://www.instagram.com/p/BrnDLAWlAwA/

@darylaiden. 2018g. 'In touch. The past 4 …'. Instagram, 16 December. https://www.instagram.com/p/BrcvY1KFXCi/

@dude.sg. 2018. 'Super proud to be launching …'. Instagram, 4 December. https://www.instagram.com/p/Bq7rHdVBoYO/

@project.tricky. 2017. '@project.tricky'. Instagram.com. https://www.instagram.com/project.tricky/

@youdidnoteatthat. 2018. 'Speaking the truth in this …'. Instagram. https://www.instagram.com/youdidnoteatthat/

@youdidnotskatethat. 2018. 'You did not skate that'. Instagram. https://www.instagram.com/youdidnotskatethat/

@youdidnotsleepthere. 2018. 'Celebrating Instagram's most illogical campsites …'. Instagram, https://www.instagram.com/youdidnotsleepthere/

@yutakis. 2018. '#fantasyvibesonly'. Instagram.com. https://www.instagram.com/explore/tags/fantasyvibesonlystudio/

Index

#funeral 70, 185–7
#nofilter 55
#PrayforParis 155
#tbt 71–2, 90–1
#ultrasound 176–7
#yellowhelmetchallenge 154

@blackstagram 34
@insta_repeat 206
@roaminggnome 149

1888 92
29Rooms 161
4chan 77

Abidin, Crystal 17, 68, 94, 103–7, 111, 127, 140, 142–3, 146, 154–6, 159, 180, 183
Addict Aide 152
advertising 1, 4–5, 12, 31–3, 39, 113–14, 126, 130, 146, 152, 173, 177, 182–3, 189, 213, 215–17
advertorial 108, 115–16, 127, 132, 146–7
aesthetics 3, 5–6, 39–74, 76, 81, 86, 91–2, 94, 96, 145–6, 156, 191–3, 198, 201, 205, 208, 210, 212, 214–15
African American 63, 105
algorithm 19–20, 25, 118, 131, 143–5, 197
  algorithmic feed 88–9, 215
  algorithmic ranking 143
  algorithmic timeline 18–19
Andrew, Mari 79, 205–6

Android 11, 54, 193
animated GIF 77
annotation 62–3
anorexia 22
app 1–4, 8–15, 25–7, 29, 33, 44–53, 73–85, 87–9, 91–8, 100–4, 128–9, 146–8, 150–1, 154, 164
Apple 10–11, 15, 78, 94, 213
application program interface (API) 8
Ardern, Jacinda 5
art and photographers 149
artificial intelligence 96, 203
astroturfing, 113–14, 146
authenticity 1, 104, 111–12, 191, 197, 199–200, 204–5, 214, 216
avatar 2, 201

Balmain 202
Barker, Jessie 163
Barthes, Roland 44, 46
Bartholeyns, Gil 53, 192
Baym, Nancy 67–8
behind the scenes posts 126, 134–6, 156, 183, 209
Berger, Joe 44
best life 104
Bestfluence 147
blog 12, 65, 101, 127–9, 133
Blum-Ross, Alicia 179–80
Bolt 4, 82, 99
Boomerang 4, 15, 29, 47, 61, 74, 83–4, 164
Boomf 195

Bow Wow 209
brand 12, 32, 73, 76, 107, 110,
    116, 118–19, 126, 130, 137,
    149, 160–1, 199–202, 208
breastfeeding 21, 68, 179
brelfies 179
Broad City 64, 199
browser 13, 75, 84
Brud FYI 203–4
Bucher, Taina 19
bulimia 22
    see also eating disorders
Bullen, Lauren 207
bullying 174
Bunn, Maryellis 160
Burbn 9, 11, 79, 85

calibrated amateurism 104,
    111–12, 156, 183
cameraphone 78
Canva 97
CanvasPop 194
children 5–6, 36, 119, 169–70,
    174, 176–84, 189–90, 211
chronic fatigue syndrome 152–3
Cive 171
clean-eating 73
Clinton, Hillary 34
co-creation 184–5, 190
Cobb, Gemma 22–3, 35
Cocoagraph 195
communication 1, 3, 6, 9, 25–8,
    32, 40–5, 75–6, 79, 81, 85,
    155, 186–7, 200, 204–5,
    214–17
communities of culture 149
community guidelines 20–2, 35,
    174, 212, 217
copyright 9, 99, 108, 180
creativity 83–4, 87, 216
cross-platform traffic 127, 147
Cruz, Edgar Gómez 44, 79
Curtis, Pixie 180–1

database 8
dating 89, 151, 160, 198–9

David, Craig 65
Dayre 129
De Rosa, Antonio 192
De Souza, Poppy 51, 53, 56
death, deceased 5–6, 36, 87,
    173–5, 185, 187–190
    see also funeral
deep learning 94, 96
DeepArt 96
Delage 152
demographic 5, 14, 26
deviantART 76
digital camera 43
Diigitals 202
disruptive 16
Dorsey, Jack 11
Douyin 30, 216
Dropbox 104

eateries 119, 163–4
eating disorders 22–3, 153
emergent teen uses 150
emoji 8, 23, 30, 60, 62–3, 73–4,
    114, 119–20, 133, 137, 152, 199
ephemerality 26, 28, 60, 82
Eurovision 70
experiential authority 107
Explore 8, 19, 22, 29, 45, 48, 65,
    67, 75–6, 84, 141, 205

Facebook 1–2, 8, 11–19, 26–7, 31,
    33–8, 40, 59–60, 66, 76–7,
    88–90, 96–100, 110–11,
    188–9, 199, 213, 217
facial recognition 60
family friendly 23
fashion spotlight 126
father of daughters (FOD) 182
Feifer, Jason 186–7
filter(s) 53
Finsta, Finstagram 16–18,
    109–12, 114
finsta snitches 18
Fisher, Tatum and Oakley 182
flatlay 72, 116, 126
Flickr 3, 40, 66, 76–7, 194

followers 4, 10, 16, 28, 34, 63,
  70–1, 74, 98, 100–7, 109,
  112, 114–19, 121, 125–6,
  131–44, 146, 148–9, 152, 156,
  169–71, 180, 182, 186, 190,
  197, 200, 203–5, 208
Ford, Clementine 181
Foursquare 9, 11, 76, 79
fraud 197
friends 13, 28, 59, 70–1, 101–3,
  151–2, 175, 177, 186–8, 205,
  211
funerals 5, 70, 185–7
  see also grief; mourning
FxCamera 53
Fyre Festival 113–14, 146

Gelardi, Piera 161
General Data Protection
  Regulation (GDPR) 188
geodata 79
geographic metadata 86
Gibbs, Martin 40, 50, 64, 70, 186
GIF stickers for Stories 29
Gillespie, Tarleton 8, 19–21, 25
Giphy 29–31, 63
  GiphyCam 84
Gizmodo 88
Goffman, Erving 112
Google Drive 104
grief 155, 157–9, 174, 185–6,
  189–90

Halpern, Megan 43, 53, 78
Hancock, Matt 36
Hand, Martin 30, 42, 72, 79, 108,
  114, 146, 163, 180, 186, 195
Harper's Bazaar 201
hashtag, 7, 19, 22–3, 55, 65,
  70, 72, 74, 85, 99, 115–16,
  118–19, 121, 127, 139, 153,
  168, 185–6, 199, 214
health 22–4, 36–7, 73, 121, 152–3,
  173, 198
Hipstamatic 2, 10, 39, 53, 78, 92
Holga 39

homes 5, 168–70, 173, 191, 209
hook-up apps 65
Hooper, Clemmie and Simon
  182–3
Horowitz, Andreessen 11
Horst, Heather 79
Humphreys, Lee 43, 53, 71–2, 78
Hyperlapse, 4, 15, 47, 74, 82–4

iconography 41, 45–8, 53, 58, 91,
  191
identity theft 108, 135
image-editing 92, 94
ImageShack 76
immediacy 9
imposter (bots and scam
  accounts) 137
Influencer 32, 94, 100–11,
  113–26, 129–49, 159,
  168–73, 180–4, 198–205,
  208, 217
  Influencer agencies 101, 115,
  141, 200
Ingrid Goes West 200
Insta 2, 5, 46, 59, 65, 87, 92, 151,
  160–2, 167–70, 172, 196–7,
  205, 209, 211, 213
Insta-famous 170, 196–7
Insta-friendly, 213
Insta-home 169
Insta-museums 160–2
Instabites 195
instablogging 129, 147
Instafood 166
Instagraham 195
Instagram Direct, 81, 213
Instagram purge 137–40, 148
Instagram vs. reality 210–11
Instagrammability 65, 160,
  162–4, 172, 210
Instagrammable foods 163,
  165–6
Instagrammable sites 160
Instapods 141, 148
Internet Research Agency (IRA)
  34

Ipernity 77
iPhone 1, 10, 42–3, 45–6, 78, 163
    iPhoneography 43, 53, 78

Jacenko, Roxy 180
Johnson, Casey 72, 177, 179

Kamon 92
Know how to talk to your teen about
    Instagram: A parent's guide 173
Kress, Gunter 45
Krieger, Mike 2, 9, 11–12, 14,
    32–3, 37–8
Kusama, Yayoi 162

Layout 4, 15, 47, 51, 74, 80, 83–4,
    97
legacy contact 188–9
LGBTQ 63, 68
lifespans 174–90
Like & Subscribe 171
like my addiction 152
Lil Miquela, 203–5
Livingstone, Sonia 179–80
location information 79, 85–6
logo 46–9, 192

MacCannell, Dean 104, 112
MacDowell, Lachlan 53, 56
McClure, Alexis and Ava 182
make-up libraries 126
Manovich, Lev 40, 68, 86
markers of ownership 108
Markoe, Madelyn 163
Mediated Memories in the Digital
    Age 43
Meitu XiuXiu (Meitu Pic) 93–4,
    97, 216
meme accounts 131
memorialize 212
mental health 36–7, 153, 198
Messenger 37
metadata 13, 86–7, 91, 176–7
Micah 404, 150
microcelebrity 105–7, 180
midwifery 182

Milner, Ryan 45, 77
Mint 132, 195
Mirzoeff, Nicholas, 90–1
mobile app 75, 104, 129
mobile device 13, 59
moderation 2, 19–22, 25, 30
Morris, Jac, 207, 211
Mosseri, Adam 33, 36–8, 194, 217
Mostik 69–70
mother of daughters (MOD) 182
Mothership 14, 208
mourning 5, 174, 185–7, 190
    see also funerals; grief
multiple accounts 16–18, 109, 112
Mumsnet 183
Museum of Ice Cream (MoIC)
    160
museums 5, 50, 159–62, 173, 213
music stickers 30–1
Musical.ly 30–1, 216

National Gallery of Singapore
    162
Netflix 53, 213
network surfacing strategy 109
networked public 103
New York Times 10, 16, 160
New Yorker 81
Noonoouri 200–1, 203
nudity 20–1, 23–5

Ocasio-Cortez, Alexandra 5,
    156–7
Olszanowski, Magdelena 23, 50
On photography 9, 41
Open Facebook 38
Osmann, Maud and Nataly 72
Outfit of the day (OOTD) 114,
    116, 125
oversharenting 179
overuse 174

Padgram 14
paid partnership 12, 32, 107, 183
parent 110, 170, 174–5, 177–81,
    184, 187–90

parental and child Influencers 5, 180, 189
parody 145, 207–8, 216
partying 126
Photo Shelter 205
Photobucket 76–7
photosharing 87
Picasa 76
PicPlz 2, 10–11
Pimenova, Kristina 181
Pinterest 208
Pixelis 195
Pixie's bows 180
plagiarism 108, 207–8
plastic surgery 197
Polaroid 3, 9–10, 39, 46, 50, 52, 192–3, 206
politician 155–6
politics 2–3, 8, 25, 33–5, 37, 63, 68, 80, 90, 143, 154–6, 158, 211, 213, 215
pornography 20, 23–4
Postman, Neil, 155
Poulsen, Søren Vigil, 45, 53
Prism 94–7
privacy 17, 23, 27, 81, 110, 177–80, 183–4, 188–9, 213
private account 16, 111, 132, 177
    private commercial account 130–1, 148
pro bono work 133, 148
pro-ana 22
pro-ED 22–3
product placement 107–9
program 8, 13–14, 61
pseudonymity 17

Quartz 205
queer communities 17

racism 30, 68
reaction GIFs 29
Reddit 77, 157
relatability, technique of 4, 106, 115, 132, 146–8, 154, 197

removal (of content) 19, 22, 25, 36
retro camera 46, 53–4, 78
Rettberg, Jill Walker 26, 30, 55
Rinse and repeat 205, 210
Rinsta, Rinstagram 16, 110, 112
Rise, Cole 10, 46
Roys Peaks (Lake Wanaka, New Zealand) 171
Russell, Molly 33, 35–6, 188–9

Schrock, Andrew 79
Seko, Yukari 175
SelfieCity 68
selfies at funerals 5, 70, 186–7
Senft, Teresas 67–8, 105
Serafinelli, Elisa 39, 66, 87, 91
sexting 26
sharenting 5, 178–80, 189
shopping stickers 32
Shudu 201–4
Shutterfly 76
simulatable aesthetics 208, 210
Skype 213
Snapchat 2–4, 15, 25–30, 38, 49, 58–60, 80–2, 209, 213
Snapfish 76
Snow 216
social awareness 151, 153–4
Social Blade 147
social communication 40, 75
Soffer, Oren 26
Sontag, Susan 41
sponsored content 100–2, 114–15, 121, 137, 147, 194
    sponsorship 4–5, 12, 32, 127, 182–3
Spotify 28, 71
stalker 207
sticker 6, 28–32, 62–3, 129, 194
Stitchta (Stitchtagram) 195
Stories 1–3, 6–7, 25–32, 49, 58–64, 80–5, 96–100, 151, 157, 177, 183, 198–9, 204, 212–15
Stories Highlights 28

Subcultures 149–50, 172–3
surveillance 13, 60, 177
Systrom, Kevin 2, 9, 11–12, 14,
    27–8, 32–3, 37–8, 46

teacher influencers 151–2
template 2, 6, 151, 191, 205–7,
    214–16
The Atlantic 151
The Guardian 187
The Independent 36
The Smart Local 162
third party application 3–4,
    14–15, 29, 38, 51, 83, 98,
    194, 212
thirst trap 151
Throwback Thursday 71
Tiidenberg, Katrin 42, 44, 52,
    67–8, 73, 80, 175
Tinder 151, 160
Tindstagramming 151
transparency 12, 146–7, 156, 183,
    215
travel bloggers 72
trolling 187, 207
Trump, Donald 34
Tudou 216
tumblr, 29, 77, 186–7
Turrell, James 162
Twitch 29
Twitpic 77
Twitter, 7, 11, 13–14, 19, 27, 29,
    33–4, 40, 47, 49, 66, 73, 77,
    84, 88–9, 98–9, 101–3, 114,
    134, 137, 159, 170, 209

ultrasound 70, 175–7, 184, 212
Unfold 97
unwanted attention, *see* bullying
US elections 33
user engagement 47–8, 75, 143,
    215

V Live 216
Vaidhyanathan, Siva 10, 13–14, 18

Valencia 56–7, 95
Van Dijck, José 16, 41, 43, 90,
    187
Van Leeuwen, Theo 45
verification 138–9, 144, 148
vertical format 3–4, 29, 49, 51,
    59, 64, 212–13
video 1, 3–4, 15, 26, 28–9, 47, 51,
    56–7, 59–62, 75, 79, 82–3,
    96, 99, 152, 164, 175, 212–13
Vine 69, 84
virtual Influencer 203–4
visibility 11, 21, 67–8, 81, 90, 98,
    104, 106, 143, 148, 175, 183,
    214
visual social media 1–3, 7, 9, 13,
    25, 29, 38, 75, 87, 212–13,
    215–16
vlog, vloggers 73, 156, 204
volunteer tourism 153
VSCO 84, 93

Wagner, Jack 33, 171
wake 33, 36, 77, 137, 155, 186
    see also mourning
ways of seeing 44
Web 2.0 3, 76
Webstagram 14
Whatsapp 33, 37, 131
Wilson, Cameron-James 201–2
Wired 33, 161
witching hour 143–4, 148

X-Pro II 55, 57, 60, 95
xenophobia 154

Yahoo 77
Yfrog 77
Yow, Daryl Aidan 208–9
Yutakis, James 168–9

Zahid 131
Zappavigna, Michele 54, 66
Zuckerberg, Mark 11, 16, 18, 33,
    37–8